CREATING OUR OWN

CREATING OUR OWN

...... *Folklore, Performance, and Identity in Cuzco, Peru*

ZOILA S. MENDOZA

DUKE UNIVERSITY PRESS DURHAM AND LONDON 2008

Printed in the United States of America on acid-free paper ∞

Designed by Heather Hensley

Typeset in Minion Pro by Keystone Typesetting, Inc.

Library of Congress Cataloging-in-Publication Data appear
on the last printed page of this book.

IN MEMORY OF

Bernard Cohn, Miguel H., Milla M., and Delia Vidal de Milla

Contents

······ *Illustrations*

...... *Preface to the English Edition*

This text was originally conceived, written, and published in Spanish. Following the advice of the readers for Duke University Press, I have modified it in a couple of ways to make it more suitable for the academic public in the English-speaking world. I am indebted to the anonymous readers for their extremely helpful suggestions. First, I introduced more references to and discussed at greater length the relevant literature, which will help the reader place my work in a wider perspective. Second, I reduced or deleted quotes and references (most of them song lyrics, descriptions of performances, discourses, or speeches) that were more directed toward the Peruvian, Spanish, and Spanish-Quechua readership.

The translation was not an easy task, but it was successfully done thanks to the arduous work of Javier Flores-Espinoza, who also translated my first book from English into Spanish. This previous experience and his thorough knowledge of Peruvian history and reality proved to be key in the completion of the task. However, I also owe much to my husband, Charles Walker, who was, as he has always been, my main consultant for editing my work in English. His patience and encouragement have always been crucial to my academic (and nonacademic!) life. For continuous help and support I am also indebted to Valerie Millholland, who made this publication possible. From the time I timidly inquired into the possibility of publishing an English version of this book until the very last steps of submission of the final translation of the manuscript she has always been generous with her time, extremely responsive, kind, and good-humored. Valerie is every author's dream editor.

When the Spanish version of the book was in the final stages of production and the translation of the modified version for the English edition was under way, Evaristo Tupa, a musician and photographer whose testimony I include in the book, along with one of his photographs, passed away. Because I have chosen to leave untouched the acknowledgments written for the Spanish edition, where I give him thanks as if he were still alive, I make this clarification here. Even though he could not see this book, his family's appreciation for the recognition that I give to him made me feel that my gratitude had reached him. I was happy to see his family, and those of several of the deceased artists and intellectuals discussed in this book, at the Cuzco presentation of the Spanish version and to hear that they, as well as many other Cuzco artists and intellectuals, thought my work had done justice to a very important but almost forgotten part of Cuzco history and culture. This made me feel that the main purpose of this book has been accomplished, since, as I explain in the acknowledgments, my commitment as a scholar is to those from whom I learn what I write about.

Acknowledgments

Although all research and every text transform us in unique ways, I feel that the stories and feelings I have tried to show in this book, as well as the process of giving it its final shape, have deeply touched me. The task of acknowledging those who accompanied me along the way is therefore very difficult indeed, not just because it always proves challenging to name all the individuals who have somehow participated in a given project but also because the latter is closely connected with previous projects. I therefore apologize beforehand because in some cases I refer to groups or institutions in the hope that all the individuals they encompass will feel acknowledged.

Bernard Cohn, my teacher during my graduate studies at the University of Chicago, drew my attention to the importance of studying the institutional aspects of the promotion of folklore. Thanks to his suggestion I entered this world in a previous research project, and it gradually became a project in itself. The teachings and writings of Cohn played a central role in my interdisciplinary adventure and helped me ease the fears and frustrations that sometimes beset anthropologists when they enter the domains of history. His invaluable advice that I should explore and interrogate different forms of knowledge of social reality changed me as a researcher. It is for this and much more that I dedicate the book in part to his memory.

The book is likewise dedicated to the memory of Miguel H., Milla M., and Delia Vidal de Milla, whose warmth, help, and enthusiasm clearly marked the book and made it possible. The long conversations we had in their home in Cuzco, the documents and contacts they facilitated, and above all the passion and emotion they transmitted to me enriched my knowledge of the world of art and folklore in the city of Cuzco. This city will never be the same without their warm presence. I deeply regret that this book was published after they passed away, but I am sure they know, wherever they are, that the dedication goes to them with all my heart and with my most sincere gratitude.

The members of two institutions in Cuzco played a central role in my exploration of the urban promotion of folklore. They are the members of the Centro Qosqo de Arte Nativo and the Instituto Americano de Arte de Cuzco. Always generous with their time and documents, they allowed me to explore the goals and ideals of their respective institutions and of each of them as individuals. My thanks go to Sr. Evaristo Tupa Lonconi, an old member and musician of the Centro Qosqo, who provided me with invaluable information and helped me locate important images in the photographic archive of the Chambi family, where he has worked for several decades. I likewise thank Dr. Manuel Jesús Aparicio Vega, a prominent leader of the Instituto Americano de Arte de Cuzco, for having given me the chance to present some of the ideas expounded in this work to the members of that institution. I am also grateful to him for his friendship and his intellectual output, which has shed light on many of the arguments developed throughout this book.

In the Centro Qosqo I was fortunate to have been befriended by the Pillco Paz family, which welcomed my family and me as their own. Through Reynaldo Pillco Oquendo and his son, Enrique Pilco, I gained invaluable access to the personal and artistic world of Manuel Pillco Cuba, the father of Reynaldo and a key actor in this book. Thanks to recordings of Manuel's music, to an interview that was recorded shortly before his demise, and to photographs and documents preserved by the family, as well as the long conversations I had with Sr. Reynaldo and Enrique, I was able to approach in a unique way the artistic activities of this harp virtuoso and lover of the various manifestations of *cuzqueño* music. Enrique also assisted me in my research, helping me scrutinize and organize the documentation of the Centro Qosqo. The cuzqueño musical art that both Reynaldo and Enrique practice, which they materialized in a beautiful recording along with other Cuzco artists, inspired me throughout the development of this text. My thanks go to Sra. Liduvina Paz, Lizbeth, Hugo, Lidú, Sofía, Edgard, and the rest of the family for their generosity, encouragement, warmth, and company.

One of the most important and hardest tasks is to acknowledge all of the cuzqueño artists, as well as other residents in this region, who enticed me into their world through their music and dance. It would be impossible to name all of them here. I have always admired their love for and devotion to their respective arts and their commitment to the task of cultivating what they consider to be theirs, often receiving financially little or nothing in return. I acknowledge the musicians and dancers of the Centro Qosqo, the old and current members of the Grupo Expresión, and Flor Canelo, Kike Pinto, Guido Núñez del Prado, Leo Casas (senior), Janett Vengoa, Claudio Orós, Manuel Ollanta Aparicio, Modesto Coli, Jaime Arias, Valentín Pillco, Alejandro Huamán, and many more artists with whom I have spent some of the best moments in my life. Here I would also like to thank the internationally renowned Cuzco composer Armando Guevara Ochoa, who was generous with his time and shed light on many aspects of this book.

Since I began to visit Cuzco frequently in the late 1980s, the Centro Bartolomé de las Casas has always given me its support. With the invaluable help of Fernando Pancorbo I found in its photographic archive many important photos, some of which are published here. It was also in the library of this institution that I had privileged access to the invaluable personal archive of Alberto Giesecke and the private library of Rafael Aguilar. Just as in previous years, Mari Chino and Julia Rodríguez were of great help when I worked with these materials, providing me with the necessary guidance and support. In this institution I was also fortunate to befriend Adelma Benavente García, the daughter of the late artist Julio Benavente Díaz, who kindly provided me with important personal and professional data on her father and granted permission for the publication of his photograph in this text. I would also like to thank here the late Srta. Julia Chambi and her nephew, Teo Allain Chambi, who granted permission for the publication of photographs belonging to the archive of the famed photographer Martín Chambi.

While examining the Giesecke archive I had the help of Marlene Cama, who had taken part in its cataloging. Marlene likewise proved to be a superb research assistant in the study of the Cuzco newspapers *El Sol* and *El Comercio*. Willie Hiatt most generously shared with me the materials he had collected from these two newspapers and provided some crucial favors when he traveled to Cuzco. Elizabeth Mamani Kjuro was essential in the translations from Spanish to Quechua, and also helped to look after my children when it proved necessary. Zuli Grandillet also helped with this last and crucial chore. Without their help and that of Charles Walker, this study would not have been possible. Thank you Chuck, María, and Samuel for your patience and good humor. I am also forever indebted to my parents, Zoila and Eduardo; it is thanks to them that I listened to and danced my first *huaynos*, and they are still moved by my interest in all things from the highlands. Without their love and devotion, our constant visits to Peru would not have been so special for my family.

I began to conceive, organize, and prepare this book while living in the city of Seville in the academic year 2001–2002. The beauty of this city, its music, dances, and people, as well as the chance to enjoy my native language for a long and continuous period, played an essential role in my development in understanding and becoming more sensitive to the aesthetic, sensual, and emotional experience connected with spoken and nonspoken languages. My stay in this city, and that of my family, were fruitful and pleasant thanks to the great support of our friend Antonio Acosta, also a scholar of Andean history. From helping us settle down, with all that this entails, to explaining the local colloquial expressions and protocols we found strange at the time, Antonio helped us like a brother. We shared unforgettable moments of entertainment with Antonio, Lola Maestro, Luis Miguel Glave, and María José Fitz, along with stimulating conversations about Peruvian society and history.

The year spent in Seville working on this book was possible thanks to a grant provided by the University of California President's Fellowship. Previous and subsequent research and writing were possible thanks to grants from the National Endowment for the Humanities and the Office of the Vice Chancellor of Research of the University of California, Davis. Parts of this study were presented at international conferences and were enriched by comments made by the participants. I am grateful to Laura Gotkowitz, Marisol de la Cadena, Carlos Aguirre, Carmen McEvoy, and Michelle Bigenho for having organized these conferences and panels. Along the way I also received the comments of Walter Clark, Brooke Larson, César Itier (who kindly shared some sources), and Raúl Romero. Raúl and Gisela Cánepa are still my main interlocutors in all the work I do on Andean music and dances, and the center headed by Raúl (recently renamed the Institute of Ethnomusicology), his house, and his family are still a crucial support during my visits to Lima. In this city I am also grateful to Dr. Francisco de Zela, Annie Ordóñez, and Rocío Reátegui in the Fondo Editorial of the Universidad

Católica del Perú for the different ways in which they supported the Spanish publication.

I am quite sure that belonging to a department of Native American studies since 1999 has had an impact on my professional work and more specifically on the perspective adopted here. In this work I have reaffirmed my conviction that we must always have a clear stance regarding our intellectual production and must not ignore the political implications of academic output that calls itself objective and scientific. Thanks to my colleagues in this department at the University of California, Davis, I have learned that the commitment a scholar has to the people he or she is writing about should come first and that one must try, as far as possible, to ensure that the knowledge engendered thanks to this community goes back to it. To a great extent it was because of this that I wrote—with the approval and enthusiasm of my colleagues, particularly Stefano Varese—a text in Spanish for the first time since I joined the English-speaking academic community, one that is therefore less burdened with academic jargon. I thus hope to make a small contribution toward the expansion of our knowledge and with it our love and respect for the Andean identity of Peru.

INTRODUCTION *Revisiting Indigenismo and Folklore*

This book aims to share some stories that illustrate the complexity and significance of a field of creative activity that began to be called folklore in Peru and other parts of Latin America in the early twentieth century. Through a detailed study of the so-called folkloric arts (music, dance, and drama in particular), I try to show the leading role these expressive practices had in the development of ethnic/racial identities (a term to be explained below), of regional identity, and in the proposals for a national and continental identity (typically called American and sometimes Hispano-American) that *cuzqueños* (the people of Cuzco) developed throughout the twentieth century. This study focuses on the first half of the century because it was during this period that the most significant canons coalesced, canons that would influence artistic output throughout the twentieth century and the early twenty-first. These canons took shape in spaces sponsored by members of the so-called *instituciones culturales,* or cultural institutions (mostly private institutions with the occasional support of the state). These institutions were based in the city of Cuzco (also spelled variously Qosqo, Ccoscco, Kosko or Cusco) and were devoted to the establishment of spaces where folklore could be developed.[1] My study focuses on these institutions and the spaces where the criteria with which "Indian folklore" was distinguished from "mestizo folklore" and where the *cholo, cuzqueñista* (a concept to be explained below), Peruvianist, and Americanist feelings of the time developed.

Although in previous scholarly works I underlined the importance of the study of the institutional aspects of folklore (Mendoza 1998, 2000, 2001), the reading public I had in mind as my new research and the corresponding text took shape was above all that of cuzqueño artists and intellectuals, as well as Peruvians in general. It was because of this, to a great extent, that the book was written in Spanish and that I tried to avoid dwelling on academic debates and references that were not strictly relevant to the points I was trying to illustrate. The fact that the book was written in Spanish allowed me to share with the people who lived this history and the families of the deceased ones the ideas they themselves had helped craft with the narratives they shared with me. For instance, I was able to discuss drafts of the chapters with some of them and to incorporate their comments. I was likewise able, while writing this book, to present sections at public conferences and on local television programs, thus incorporating feedback from other members of Cuzco society. In general, what proved crucial to the perspective adopted in this text was intense interaction with individuals (some now deceased) and their families together with the long conversations we had and the festive and artistic events I shared with them throughout the process of research and writing. It was thanks to the enthusiasm and pride with which the artists, their families, and the cuzqueños in general spoke about the field of artistic creation known as folklore that this study began to take shape and found the drive it needed to reach its completion.

But even though the text was specifically designed and developed with the foregoing public in mind, I hope it will also prove to be of interest to anyone, in other parts of Latin America or the world, who wants to reformulate the study of the relations between artistic, political, and intellectual activities in the midst of major social and cultural change. It thus joins studies that have shown the crucial relationship between so-called folklore, the development of national identities, concepts regarding cultural legacies and heritage, and the worldwide phenomenon of tourism (Herzfeld 1986; Cantwell 1992; Kirshenblatt-Gimblett 1998). In the specific case of Latin America, I hope this study will help foster a better understanding of the significance and strength that the indigenista movement had in the early twentieth century, the impact of which is still quite clear in the countries of the region. Finally, I hope that the cuzqueño social processes documented here will encourage us to rethink the often undervalued role that art—particularly what is known as folklore—and feelings have in understanding a society and its history.[2]

Although public forms of expression—music, dance, and drama—are privileged areas where one can understand the experiences lived by the members of a given society—since they embody and give shape to many of these experiences—it is no less true that close study often reveals paradoxes and contradictions. It is therefore crucial, as was noted by Veit Erlmann, that our analysis does not try to find a core principle that underpins these performances but instead "accepts the challenge" posed by these discrepancies and disjunctures (1992, 689). We have to understand these performances on their own terms, not as a reflection of other social realities but as important realities in their own right (Fabian 1990; Erlmann 1992, 1996). This is why, unlike previous approaches, my study emphasizes the fact that the significant "artistic-folkloric" output that appeared in Cuzco throughout the first half of the twentieth century cannot simply be understood as a reflection of other social and political processes that led to the development and flowering of a cuzqueño regional identity and also to the proposals for a national and continental identity developed by Cuzco artists and intellectuals. It is my belief that this output must be understood as an integral and significant part of these processes. I further insist that it was to a large extent thanks to this artistic output that these longings for a regional, national, and continental identity coalesced and took a specific shape.

In this same perspective, and as part of a discussion of the undervalued role assigned to public forms of expression—and to art in general—when analyzing society, I use some concepts proposed by Raymond Williams (1977) in favor of the crucial role artistic-folkloric activities had in the early twentieth century's development of indigenismo (and neo-Indianism within it), of the cuzqueño regional identity, and of the proposals for a national and continental identity. Through a close look at music, dance, drama, and some other kinds of public celebrations held in Cuzco in the first half of the twentieth century, I try to understand the "affective elements of consciousness and relationships" (structures of feelings) shared by the cuzqueños in order to approach what was "actually being lived" (practical consciousness) throughout the time when such significant social processes were taking place (Williams 1977, 131–32). I seek to understand the qualitative changes that took place in Cuzco in the first half of the twentieth century by placing significant and inspiring artistic-folkloric activities squarely in the foreground and understanding "thought as felt and feeling as thought," thus leaving behind the dichotomy of "feeling against thought" (131–32).

FOLKLORE AND ETHNIC/RACIAL IDENTITIES

In Latin America, the concept of folklore was inherited from a European tradition in which it acquired a formal meaning in regard to the study and teaching of a people's or community's lore (hence the term *folklore*), as well as a political connotation because it was used to propose the development of new national communities (Herzfeld 1986; Rowe and Schelling 1991, 4). In Cuzco and the rest of Peru, the use of this concept was shaped by the definition given by an Englishman, William J. Thoms, in 1846. It possessed these connotations and was also associated with the idea that the life of the peasantry represented a sort of ideal (or idealized) communal existence as opposed to the emergent industrial society and the culture of the formally educated (Rowe and Schelling 1991, 4). This concept proved useful to intellectuals and artists in Cuzco in the early twentieth century for at least three reasons. First, they sought to foster a regional identity and derive from it a national identity—in other words, to develop communities with a common tradition, a regional and national folklore.[3] Second, they wanted the Andean traditions they appreciated, and that so many of them performed, to be likewise treasured by those who despised them and did not want to accept them as representative of a common identity. Finally, in the face of industrialization and urban growth, as well as the expansion of the means of communication and the overall development of capitalism, those forms of expression that came from the countryside were more highly valued, and even more romanticized, than urban or cosmopolitan forms, as in Europe and many other Latin American countries.

Although it cannot be denied that the very concept of folklore tends to make one think in terms of communities unified by common traditions, and thus to minimize the differences within these communities, it cannot be claimed that the intellectuals and artists in Cuzco who fostered folklore in the early twentieth century wanted to silence the different traditions that existed there.[4] Although they linked the Indian identity with the traditions found in the countryside, which some believed were closer to the pre-Hispanic past, they also valued urban and colonial traditions and made extensive use of them (particularly after the 1930s) in order to consolidate a regional identity that would place the "mestizo" and/or the "cholo" squarely in the center of the regional and national tradition. In addition, the individual creations (compositions, arrangements, *captaciones*,[5] etc.) and styles of the folkloric performers received wide recognition among folklore promoters.

As in other studies, I use the terms *Indian, indigenous, mestizo*, and *cholo* as ethnic/racial categories because, although in the Andes these categories once formed part of the "racial" hierarchies that were legally established in colonial times, and were reinforced in extralegal ways in the Republic, it is also no less true that phenotypes had less to do with these categories than did other "ethnic" characteristics of the subject since at least the eighteenth century (Mendoza 2000, 9–18; 2001, 30–42). Race and ethnicity are historically defined categories, but the first of these concepts tends to emphasize somatic indexes while the latter stresses lifestyle elements such as language, clothing, and occupation. Both analytical categories have a lot to do with social class, both in the Andes and elsewhere, because the identity of an individual in any given society is related to the resources to which this individual has access.[6] Thus, indicators such as kinship relations, material resources, and educational levels, among others, also play a significant role in defining the identities of individuals, as does their gender identities.

Cuzqueños have used the categories of mestizo, Indian, and cholo for centuries to establish differences in status among themselves. However, this status is not fixed in everyday practices, and cuzqueños have used different resources to pass from one status to another, albeit sometimes in a most conflictive way. As I have shown elsewhere, for instance, contemporary cuzqueños actively define their social, and ethnic/racial identities through the performance of certain styles of music or dance (Mendoza 2000, 2001). Certain markers that separated what was indigenous from what was mestizo materialized in the first half of the twentieth century to a great extent through musical and dance styles. What was indigenous thus became associated with the countryside, with what was farthest from the city of Cuzco, with what was most rustic or less elaborate, with the Quechua language, and with everything that was envisaged as being closer to the pre-Hispanic or Inca past. Mestizo identity was linked more with the city and its culture, with what was more elaborate and/or artificial, with the use of Spanish or the alternate use of Spanish and Quechua, and with the colonial and republican legacy. Of course, in practice, as we shall see throughout this book, enforcing this separation proved to be problematic when it came to classifying folkloric art.

Analyzing or describing the use of the category of cholo in Cuzco and Peru is difficult, but it is always important both to acknowledge its colonial roots (Varallanos 1962; Seligman 1989) and to be specific with regard to the connotations this category has at any given time. As Seligman (1989, 697) explains, the category *cholo* acquired pejorative connotations in colonial society once miscegenation began to undermine the caste system. These connotations became more clear nationwide during the first decades of the twentieth century when people from the highlands began to migrate to the cities in far greater numbers (especially to Lima, the coastal capital city of Peru). The term gradually began to imply an incomplete transition from a rural to an urban culture, as well as a marginal position within the economic structure. The material indicators of the cholo have varied throughout time and change depending on their context, but they tend to cluster around the preferences shown in language, attire, and economic activities, as well as musical and dance styles.

The category *cholo* had strong pejorative connotations by the time the neo-Indianist proposal emerged in force, as it was linked to low social status and an identity as highlander. This cholo identity was adopted by the intellectuals and artists in an attempt to give it a positive connotation and convert it into a symbol of pride in being a highlander (a *serrano*). The reader will see throughout the book that the categories *cholo* and *mestizo* were used as synonyms by the artists and intellectuals who proposed these categories as the basis for regional, national, and American identities, above all from the 1930s on.

FOLKLORIZATION, INDIGENISMO, NEO-INDIANISM, AND CUZQUEÑISMO

It should come as no surprise that the art called folklore was of vital importance in the proposals made by the intellectuals and artists of Cuzco in the early twentieth century regarding individual, regional, national, and continental identities. In the Andean countries, the public performance of dance and music has provided an opportunity for the confrontation and negotiation of identities since the early colonial period (Ares Queija 1984; Estenssoro 1990, 1992, 2003; Poole 1990; Mendoza 2000, 2001). The dynamic thus developed turned these forms of expression into highly significant elements for the configuration of individual and group identities. Since the early twentieth century, a process that could be called "folklorization" added a new and powerful dimension to this dynamic in much the same way as had happened in other parts of Latin America (Rowe and Schelling 1991; Guss 2000). This process, whereby public forms of expression are selected as being representative of a whole region or nation and are staged and promoted as such, has proved essential to the promotion of these identities in various Latin American contexts (Wade 2000; López 2004, 2006). We are in the process of folklorization when these forms of expression become known as folklore.

But this process may also have different connotations, depending on the historical circumstances under which it takes place and the intentions of the individuals who push it forward. In the case of Cuzco, the artists and intellectuals who promoted the development of the field that would later be called folklore acknowledged the significance of this type of practice in the everyday lives of the inhabitants of the region and thus found in it inspiration for their proposals for a regional, national, and continental identity. When these forms became classified as folklore, they were elevated to the status of art and lore, which were considered worth cultivating. In fact, the artists and intellectuals whose activities are studied in depth in this book often called their work folkloric art—which is why I refer to it as artistic-folkloric activity.

Cuzco—its history, its cultural elements, its pre-Hispanic and colonial monuments—has inspired several proposals for a national identity throughout Peru's republican history. We find an early example of this in the nationalist efforts led by the cuzqueño Agustín Gamarra, a military caudillo who served as president of Peru in 1829–33 and promised to recover the past glories of Cuzco (Walker 1999, chap. 5). However, it was in the first half of the twentieth century that the cuzqueño intellectuals and artists had a major opportunity to provide Peruvianness and Americanness with specific forms and content. Contrary to what has been claimed regarding the folkloric art that was meant to foster a regional, national, and continental identity in this period, I insist here that this creation was not the result of a plain and simple manipulation and stylization on the part of intellectual and artistic elites of elements belonging to rural groups and low-class urban groups. This art was rather the result of a complex and fluid interaction, both social and cultural (an exchange of styles and aesthetic preferences), between artists and intellectuals who came from different rural and urban sectors of Cuzco's society. This interaction and exchange led to a prolific artistic-folkloric production that shaped a strong regional identity and attractive proposals for a Peruvian identity. In other words, I claim that the proposals for a regional and national identity developed by indigenismo were to a great extent inspired and given substance by these important artistic activities. This early-twentieth-century artistic output cannot be understood, therefore, as a simple reflection of social and political processes that led to a burgeoning regional cuzqueño identity and of proposals for a national and continental identity; it must be understood as an integral and key part of those processes.

The period 1920–50 was a key period in the development of the canons that would exert a strong influence on artistic production of this kind in Cuzco. It roughly coincides with the development of an important movement within indigenismo, which in the case of Cuzco is known as neo-Indianism (Poole 1997; De la Cadena 2000), *indigenismo práctico* ("practical indigenism"; see Tamayo Herrera 1981), or, at the national level, *indigenismo–2* (Lauer 1997). Although some of the studies that focus on this period have a different understanding of the relationship between this movement and the previous one, which is usually called indigenismo and sometimes sociopolitical indigenismo (Lauer 1997), it is clear that the movements are linked in various ways.

As I have shown elsewhere (Mendoza 2000, 51–55; 2001, 86–93), even in Cuzco itself indigenismo—a movement that tried to place the "Indian" or the "indigenous" population squarely in the center of the debates—was a complex movement the development of which can be traced to 1848, spanning at least four generations (Deustua and Rénique 1984; Kristal 1987). Traditionally, students of cuzqueño indigenismo (see, e.g., Tamayo Herrera 1980, 1981; and Deustua and Rénique 1984) have focused on the development of this movement as a part of the expansion of capitalism and the state in Cuzco and throughout Peru, particularly during the administration of President Augusto B. Leguía (1919–30). More recently, an effort has been made to recover some aspects of the previous approach and analyze this movement by focusing on the political content or implications of the concepts of race and culture, which representatives of the movement developed in order to apply them to the categories *Indian* and *mestizo* (De la Cadena 2000).[7]

As several studies have noted, there was a marked difference in the way the identity of the contemporary Indian and indigenous culture was understood by indigenistas such as Luis Valcárcel—one of the major leaders and ideologues of this movement—and by neo-Indianists such as José Uriel García (Aparicio 1994; Poole 1997; De la Cadena 2000). Valcárcel was born in Moquegua and raised and educated in Cuzco. His vast intellectual output includes several publications on Inca life, political principles, and myths and rituals, as well as contemporary peasant problems. In them he tried to connect some aspects of the ancient and admirable Inca culture to the vestiges of it that could still be found (according to this perspective) in Cuzco's indigenous present. Furthermore, his artistic activities connected Cuzco's contemporary folklore with the idealized images of a glorious Inca past.[8] As other studies have shown, these efforts to connect the contemporary practices of peoples that are politically or socially marginalized to an idealized past, in an attempt to build either a national or an ethnic identity, are also found in other historical periods and other parts of the world (Herzfeld 1986; Kirshenblatt-Gimblett 1998). Valcárcel's ideas and work attained nationwide recognition, as is shown by the fact that in 1931 he moved to Lima to become the director of the Museo de Arqueología Peruana and then the dean of the Faculty of Humanities at San Marcos University. He later represented Peru at the United Nations Educational, Scientific and Cultural Organization (UNESCO), at the Organization of American States (OAS), and in many cultural events outside Peru. He even served as the minister of education in 1945. However, although the idealized image of the Inca empire has rooted itself in Peru's consciousness (Portocarrero and Oliart 1989), it cannot be claimed that the indigenista project succeeded in establishing a national identity that is based on an indigenous or highland identity.

In his book *El Nuevo Indio* (*The New Indian*, 1930), which gave rise to the term *neo-Indianism*, José Uriel García diverged from the way in which indigenista leaders such as Valcárcel understood indigenous identity and culture. In Poole's words, in the first half of the twentieth century cuzqueño artists and intellectuals "lived in the complex urban-rural environment of the city of Cuzco, and were all aware of the multitude of ethnic gradations existing between the ideal states of pure mestizo and pure Indian" (1997, 186). Whereas for Valcárcel the true Indian still lived outside the city in some remote part of Cuzco department as a living testimony to what the Inca past had once been like, for García the differences between the Spaniard and the Indian had faded away due to the miscegenation of colonial times. In his view, the "new Indian" was a result of this very miscegenation. In chapter 3, I show that Valcárcel himself acknowledged this clear ideological discrepancy.

Neo-Indianist artists and intellectuals such as García and Humberto

Vidal Unda put forward a highland cholo or mestizo identity that they hoped would be adopted as the continental identity of the future not just by the cuzqueños but by all Peruvians and all Americans, too. The neo-Indianists were not alone in promoting a mestizo identity as a national and American symbol, nor were they the first to do so (De la Cadena 2000; Wade 2000), but what I try to show here is that their proposed *mestizaje* was strongly inspired by the complex cultural reality perceivable through a rich artistic-folkloric output. Perhaps this was also the case in other parts of Latin America. This complexity led them to feel the cuzqueño and Peruvian identity as one in which the pre-Hispanic and the European traditions had fused to form elements of the popular culture that prevailed among both the peasantry and urban groups. Thus, in promoting areas of fluid exchange between artists from different rural and urban social sectors, the neo-Indianists contributed to the consolidation of canons and repertoires with which all cuzqueños were able to identify for decades.

But the neo-Indianists encountered multiple paradoxes and contradictions in their efforts to promote a folkloric art that comprised all sectors of cuzqueño society and in proposing mestizo art as a symbol of this movement. One of the main paradoxes they faced in their proposal of mestizaje as the epitome of a unified future for Cuzco and Peru was the fact that the representatives of this movement reproduced the Indian-mestizo dichotomy, which was clearly shown when they used these categories to distinguish the genres of music and dance in contests. The reemergence of the differences between racial or ethnic groups also occurred during attempts to build a mestizo national identity in other parts of Latin America (Wade 2000, 6–7). But once again the specific meaning this takes in each case must be carefully examined. The neo-Indianist artists and intellectuals distinguished these styles not in absolute terms through a classification of music and dance styles as either indigenous or mestizo but in relation to degree. Ideally, the farther away from the city, the more rustic, the more pre-Hispanic, and the more rural they were the more Indian these performances were considered to be. On the other hand, the artistic output was deemed to be more mestizo the more obvious its colonial and republican influences were, the closer to the city of Cuzco it was produced, and the more stylized and elaborate it seemed.

But this classification weakened in the face of the complexity of the musical pieces and of the identity of the contestants. In fact, it must be clearly understood that when the people who organized these events—the contests in particular—insisted that both mestizo and indigenous artists should participate they were endeavoring to include the widest possible range of art so as to revalue peasant styles hitherto despised and allow the folklore they themselves practiced to participate in the development of a regional and national identity. The use of the term *cholo* to describe both the art of the peasantry and that of urban artists belonging to social and artistic elites was apparently an attempt to solve the contradiction of having to separate the categories of indigenous and mestizo.

Finally, no reference can be made to the proposals the cuzqueño artists and intellectuals made in the first half of the twentieth century for a regional, national, and continental identity without first understanding some basic tenets of what they began to call cuzqueñismo. Aparicio (1994) notes that this feeling was explicitly stated by Ángel Escalante in a famous article he published in 1929, while serving as a congressman in Lima, in a special issue of the journal *Mundial* devoted to the declaration of Cuzco's cathedral as a basilica, a fact that drew the attention of the public to Cuzco and probably influenced the religious language he used (134). He wrote:

> Cuzqueñismo is what this new creed must be called. Because Cuzco is the heart of the continent, the admirable coffer of the American tradition, the holy altar of the race, the secular temple where the Eucharist of Americanism alone can be consumed. Because Cuzco is the monument raised by the ages to the glory of those incomparable warriors and legislators who exhibited their magnificent and gallant victorious banners all over South America. Because from there at all times men emerged, spreading ideas, sprouting seeds and expanding perfumes with the unmistakable seal of a high spiritual beauty and a clear-cut Peruvianness . . . Cuzqueñoness (*Lo Cuzqueño*) does not and cannot refer to the departmental political demarcation because Cuzco is the soul itself of nationhood and cuzqueñismo is the fullest and most typical crystallization of the national ideology.[9]

This feeling, which places Cuzco at the center of the national and continental ideology, took shape and was nourished thanks to prolific artistic-folkloric production and international interest in the archaeological and colonial monuments of Cuzco. Both elements were entwined with the growing interest of national and foreign tourists in this region. The characteristics that cuzqueñismo would take were also strongly related to the material changes the city of Cuzco underwent in the first part of the twentieth century—what Tamayo (1981) calls "the first modernization." Industrial development, migration to the city, sanitation measures that met new standards of hygiene, and the arrival and expansion of means of transportation and communication (trains, trams, the telephone, radio, automobiles, and highways) all exerted a strong influence on the experiences, feelings, and ideas of those who posited a new regional and national identity. As we shall see, cuzqueñismo was constructed and lived in different ways by the various groups and individuals that took part in the manifestation of this feeling.

The neo-Indianists had a somewhat paradoxical and ambiguous relationship with modernization, as well as with the modernist and avant-garde literary and artistic movements that arrived, mainly from Europe, during the first decades of the twentieth century. Neo-Indianists, as noted by Poole, on the one hand adopted avant-garde language by rejecting the idealization of the Inca past that previous indigenistas had favored, but, on the other hand, faced with the contemporary, Lima-centered proposals for a national identity, these cuzqueño artists and intellectuals clung to the landscape and Andean traditions as a source of "spiritual and emotional strength" (1997, 184–85). Poole adds that, for many neo-Indianists, "modernity, and in particular the rhythm or velocity of modern life, was perceived as a threat to the very landscape" from which they drew this spiritual and emotional strength (185). Hence the concept and practice of folklore proved important for their proposals. It was in this field that the neo-Indianist intellectuals and artists met with cuzqueño intellectuals and artists who likewise emphasized the significance of "feeling" and dedicated their efforts to creating and feeling, as well as to helping the remaining people of Cuzco and Peru identify with something that could characteristically be called their own.

This introduction is followed by a chapter in which I explore the origins of the process of folklorization through the tour of a performing troupe, the Misión Peruana de Arte Incaico (Peruvian Mission of Incaic Art), thus allowing a first approach to the complexities of this process. The success of this tour, which was undertaken by a group of cuzqueño artists led by Luis E. Valcárcel, in representing Peru in Bolivia, Argentina, and Uruguay from October 1923 to January 1924, with no governmental support whatsoever, had definite repercussions in the establishment of the first cultural institution in Cuzco. The chapter shows that in the *misión* we find the same mechanisms at work that were fostering a convergence of styles, traditions, individuals, and themes derived from different urban and rural sectors of the cuzqueño society of the time.

Chapter 2 takes a close look at the origins of the first cultural and folkloric institution in Peru, the Centro Qosqo de Arte Nativo (Cuzco Center of Native Art or Centro Qosqo for short); the contests organized by this institution at the regional level; and the presentations cuzqueño groups made nationwide in the first contests, which were held in the Pampa of Amancaes in Lima, in the late 1920s. Using as an example the path followed by the self-taught musician Manuel Pillco Cuba, a founding member of the Centro Qosqo and a member of the misión, I show that from the beginning the self-educated musicians of popular extraction interacted with musicians of a higher social origin who had a formal and cosmopolitan musical education, thus influencing the rise of the new styles and repertoires that materialized as typically cuzqueño.

Chapter 3 describes in depth how the development of a regional identity and the proposals for a Peruvian and American identity among the cuzqueño people were entwined with the rise of Cuzco as a center of archaeological and touristic interest at both the international and national levels. I show how, from the "discovery" of Machu Picchu (1911) and the declaration of Cuzco as the Archaeological Capital City of America (1993) to the celebrations for the Fourth Centennial of the Spanish foundation of the cities of Cuzco (1934) and Lima (1935), the cuzqueños who participated in artistic-folkloric production were quite aware of their significant role as representatives of the regional and national traditions. As the spaces where this tradition could be performed at the regional and national levels expanded, the cuzqueño intellectuals and artists positioned within the neo-Indianist movement, such as José Uriel García, its leader, saw in folklore an example of the miscegenation that had given rise to the identity of the current inhabitants of the Andes. The key image of the Inca was gradually abandoned in the repertoire that consolidated itself as typically cuzqueño and instead a more important role was accorded to the contemporary urban and rural practices perceived as cholo and mestizo.

Chapter 4 is a detailed study of a space of artistic-folkloric output that proved to be a landmark in the acceptance of Andean rural music in some parts of the region—and Peru—where it had been hitherto excluded: *La Hora del Charango* (*The Charango Hour*). Using means of communication that had just recently reached the region, in 1937 this radio program took the small Andean guitar known as the *charango* as its symbol and gave an even stronger stimulus to the cuzqueñista, Peruvianist, and Americanist feelings that were envisaged as a defense of the highland cholo or mestizo culture. The artists and intellectuals who participated in this program would often speak of *lo nuestro* (what is our own) with regard to the folklore they promoted but without restricting this term to Cuzco's folklore and instead making an effort to expand it to mean "Peruvian." This was an effort that aimed to provide the rest of Peru with specific referents based on Andean traditions—such as charango music—that would shape the national identity. These cuzqueñista and Peruvianist feelings developed under the perceived pressure of an "invasion" of foreign cultural elements and in the face of the *criollo*[10] coastal proposal, focused in Lima, which also presented itself as an alternative source of a national identity. The chapter also shows how this space for the interaction of artists from various sectors of cuzqueño society stimulated the creation of new musical styles and techniques within the charango tradition. I include an account of the careers of the two most important self-taught musicians who left their mark on the cuzqueño tradition: Pancho Gómez Negrón and Julio César Benavente Díaz.

Chapter 5 chronicles the rise and development of another major cultural institution in Cuzco that actively promoted folklore during the first half of the twentieth century: the Instituto Americano de Arte de Cuzco (American Art Institute of Cuzco or IAAC). Established in 1937 by José Uriel García, it replaced in several respects the momentarily deactivated Centro Qosqo by promoting contests and other spaces for artistic production. This institute gave initial support to several folkloric groups formed mostly by self-trained musicians of rural and popular urban extraction who were seeking an opportunity to join the thriving folkloric life of the city of Cuzco. This was the case with the Asociación Folklórica Kosko, which led to the definitive revitalization of the Centro Qosqo and its growth. A discussion of the origins of this group illustrates the heightened presence these popular artists had in the cultural institutions of the city of Cuzco.

In the same chapter I also explore some aspects of the career of Armando Guevara Ochoa, the Cuzco musician and composer most widely recognized in Peru and abroad, whose art while he lived in Cuzco was developed in spaces fostered by the IAAC. This world-renowned artist, who is acknowledged as the creator and practitioner of a nationalist musical tradition, was a disciple and friend of Manuel Pillco, from whom, according to the testimony of Guevara Ochoa himself, he learned "the purest Andean folklore." Finally, the chapter returns to the issue of the growing importance of national and international tourists in Cuzco and examines the ways in which this is entwined with the rise of the Día (June 24) and the Semana del Cuzco (Cuzco Day and Cuzco Week), as well as with the ritual that would become the icon of these celebrations—the Inti Raymi. This week, and later the entire month of June, became the major site for the creation and re-creation of Cuzco's folkloric traditions.

The epilogue revisits some of the major conclusions reached in this book and explains how the trends and canons developed in the first part of the twentieth century have left their imprint on Cuzco's artistic-folkloric production to the present day. Whereas in the late 1960s the state had a more active and direct role in the promotion of folklore, and the number of folklore contests and festivals increased, the characteristics of what was considered typically cuzqueño remained rooted in what had been developed in the first part of the twentieth century. I briefly review the failed efforts of the major folkloric groups of Cuzco to have their art recognized as representative of the national identity. This happened in 1968, when the Peruvian government for the first time ever officially sent a folkloric group to represent Peru abroad. The group chosen, which was sent to Mexico, was one based in Lima that represented criollo musical traditions, Afro-Peruvian ones in particular. I likewise review the paradoxical situation Cuzco's artists, and Andean artists in general, found themselves in vis-à-vis Ima Sumac, an internationally acclaimed singer who presented her music to the rest of the world as a legacy of Peru's Incaic tradition. I finish with some reasons why it is still important to understand the complexities of the intellectual, sentimental, and artistic creative process that took place in Cuzco throughout the first part of the twentieth century.

1

. . .

THE MISIÓN PERUANA DE ARTE INCAICO AND THE DEVELOPMENT OF THE ARTISTIC-FOLKLORIC PRODUCTION IN CUZCO

A key moment at which to begin our exploration of folkloric art in Cuzco is when the production of the music and dances that would shape a regional identity, as well as regional proposals for a national identity, previously closely connected with the development of the "Incaic theater," took on independent and active lives of their own and began to displace drama. Without completely abandoning the theater, many artists became creators and the driving force behind the cultural institutions and events that would promote artistic-folkloric creation throughout the twentieth century. At first, many of the *cuadros costumbristas* (traditional tableaux), musical pieces and dances that began to be depicted as representative of the Peruvian and cuzqueño identity, had been a part of these dramas or were directly derived from them and thus still had the Inca or Incaic as their central symbol. But, although it never completely vanished, the Inca theme gradually ceased to dominate the artistic scene while a more prominent role was awarded to themes that were recognized as representative of the contemporary world and/or cultural miscegenation.

It must be noted that in order to materialize the Inca aesthetic, from the beginning the renowned musicians of Cuzco and other provinces had used some elements derived from the contemporary rural repertoire (Romero 1988, 223–24). However, it was around the 1920s that the artists, themes, instruments, and styles belonging to the contemporary rural and popular urban worlds began to appear more openly and in force. Finally, it was also at this time that the artistic output took on a leading role in the efforts to develop the genuine cuzqueño and national identity.

The best way to illustrate this moment is to review some aspects of what was called the Misión Peruana de Arte Incaico (Peruvian Mission of Incaic Art), a performing troupe headed by the renowned indigenista Luis Valcárcel. Between October 1923 and January 1924, this artistic group, which was hailed as a Peruvian cultural embassy in both the national and foreign press, successfully took a repertoire of cuzqueño art to Buenos Aires, La Paz, and Montevideo, where audiences assumed that it was representative of Incaness, Peruvianness, and Americanness. The misión's experience, which was formed mostly by cuzqueño artists, is worth recalling for at least three interrelated reasons. First, it remains engraved in the memory of cuzqueño artists as a glorious moment when cuzqueño traditions, and Andean traditions in general, received well-deserved recognition both in Peru and abroad. Second, in the misión, as I try to show here, there were already mechanisms at work that would foster a convergence of the styles, traditions, individuals, and themes that would become more fully developed once Cuzco's cultural institutions took shape. Finally, everything seems to indicate that the successful experience of the misión stimulated not only the establishment of the Centro Qosqo de Arte Nativo, which was the first institution of this kind (and the most important and respected one in Cuzco nowadays), but also the establishment of all the institutions that followed it.

We must not forget that the misión was formed in the midst of the social and political changes brought about by President Augusto B. Leguía during his eleven-year administration in 1919–30 (what is now known as the Oncenio). These changes were intrinsically connected to the expansion of the state and capitalism in Peru, as well as with Leguía's dream of building a Patria Nueva (New Fatherland) that would modernize Peru through the transformation of its ancient political and economic structures. Leguía tried to gain the support of the proletariat, the peasantry, and the middle class in order to consolidate his position vis-à-vis the old landed oligarchies. This led him to develop a populist rhetoric that echoed indigenista ideas. For instance, his administration supported the establishment of the Comité Pro-Indígena Tawantinsuyo (Tawantinsuyu Pro-Indian Committee), which was a pivotal actor in the political arena of the time and was formed by pro-Indian ideologues based in Lima, radical indigenistas from the provinces, and Indian leaders who identified themselves as such and came from different political backgrounds (De la Cadena 2000, 89). Leguía likewise gave legal recognition to the communal property, agricultural land, and pastures of "Indian communities" and established the celebration of the Day of the Indian on June 24. During his second term of office he likewise actively promoted the music and dance festival held on this date at the Pampa de Amancaes in Lima, which until then had only taken place as part of the feast day of Saint John.

This study of the Peruvian and cuzqueño experience of the misión will show that, although this group was led by intellectuals and artists with formal musical or artistic educations and some cosmopolitan influences (a knowledge of the classical and contemporary repertoires of Europe and the United States), it also included artists who came from a more popular, rural, and self-educated cuzqueño tradition. I will emphasize that the artistic output of the formally educated artists was strongly based on popular Andean urban and rural traditions that were considered indigenous from the standpoint of the city. I will likewise stress that in the misión's performances we have an early example of the convergence of individuals, themes, genres, and forms and in general a fusion of aesthetic elements from various traditions derived from both a formal and a cosmopolitan artistic upbringing and Cuzco's self-educated rural and popular-urban tradition of the time. However, in order to understand the nature of the misión and the work done by the artists that led it, a brief reference must be made to the previous development of the drama and music that had been called Incaic and were synonymous with a nationalist and Americanist art in Cuzco and the rest of Peru, as well as in other South American countries.

INCAIC THEATER

César Itier, the author of the major study of Quechua theater in Cuzco (1995, 2000), emphasizes the fact that the Incaic drama fostered and developed above all in Cuzco was a "comprehensive proposal of a national culture" that "meant to renew the development of the pre-Columbian drama, linguistic, musical and choreographic tradition interrupted for four centuries" (2000, 11).[1] Itier identifies four major stages in the development of this tradition, during the third of which (1917–21) this art form was acknowledged "by a vast public as the national theater par excellence, not just in Cuzco but in other provinces, as well as in Lima" (2000, 87).[2] In this period, too, the work of Cuzco's theatrical companies crossed national borders and turned the Incaic theater into a pan-Andean phenomenon (Itier 1995, 11). It is worth noting that at least by 1913 the interest in this type of drama was not limited to the upper and middle classes of the city of Cuzco but was very popular among members of the general population who were monolingual Quechua speakers.[3]

According to Itier, Incaic dramas were "set in Inca times, [and their] arguments came either from contemporary regional legends or from the sixteenth- and seventeenth-century chronicles. [They] often portray loves gone awry due to historical circumstances. The characters are always Incas, that is, members of the elite. In general, Incaic dramas sought to show the virtues that made Tahuantinsuyo great and the vices that brought about its ruin; the authors thus hoped to morally instruct their public" (1995, 26–27).

The play that marked the peak of this tradition was known as *Ollantay,* but its original title was *Los Rigores de un padre y generosidad de un rey* (*The Harshness of a Father and the Generosity of a King*).[4] The possible origin of this play generated a long and interesting debate.[5] Some even argued that it was a legacy of the Inca period (though not written at the time, of course, as the Incas had no form of writing). This play, which was possibly written in the late eighteenth or early nineteenth century by the Catholic priest Antonio Valdés, has been the subject of several translations (not just into Spanish but into other languages as well), versions, and reinterpretations by many literati and playwrights, both Peruvian and foreign. *Ollantay* eventually became the most popular play performed by the members of Cuzco's cultural institutions.

This play tells the story of the forbidden love between Kusi Ccoyllor, a princess of the Inca nobility and the daughter of Inca Pachacutec, and Ollanta, a general in the Inca army who was not of noble status. The secret union of Kusi Ccoyllor and Ollanta, forbidden by Pachacutec, produces a child named Ima Sumaq, which results in a ten-year jail sentence for Kusi Ccoyllor. Later Ollanta takes up arms against Pachacutec, but the old Inca dies before a direct encounter takes place, and his son, Tupac Yupanqui, succeeds him. The new Inca, unaware of the history of the liaison between his sister and Ollanta, faces the latter in person and not only forgives his rebellion but also acknowledges his military feats on behalf of the empire and appoints him "second Inca" (Calvo 1998, 307), the official in charge whenever the Inca leaves Cuzco. When this happens, Ima Sumaq, who has recently discovered her imprisoned mother and is unaware of the identity of her father, leads Tupac Yupanqui and Ollanta to her prison. The quandary is resolved, and Tupac Yupanqui sanctions the union between Ollanta and Kusi Ccoyllor.

The music and dances in these plays were part of their great appeal. The classical musical theme in the first performances of *Ollantay*, which were staged in the late nineteenth century and the early twentieth, was composed by Manuel Monet, one of the pioneers of Cuzco's music in a regionalist and nationalist vein.[6] In the late nineteenth century Monet, along with other cuzqueño musicians,[7] was collecting indigenous melodies in order to incorporate them into his compositions, which were likewise based on musical styles from the pre-Hispanic tradition such as the *harawi*[8]. In the following section we shall see that other provincial musicians who composed this type of music also followed this strategy, albeit with variations in degree and the ways in which the materials derived from the contemporary rural and popular-urban repertoires were used.

It must be noted that the choreographers of the theatrical companies also used contemporary rural traditions to a greater or lesser extent. This was acknowledged in a newspaper comment published in 1919 about the performance in Cuzco of the play *Yawarwaqaq*, written by the famed cuzqueño author José Félix Silva, which claimed that all of the dances were "modern stylized creations of the indigenous tradition, as should be the case in all reconstructions of this kind of the past, which must not be a servile copy of it but an aesthetic depuration" (Itier 1995, 33).

The fact that a journalist acknowledged that the music and dances presented as Incaic were to a great extent based on the contemporary peasant repertoire should come as no surprise, as the prevailing idea among the most renowned artists and students of the time was that "the peasant music of the time was an extension of Inca music" (Romero 1988, 224).[9]

INCAIC MUSIC

As with theater, the development of so-called Incaic music in Peru must be understood within the context of a nationalist effort of an indigenista kind that swept all of Latin America in the early decades of the twentieth century (Béhague 1996, 311–24). Although at first most of the productions of the composers who spearheaded the creation of this music were associated with theater, it had already developed a parallel life of its own. By 1917 it was acknowledged throughout Peru as a genre in itself (Itier 2000, 9).

The extent to which the individuals who were the driving force behind this music based their creations on contemporary rural and popular-urban musical forms varied from one case to the next, as did the extent of their formal musical education. Nonetheless, their work had much in common. These nationalist productions, in which provincial composers such as the renowned Huánuco-born Daniel Alomía Robles were preeminent, had a major influence on the members of what was already known in the early twentieth century as the Cuzco School.

One of the few efforts thus far to systematize what is known of Peruvian music considers that the work of most of the pioneering members of this school (Mariano Ojeda, Pío Wenceslao Olivera, Manuel Monet, José Calixto Pacheco, Leandro Alviña, and José Domingo Rado) "did nothing more than collect popular melodies that were copied in full on their scores and harmonized with great simplicity" (Pinilla 1988, 143). Regarding composers such as Juan de Dios Aguirre, Roberto Ojeda, and Baltazar Zegarra (three of the musicians known in Cuzco as the "Big Four of Cuzco Music"), who were notable somewhat later,[10] Pinilla notes that, "although they wrote compositions for orchestra, chamber groups, and piano with slight variations vis-à-vis the folkloric original, they were clearly still more on the popular than on the erudite side" (143).

This type of comment, which stresses—sometimes condescendingly—the fact that these cuzqueño musicians relied heavily on the repertoire of the rural and popular-urban culture of their time and did not undertake any major musical elaboration, is considered offensive by Cuzco artists, who even now defend the development of a regional and national music of the sort composed by the classic composers of cuzqueño music (Ojeda 1987, 43). Pablo Ojeda (the son of Roberto and grandson of Mariano), for instance, rejects the "technicist" approach within which some of these comments have been made not just of Cuzco composers "but also against the composers from other parts of Peru who worked with 'melodic phrases' [taken] from Andean folklore" (1987, 44). In addition, "Many believe that to create based on an indigenous melody is simply a matter of technique, [but they do not] realize the trove of indigenous and indigenista spirit one needs for such a delicate task. Some eminent musical technicians have a European influence which often makes them break the beat when working with Andean folkloric music, thus producing flawed versions. . . . Many likewise believe that the creations of Peruvian composers with an Andean orientation are no more than compilations. Nothing could be farther removed from the truth" (46–47).

The assertions made by Pablo Ojeda, on the one hand, confirm that the musical work of the members of the Cuzco School, like that of other composers of Incaic and nationalist music, was based to a large extent on the contemporary popular rural or urban repertoire. On the other hand, his allusion to the "trove of indigenous and indigenista spirit" also reminds us that one of the major concerns of these musicians was to find elements in the rural and popular-urban traditions that would provide a solid base with which to develop a type of music wherein all sectors of Cuzco's society, and, if possible, all of Peruvian society, would find elements they could consider their own. In this way what was essentially "our own," cuzqueño and/or Peruvian as the case may be, should be strongly rooted in the Andean or highland tradition.

Although it is not easy to reconstruct the different processes through which the abundant pieces in this genre were created, the following is a transcription of parts of an account that partially illustrates some of the ways in which these processes worked. It tells of the origins of the *himno al sol* (hymn to the sun), one of the melodies harmonized by Daniel Alomía Robles, which became a classic piece in the repertoire of what can simultaneously be considered Incaic, nationalist, and cuzqueño music.[11] While Daniel Alomía Robles was not a native of Cuzco and his work as a composer and compiler included melodies from various departments in Peru (e.g., the melody on which this hymn is based was collected in Jauja, Junín), the two years he spent in Cuzco (1915–17) were of great importance both for his own work as a compiler and composer and for the cuzqueño musicians who were stimulated by the work of this remarkable supporter of nationalist music. As Alomía Robles wrote:

> In the year 1897, Dr. José María Dianderas, the old priest of Jauja, introduced me to a tall Indian of well-developed muscles which enabled him, despite his advanced age (117 years), to walk with the erect body and the military bearing of a good soldier, which he actually was in the liberating army. . . . His name was José Mateo Sánchez. . . . It was he whom I first heard singing this beautiful hymn, whose delicate notes I was unable to understand at the time because the throat modulating them, worn by time, only produced a hoarse, cavernous, unpleasant voice. . . . He certainly realized I had not understood his music. One day I went

hunting to Lake Marco on his invitation; that morning, after presenting me with a precious heron he had caught, he said to me, "Wait, you are going to hear what we sing to the Sun." Moments later, two girls with two men from the same community entered the *choza* (a small hut in which Indians live). One of them brought a violin (this instrument has become widely spread among the Indians), and the other a *pincullo* (a small *quena*) and a *tinya* (a small drum).

I was finally able to listen to this mysterious melody, so heroically saved from oblivion by these silent inhabitants of our *puna*.

Later I ascertained that [this same melody] is also known in the provinces of Huamalíes and Dos de Mayo, in the department of Huánuco. Finally, when the reverend Jesuit fathers Margañón and Perier were in my house to see my collection, they assured me they had heard it in the highlands of Ecuador, where they had lived for over fifteen years. (Eco Musical 1943, 23–24)

The final comment reminds us that Robles and other musicians and musicologists of his time yearned to reconstruct a type of music they believed was an extension of the Inca tradition and therefore must be widespread throughout the Andean area. It was on this basis, after instilling in them above all a harmony,[12] and in some cases turning them into symphonies, operas, or zarzuelas, that these musicians were able to develop the nationalist music of the time.

Several styles, themes, titles, and melodies repeatedly appear in the works of these musicians. This may have been due to the fact that in this period musicians sought a common source of inspiration in the Inca and contemporary rural and popular urban cultures, to the presence of common musical elements throughout the Andean area, or because they borrowed from one another (albeit without always admitting so openly).[13] It is true that the music that would eventually be identified as typically cuzqueño continued to acquire new characteristics and nuances throughout the twentieth century, but what ultimately became the model to follow was the repertoire of the first two decades in which the most renowned themes were the ones acclaimed at the national and South American level as part of the "misión."

THE MISIÓN: MEMBERS, REPERTOIRE, AND STYLES

It was during their participation in the tours undertaken by the misión, that the cuzqueño artists who had devoted themselves to the creation of an Incaic art attained "their greatest recognition" (Itier 2000, 75). Paradoxically, this was also the moment in which the Incaic theater became restricted to the Cuzco region, having been abandoned by the local and national intellectual elites of Peru.[14] The misión, which was also known as the Compañía Peruana de Arte Incaico (Peruvian Company of Inca Art), was actually not a theatrical company, as its repertoire included a large range of musical pieces, dances, *cuadros costumbristas* or *de costumbre* (traditional tableaux), reconstructions of Inca festivals, and exhibitions of textiles, paintings, and photographs alongside lectures on so-called Inca art and other subjects.[15] The plays performed in the shows were often abridged and reduced to just one scene, and the music, dances, cuadros costumbristas, and reconstructions of Inca rituals (with abundant music and dances) predominated. In fact, what the foreign press hints at is that the music and dances were apparently in greatest demand and most acclaimed.

Briefly, the misión was born thanks to the resourcefulness of Roberto Levillier, the Argentinean ambassador to Peru (and also a Peruvianist historian), who provided the funds that the Comisión Nacional de Bellas Artes had sent from Buenos Aires in order to have a Peruvian art group perform Peruvian art (in turn labeled "Inca," "autochthonous," or "indigenous") in that city.[16] The funds were meant to provide for "the organization of the company, the purchase of wardrobe and props, the support of the artists, and defrayal of their traveling expenses in Argentina," with transportation to the Argentinean frontier the only expense not covered.[17] Despite appeals in the Lima press requesting support for this "patriotic effort," the Peruvian government did not provide any economic support for the group.[18]

What lay behind this initiative was the desire of some Argentinean artists and intellectuals to promote a nationalist and Americanist art based on the Indian at a time when their country was still debating whether to define itself as a land with either an Indian or an essentially white and European heritage.[19] The presence of some interest in, and support for, indigenista visions of the nation in Argentina are clearly shown not just in the absolute triumph of the misión's performances, which were attended by the president of the republic and major political and cultural figures, but also by the newspaper coverage.[20] These comments demonstrate that, although it was acknowledged that the leaders of the group were renowned artists and intellectuals with formal training in their respective fields, the group was perceived—

particularly with regard to the performance of music, songs, and dances—as representative of a simple art form devoid of any major influence from Western aesthetics and thus closer to what was considered "authentic" or "indigenous." Consider the following comment:

> Last night in the Colón [Theater], our public attended a spectacle which, for *its significance*—as a manifestation of autochthonous Peruvian art—and *the influence that it will exert on our creative artists, providing them with a purely American element of inestimable value, has assumed great importance.*
>
> A succession of tableaux, dances, choirs, and songs revived for an instant the past splendor of so powerful a race. The fierceness of its warrior dances, the gentleness of the songs, the poetry of its tableaux, the dazzling polychromy of the costumes, *and the naive and natural art* of its interpreters gave this spectacle a *stamp of authenticity* to which, by the way, we have not been accustomed by better-organized companies.[21]

The perception of the misión's art as minimally ornamented and elaborate was not limited to Argentinean observers but was also common to those in Bolivia and Chile.[22] For instance, it was noted that the choirs were "always in unison" (i.e., there was no polyphonic elaboration) and that the voices were "natural, unstudied, with a guttural timbre and colorless at times."[23] Other comments hint more clearly at the combination of traditions and styles present in some of the pieces performed. According to one account, "The Inca pastorella of Ccosco Llaqta,[24] a song from the mountains of Cuzco; the eclogue of Inti-raimi, a sacred hymn from the festival of the Sun; the Ahuaccuna, which males and females from the humble tribe dance and sing, while they knit and cook their domestic wares, is a plastic-exotic tableau (*cuadro plástico-exótico*) that catches the attention, even though this strident and noisy music is discordant in the ear, but the sweet chords bring forth deep feelings of a sweet and pleasant well-being that drown the fortissimo of the orchestra in crescendo."[25]

The music and lyrics of the *awajkuna* or *ahuaccuna* (the weavers), the example par excellence of what was considered a cuadro de costumbre or costumbrista; the music of the reconstructed Inti Raymi, the Inca ritual held during the winter solstice in honor of the sun;[26] and other themes and dances interpreted by the misión were the creation of Roberto Ojeda (1895–1983), the musical director of the group and a prolific cuzqueño musician

1. Roberto Ojeda, Manuel Pillco, and an unidentified musician (Sacsayhuamán, 1920–30). (PHOTO BY THE CABRERA BROTHERS, FOTOTECA ANDINA ARCHIVE, CENTRO BARTOLOMÉ DE LAS CASAS, CUZCO.)

see fig. 1). The music of Roberto Ojeda, both the earliest, which possessed an Incaic tone (*tónica*), and his later works, which were more openly costumbrista, always relied heavily on the contemporary rural and popular-urban repertoire (Ojeda 1987, 68–72). This famed cuzqueño musician, who came from the urban middle class of the city of Cuzco and had been musically educated by his father, Mariano Ojeda (a composer of sacred music and the organist at the cathedral), attained his artistic recognition during the misión's tour (68).[27] Like other members of the misión, Ojeda became one of the major founders and driving forces of Cuzco's cultural institutions, including the Centro Qosqo.

Roberto Ojeda's musical work includes above all compositions that were widely known as his creations (like the ones mentioned above and others that were part of Incaic dramas), which were constructed from melodies he collected, and incorporated peasant genres such as the *qaswa*, the *hu-*

anca, and the *pastoril* (Ojeda 1987, 69). Second, the so-called captaciones are also dominant among his musical works; they consist of personal arrangements of whole themes that were popular in the contemporary repertoire but had no known author, themes that were called "folkloric" or "anonymous" (49–50). Roberto Ojeda, who began to take notes on the popular and rural music of Cuzco when he was very young while traveling through the provinces of this department, also possessed from the beginning the materials compiled by his father (70). One of his most famous compositions is the *awaqkuna*, which for decades would remain an almost essential piece in performances of Cuzco "folklore" both inside and outside the region (see fig. 2). The following is a transcription of the first three stanzas of the main *huayno* that accompanies this scene, which show some characteristics in common with many cuzqueño huaynos of this and other periods, that is, it is a song of love that at the same time evokes the Andean landscape.[28]

Ñan Pacha paqarinña	So the land begins to revive
k'anchayninta illaricheq	its brilliance dawns
kaqninta kusichinanpaq	to cheer its creator
Llaki phuti sonqoipiña	In my saddened heart
urpillaitan chinkachini	my little dove I've lost[29]
weqetaña ujiarini	tears I've already drunk
ch'akyinipi yuyarispa	remembering when I am thirsty
Orqontan q'asantan wasapamuni	By mountains and ravines I go
mayuntan waiq'ontan kinraikamuni	through the river and the gorges I come
urpichallaytan chinkachimuni	my little dove I've lost
sonqochallaitan chinkachimuni	my little heart I've lost[30]

Indeed, even if we leave aside the fact that Ojeda's music throughout the tour already showed a convergence of styles and traditions and had a strong component of contemporary rural and popular-urban music, this convergence will be more noticeable if we examine closely the repertoire and the members of the misión. The group had about forty-seven members.[31] The names most commonly mentioned in the writings and discussions about the misión include Luis Valcárcel, its director, who, with Luis Velasco Aragón, the secretary and a well-known cuzqueño writer and journalist, was in charge of presenting the group and giving lectures; Luis Ochoa and Julio

2. Cuzco actors, possibly from the Asociación Folklórica Kosko, performing a scene from the *awaqkuna* (Cuzco, 1940). (PHOTO BY EULOGIO NISHIAMA, FOTOTECA ANDINA ARCHIVE, CENTRO BARTOLOMÉ DE LAS CASAS, CUZCO.)

Rouvirós (famed figures in Cuzco's Incaic drama) as theatrical directors; the renowned artist and photographer Juan Manuel Figueroa Aznar (a Spaniard who lived in Cuzco) as the art director in charge of the props; Roberto Ojeda Campana as musical director; and Victor Guzmán, also a native of Cuzco, who was a virtuoso pianist and assisted in the musical direction.[32]

The names of the actors, some of whom were both singers and dancers, are much less well known, at least with regard to their participation in the misión, although they did appear in the press.[33] These individuals comprised about two-thirds of the artistic troupe, not counting the leaders, and most of them came from upper- and middle-class families in the city of Cuzco judging by their names and the fact that they were called *señoritas* and *señores* (ladies and gentlemen).[34] Finally, there were those who comprised about one-third of the artistic troupe whose names are not even listed, as they were considered "natives" or "aboriginals" from either humble urban backgrounds or rural areas. The harpist Manuel Pillco probably was one of these. He gradually made himself known in the art circles of the city of Cuzco and founded more than one cuzqueño cultural institution.[35]

Most of the music performed either alone or as part of the cuadros costumbristas, historical reconstructions, and scenes from plays, was apparently comprised of selections sung by choirs (probably formed by the abovementioned "señoritas y señores"), solo songs accompanied by traditional instruments such as the *quenas* (native flutes), and performances by a traditional ensemble (*orquesta típica*) "formed by a small harp, quenas, small drums, pinkuillus, and the tinya," the latter a small drum of pre-Hispanic origin.[36] It is likely that the members of this traditional ensemble were among those the press considered aboriginals or natives whose names were omitted. Judging by the comments made in the press regarding the voices and music, many of the performances showed the traditional characteristics of rural Andean music (which is based on pre-Hispanic traditions) such as "the preference for high-pitched sounds at the limit of the vocal range," the use of musical scales different from those commonly used in European music, and the absence of harmony or its limited use (Romero 1988, 229–35). This type of music contrasted with more harmonized and orchestrated compositions such as the theme from *Ollantay* or the hymn to the sun. It can be said, in fact, that these musical creations belonged to a mestizo style that was then taking shape, which later evolved into the music played in institutions such as the Centro Qosqo.[37] This style shows to some extent the aesthetic preferences present in traditional Andean music. Here I must stress the fact that the comments regarding the characteristics of the voices and music were not limited to the performances of the musicians considered Indian but also included those of the urban mestizos who performed music as part of the choirs, costumbrista tableaux, reconstructions of Inca rituals, and solo songs accompanied by traditional instruments. One solo sung during the tour and accompanied by two quenas, which, according to the Argentinean press, articulated "the Andean nostalgia,"[38] was a love song of unknown authorship (or a part of folklore, as it was called) that used the metaphor of the *pariwana*, the Andean flamingo, to depict the man loved.[39]

Although themes derived from the classic repertoire of Incaic music were performed—usually the most harmonized ones, which were sometimes orchestrated—this type of music did not dominate the programs. This is likewise true in the case of the performances held in Argentina, where the symphonic orchestra of the Colón Theatre of Buenos Aires interpreted some pieces under the direction of Roberto Ojeda. In the themes performed, what prevailed were compositions that had no symphonic arrangement, the captaciones, and finally the music of the dances, which were considered to be folklore because they formed part of the popular urban and peasant repertoire.

As for the dances performed by the misión, very little is known of those that formed part of scenes taken from plays, reconstructions of Inca rituals, or costumbrista tableaux, but it is likely that these dances were the most stylized ones and that their performers were members of the choir and likewise acted in the dramatic scenes. What we do know is that many were called *qaswas*, a genre representative of the Indian rural tradition (Romero 1988, 229–35). On the other hand, it is clear that the misión performed a series of dances belonging to the repertoire of rural and popular-urban festivals, most of which made no direct allusion to the Inca world, even though some believed they did so. These included the *k'achampa,*[40] *sijlla, waylaka, sajsampillo, sursurwaylla,* and several qaswas. These dances were probably performed by the people called "couples of cuzqueño aborigines" or an "indigenous dance troupe," which most certainly was a different group than that composed of the "señoritas y señores."[41] We thus find that dances such as the *sijlla,* which parodies the behavior of the colonial and republican authorities, and the *waylaka,* a transvestite interpretation of a carnivalesque nature, began to appear with the Inca theme as representative of the cuzqueño and Peruvian traditions.

A third type of dance comprised those pieces that were not connected with any tableaux or representations. Although they were new creations and had a stylized choreography, their musical style in fact incorporated rural traditions. The two dances of this kind that were most successful in the misión's performances, and later became classical pieces of the cuzqueñista tradition, were the *wach'ij tusuy* (dance of the arrow) and the *warak'a tusuy* (dance of the sling), which are widely known to be the creations of Roberto Ojeda. The press in Buenos Aires described these dances as the " 'Waraka-Tusui,' the dance of the sling, which reproduces the games the Indians of Peru play in the open air after their work, performed by women in whose hands the deadly sling becomes a picturesque ornament, and the 'dance of the arrow,' which had to be included in this program by request, [and has] a rough character, an obsessive rhythm, and is highly colorful."[42]

A close look at the program of the misión's opening night in Buenos Aires shows even more clearly the convergence of styles and traditions. The way in which each of the three parts of the program was structured hints at an inclination to present first what was most stylized and harmonized and include what was less so at the end. Consider, for example, the following sequence of the first part.

1. The hymn to the sun, performed by the symphonic orchestra of the Colón Theatre, was collected and arranged by Daniel Alomía Robles. It is a classic piece of Incaic music.
2. *Qosqo llaqta* (*Song to Cuzco*), performed by the choir, was composed by Juan de Dios Aguirre. This melancholic homage to the city of Cuzco was also in the Incaic vein. The musical production of this cuzqueño artist (another of the Big Four of Cuzco Music), like that of Roberto Ojeda, relies on the repertoires of Cuzco's rural and popular urban music.
3. *Suray Surita* is a solo song accompanied by quenas. This is an anonymous theme from Cuzco's "folklore" arranged by several musicians, including Roberto Ojeda, who presents his own version in this program.
4. *K'achampa* is a dance from the repertoire of rural and urban festivals in Cuzco with a rich choreography. In it the men face one another with their slings, or *warak'as*. The most commonly held interpretation in present-day Cuzco, which perhaps is derived from this performance by the misión, is that these are Inca warriors showing off their skill and bravery. The music and choreography of the dance were subsequently collected and arranged by several musicians and choreographers.
5. *Sumaj ñusta* (Beautiful Princess) is an anonymous musical piece interpreted by a traditional indigenous ensemble. It is considered to be folklore.

The second and third parts of this program show that what was presented—which only included "a scene from the climax of the drama *Ollantay*" (Aparicio 1994, 133)—went from the most harmonized and orchestrated, such as the score of this drama, to the least elaborate, which was closest to the rural and popular urban world, such as a qaswa, with arrangements of folkloric themes such as *Qosqo piris* and costumbrista tableaux such as *awajkuna* in between.

Finally, another way to show the confluence of styles and traditions present in the misión's repertoire is the genre in which many of the classical pieces of Incaic music and Cuzco's urban musical tradition were composed—the *yaraví*. This was a mestizo genre developed during the colonial period based on the pre-Hispanic harawi; by the eighteenth century it characterized what was considered the typically gloomy music of the "Indian" (Estenssoro 1989, 34–35; Romero 1988, 245).

It was not just cuzqueños and Peruvians in general but also the misión's audiences in Argentina that perceived the classical pieces of the Incaic and cuzqueño repertoire composed within the genre of the yaraví or harawi (e.g., Monet's *Ollantay*) as having great "emotional intensity." In Buenos Aires, the journal *La Nación* said of the misión's opening night, "The program began with the performance of the hymn to the sun, which was transcribed by Alomía Robles and bears a curious analogy with a Chinese hymn to Confucius; it is of a rare musical beauty because of its nature and its emotional intensity, qualities also found in the melodies of "Ollantay" and "Atawalpa," which were performed."[43]

Throughout the twentieth century, the cuzqueño tradition sought and managed to attain this intensity in various styles, but the privileged position of the yaraví has persisted to the present day. It was perhaps due to the fact that this genre and its different nuances were a common element shared both by the rural and the popular urban cuzqueño traditions, as well as by that developed in the middle- and upper-class artistic circles with a greater formal musical education, that Manuel Pillco, a self-taught harpist of popular extraction, eventually became a member of the artistic circle that spearheaded the establishment and development of the cultural institutions of the city of Cuzco. Pillco presumably joined the misión as a member of the "indigenous orchestra" or ensemble. The interesting trajectory of this musician, whose art characterizes the confluence of styles and social classes in Cuzco's artistic-folkloric production, is examined in more detail in the following chapters.

The misión was a significant and successful experiment that stimulated future Cuzqueño artists to persist in creating something with strong Andean highland roots that all Peruvians and even other Americans could feel was "their own." The misión's performances in fact had a greater dose of stylization, arrangements, and Incaism than can be found in later creations. However, as I hope to have shown, the misión is an example of the confluence of traditions, individuals, and styles derived from different sectors of the cuzqueño society of its time. The artistic output present in the misión, as much as that which flourished in the city of Cuzco in the following decades, cannot be understood as a simple stylization and manipulation by the elite or middle strata of the city of cultural and aesthetic elements derived from the rural and popular-urban populations. Rather we must study how the result of such a complex mix of traditions, comprising a significant part of the social and political interactions of the different sectors of Cuzco, took on a life of its own and developed its own rationale. The art that developed in this context gave a specific form to the regional identity of Cuzco and to proposals for a national identity.

This regional identity and the proposals for a national identity stimulated by a series of local, national, and international factors (such as the development of academic disciplines, the development of tourism, and state support) would increasingly build on the weapons of artistic creation. This took place above all in spaces such as cultural institutions, contests, and radio programs, all of which made the artistic-folkloric creation ever more fluid and led to the participation of a constantly growing number of self-taught artists from rural and popular-urban traditions. If we see this artistic-folkloric tradition merely as a result of the manipulation or co-optation of popular traditions, we cannot explain why it has remained deeply rooted to the present day. However, its popularity and deep roots can be understood if we realize that many of the musical pieces, dances, and tableaux are in fact the result of a confluence of individuals, styles, and repertoires that to some extent was already present in the misión and developed even more with time.

2

...

THE RISE OF CULTURAL INSTITUTIONS AND CONTESTS

The successful experience of the Misión Peruana de Arte Incaico stimulated Cuzco's artists and intellectuals into extending and institutionalizing the artistic-folkloric creation that was shaping their regional identity. This output could in turn be transformed into a national art rooted in Andean or highland traditions, as had happened in the performances of the Misión Peruana. As was noted earlier, this cuzqueño effort to develop a regional, national, and American identity must be understood within the wider context of the development of other Latin American nationalisms, which also endeavored to find the basis for their consolidation and a common American identity in the various American Indian groups (or in groups of African descent, as was the case in Colombia and Brazil).[1] As this chapter shows, the intellectuals also found inspiration in European nationalisms such as that of Russia, which had given great significance to the artistic output based on popular or folkloric traditions. Finally, we must not forget, as I have shown elsewhere, the impact that the scholarly interest in "folklore" (likewise derived from European currents), as well as the development of the identity of the people of Cuzco as a focus of archaeological studies and a potential tourist center, had on cuzqueño artistic-folkloric production.

Acknowledging that the cuzqueño artistic-folkloric production here studied developed within a context of nationalist political and cultural efforts by leading politicians and intellectuals should in no way be construed to mean that this prolific output was due to the mere manipulation and stylization that these same leaders made of cultural elements belonging to the rural or popular-urban populations. These creations were the result of a complex interaction among individuals and styles belonging to all of these social sectors. It can furthermore be argued that a great part of the artistic-folkloric drive and creative enthusiasm came from those in the rural and popular-urban sectors, who actually managed to give the institutions and spaces fostering this output their continuity. It is therefore important to analyze the different individual or group motivations that made people from the different social sectors of Cuzco join in the effort to consolidate and spread their art.

The origins of the Centro Qosqo de Arte Nativo—the first cuzqueño cultural institution dedicated to promoting the development of regional and national folkloric art, which to the best of my knowledge was also the first institution of its type in Peru—are clearly and directly connected to the Misión Peruana de Arte Incaico. Furthermore, this and the following chapters show that both groups are often treated as if they were one and the same. Just as with the Misión Peruana, the Centro Qosqo would in time become a space where individuals, styles, aesthetic preferences, and cultural elements from the different urban and rural sectors of Cuzco would meet. This, I believe, enabled a rich artistic-folkloric production to unfold within this institution, which has in turn acted as a landmark for productions of this type throughout the department in the twentieth century and early twenty-first. Cuzqueños, in fact, still consider the Centro Qosqo to be their most significant and respected cultural institution among those devoted to the promotion of folklore.

It is difficult to document the participation of self-educated artists of rural or popular urban extraction in what the members of the Centro Qosqo themselves recognize as the first stage in the development of their institution (1924 to the late 1930s). Most of the documentation of this period unfortunately records above all the participation of those who were conspicuous in the Misión Peruana or other intellectual and artistic personalities who had in one way or another gained prominence by then.[2] However, the path followed by Manuel Pillco (see fig. 3) sheds some light on the role this participation had in the creation and development of the Centro Qosqo.

Some aspects of the artistic life of Manuel Pillco, a harp virtuoso who was a cofounder of more than one cultural institution, as well as an active supporter of several more and in general a participant in almost all types of cuzqueño musical activities, will allow us to explore—in this and the following chapters—the development of other institutions and spaces for the creation and development of artistic-folkloric art. In these institutions and

3. Manuel Pillco and his *domingacha* harp. (PRIVATE ARCHIVE OF THE PILLCO FAMILY.)

spaces we will also find the growing participation of artists from a self-taught tradition of popular extraction in the mainstream development of this art in Cuzco. This growing participation coincided or fused with the state promotion of folklore as a way to foster nationalism; with the development of the neo-Indianist intellectual movement, which sought to reject Incaism while exalting cholo and mestizo identities; and with the growing national and international interest in Cuzco as a tourist center.

POINTS OF ENCOUNTER: MANUEL PILLCO, THE YARAVÍ, AND THE ORIGINS OF THE CENTRO QOSQO

I still do so, I still do, I will have to continue doing so even right up to my burial. Even dead, even in my grave I will still be playing the harp." MANUEL PILLCO

Manuel Pillco Cuba was born on December 25, 1903, in the district of Zurite, province of Anta, department of Cuzco. His godmother, Señora Carmen

Lira, took him to the city of Cuzco just before his seventh birthday so that, in the words of his relatives, "he would have a better future, as his parents understood it."[3] His first and possibly the dominant language throughout his life was Quechua.[4] It is not clear what level of formal education he attained, but his son Reynaldo believes that he may have had the equivalent of a primary education.[5] What we do know is that he began to work as an assistant to various tradesmen such as a baker, a barber, and a pyrotechnician from the moment he arrived in the city of Cuzco. His experience as a pyrotechnical apprentice had a major impact on his life, for in time he gained wide recognition in this activity and his fireworks were widely sought for all types of cuzqueño festivals. His family recalls that "his work in this field was officially recognized by the community starting in 1940 through diplomas repeatedly presented on various occasions by the Cuzco municipal council."[6] His work in pyrotechnics was his major source of income throughout his life.

Toward the end of his life Manuel Pillco fondly and gratefully remembered the treatment and education he received from Señora Lira, his godmother and the mother of Mariano Fuentes Lira, a famous cuzqueño painter and intellectual. Other than the fact that they grew up in the same house, we do not know what kind of social interaction there was between Mariano and Manuel outside the home, but Manuel's entry into bohemian and art circles may have been facilitated by this family contact. Even so, I believe that the yaraví, the main musical genre in which Manuel Pillco developed his art, and the particular style in which he played the harp were more significant and determinant points of contact between Pillco and the artistic and intellectual circles. In his interpretation of the yaravíes, and in general of all the themes that became popular in the repertoire of Cuzco music, Manuel Pillco developed an inimitable style that was remarkable due to a unique and elaborate sense of harmony and rhythm.[7]

Although some studies do discuss the musical and historical aspects of the yaraví, a detailed study of the characteristics, varieties, and development of this genre has yet to be written.[8] The existing studies agree that the yaraví was derived from, and retained significant characteristics of, the harawi, one of the most widespread genres in the pre-Columbian Andean world that presumably was of an "evocative and nostalgic nature" (Romero 1988, 243). It is worth noting that the harawi, as a genre distinct from the yaraví, still survives in rural areas of Peru such as the departments of Ayacucho, Cuzco, and Lima, and its performance still retains a close connection with specific contexts in agricultural and life cycles (planting, the harvest, marriage) and major ceremonial moments (the welcome or farewell given to prominent individuals) (243).[9]

Although there are several kinds of yaraví, in general those who have studied this genre believe it is a mestizo genre insofar as it incorporates pre-Columbian elements as well as others imported from Europe. In the words of Carlos Raygada, the yaraví "is the starting point of all scholars, doubtlessly because it is the form that best condenses the characteristics of the Indo-Hispanic miscegenation" (cited in Pagaza Galdo 1963, 97). The yaraví is likewise a genre that is believed to have originated in Peru, even though it has spread to other countries in South America. Thanks to a debate published in the *Mercurio Peruano,* it is also known that it was already recognized as a genre in the late eighteenth century (Raygada 1936; Pagaza Galdo 1963; Estenssoro 1989; Romero 1988). Interestingly, although students of the yaraví agree on its mestizo nature, its sad and melancholic tone when the debate took place in the eighteenth century was "strongly related," as Romero (1988) notes, "with the stereotype the Creole people had developed, wherein Andean music is sad and melancholic and thus reflects a presumed Andean pessimism and fatalism" (245).

The yaraví developed in various religious and secular spheres in both rural and urban areas and thus gradually acquired its own characteristics in accordance with this development. The religious sphere, wherein Manuel Pillco developed a great part of his art, was particularly important.[10] When assessing his own musical trajectory toward the end of his life, Manuel Pillco noted, "It was my lot to play the harp in religious matters—in church all of my youth. All that I learned, my dedication, it was to play in the temple . . . plus the devotion I had for the temples, [for the churches of] the Virgen del Carmen, the Reina de Belén, the Reina del Rosario—almost the biggest part—Santa Ana—I dedicated myself to playing my harp, to learn [how to play it] in church and not for festivals. I did play in festivals but not much."[11]

Pillco stressed two points when answering a question regarding his musical training with the harp. The first was that, although his father, Juan Pablo, had been a harpist, he had never taught him how to play it. He insists that he learned when he was fourteen and already living in the city of Cuzco by playing with other musicians, among whom he mentioned Cosme Licuona, with whom he played in the San Sebastián district. Decades later, both would be among the founding members of the Asociación Folklórica Kosko (Kosko Folklore Association), the institution that merged with the faltering Centro Qosqo, which led to the latter's revitalization.

The second point Manuel Pillco emphasized is the fact that his musical development took place in the religious arena, where he mostly played accompanied by a violin. Pillco's musical development was intrinsically connected to the strong religious faith he had in some of the major images worshipped by the people of Cuzco. Some of these images are listed in the passage cited above, and they also included the image of the Señor de los Temblores (the Lord of Earthquakes), which is housed in the Cuzco Cathedral and is sumptuously celebrated every Easter Monday. Manuel Pillco was also the major organizing force behind the associations of musicians dedicated to playing music in honor of these images in their major festivities.[12]

We know that the music and dances performed by native people in Catholic rituals during the colonial period became spaces of contention wherein identities and symbolic practices were negotiated (Ares Queija 1984; Estenssoro 1990, 92; Estenssoro 2003; Poole 1990). The position of the Spanish evangelizers vis-à-vis the rich tradition of ritual music and dance among the Andean population varied throughout this period, depending on which religious order was in charge of evangelization and the political circumstances. Even so, it is clear that this rooted tradition of music and dance was a major way in which the church incorporated native peoples into the Catholic world (Ares Queija 1984; Estenssoro 1990, 1992, 2003).

The musical forms and instruments utilized by the evangelizers changed as the local styles developed. The religious hymns taught in the European polyphonic tradition gave way to those of the monodic genre (*género monódico*) of the yaraví. The harp, which, along with the violin, was one of the instruments most popularized by the Spanish missionaries, was adapted until it gave rise to local forms such as the *domingacha*.[13] This small, pear-shaped, diatonic harp, usually tuned in C major, was Manuel Pillco's favorite instrument (see fig. 3).[14]

Thanks to his command of multiple repertoires, Señor Pillco moved with ease from the religious to the secular spheres and from remote rural areas to the places favored by the artistic bohemians of the city of Cuzco. Although

Manuel began to play the harp after he moved to the city, it is clear that his music was strongly influenced by rural styles. Not only did he remain in contact with his hometown, but he also played in festivals and ceremonies in small towns far removed from the city of Cuzco. His son Reynaldo believes that his father "was the bearer [of] the music from the countryside" to the city, where he "played music from the countryside and even imitated the charango with a special tuning of his. But at the same time he was also to fit in with the music played here [in Cuzco city]. So he had no problem even in changing tonality; he tuned the harp. It always had to be tuned to another tone, the major and minor tones, right? . . . The tuning was different for each theme."[15]

In the bohemian circles in the city of Cuzco, Manuel Pillco was in great demand for serenades and on festive occasions because, as his son Reynaldo said, "he got everybody going."[16] Apparently one of the reasons his music was a hit in these circles was that Manuel Pillco had an inimitable ability to harmonize melodies. According to his son, he "acquired his own style. His harmonization was most peculiar; it was pleasant (*da gusto*), and it matched the melody."[17] Enrique Pilco Paz, Manuel's grandson and disciple and a violinist and student of the traditional religious music of Cuzco, likewise stresses this ability.[18] Enrique made the following comment about the way his grandfather played yaravíes and other themes that were popularized as classic pieces in Cuzco's urban tradition:

> The interplay of the bass (*el juego de bajos*) in harmony (*concordancia*) with the melody was masterful. The harp is a harmonic instrument comparable to the piano, so one can develop the melody and accompany it at the same time. . . . This feature, little cultivated nowadays, is clearly notable in the solos recorded in the albums made with the Centro Qosqo and [the] Danzas del Tahuantinsuyo [folklore group]. It is therefore clear that his music had harmony—it actually was more harmonious than melodic or had a special harmonic richness. If you listen carefully to any of his recordings you will realize that the interplay of parallel notes was abundant. To this was added a no less complex rhythmic base (*base rítmica*). It was in sum a style that I have not heard again—nor will ever again hear—live.[19]

It has been noted that one of the things sought by the creators of the emerging styles of "Incaic," cuzqueño, or national music in the late nineteenth century and the early twentieth was to develop the harmony in their compositions and captaciones. This was not characteristic of the majority of the popular rural and urban traditions on which they based their creations. On the other hand, the yaraví was one of the favorite genres in which several of the classical pieces of this tradition were created (e.g., Manuel Monet's *Ollantay*). This was also the style Manuel Pillco preferred for his compositions, including *En mi pobreza.*[20]

It thus seems that Manuel Pillco's identification with the yaraví genre, as well as his particular harmonic style, were major points of contact between him and the members of Cuzco's musical bohemia who formed the Misión Peruana de Arte Incaico and later spearheaded the establishment of the Centro Qosqo. The family of Manuel Pillco claims that he participated in both events, although the written documentation I have found does not always support this.[21] In the case of the misión, we know that the documentation does not list all of the names, particularly those of the individuals who were considered part of a "traditional ensemble," "instrumentalists," or a "native dance troupe."[22] It is clear, however, that the harp was present in the performances given by the Misión Peruana, as is shown in several newspaper comments, including one published after the misión's debut in Buenos Aires that read, "An interesting number was the traditional ensemble comprising a small harp, quenas, tabors, pinkullus, and the tinya, playing popular cuzqueño songs."[23]

Manuel Pillco was already a renowned harpist in Cuzco by the time the misión was formed, and he mingled with the members of this group of cuzqueño artists. He was then twenty-one and had been playing the harp since he was fourteen. Another possible indication that he participated in the misión is the fact that he was asked to join the Centro Qosqo, which was established in the same year that this group of artists returned to Cuzco after its successful tour.

In a historical account of the Centro Qosqo, Diómedes Oróz Villena (1989), a current member of the Centro, included the following story taken from the recollections of Roberto Ojeda Campana, the musical director of the Misión Peruana:

> On November 6, 1924, eight artist friends who had met inside a coffee or tea shop (*tetería*) called LA ROTONDA (in the *barrios altos* of Cuzco), decided to establish a vernacular music and dance group, which they named CENTRO CCOSCO DE ARTE NATIVO. Its first board was installed some days later at a formal meeting

held on November 10 and presided over by Dr. Luis Alberto Pardo Durand, an eminent archaeologist and cuzqueñista who laid the foundations for many cultural and scientific institutions. This select group included Baltazar Zegarra P., Roberto Ojeda C., Juan de Dios Aguirre Ch., César Valdivieso, Humberto Vidal U., Santiago Lechuga, Manuel Palomino, Martín Chambi, Horacio Fortón, Avelino García and others (Oróz 1989, 1).[24]

Reynaldo Pillco admits that the inclusion of his father in this "select" group of intellectuals and artists was "somewhat special" and was perhaps due to the fact that "his performance of folkloric music had impressed them."[25] Señor Reynaldo likewise believes that the friendship between Manuel and Martín Chambi, the world-renowned photographer whose name was listed by Ojeda, may have been a reason for his inclusion in this group of founding members. Finally, since it is quite likely that Manuel took part in the Misión Peruana this may have been a major reason for his inclusion in the group.

In fact the Centro Qosqo—which was known as the Centro Musical Cuzco prior to 1933—was a cultural institution that attracted both artists and intellectuals who, due to their keen interest in music, dance, or theater, believed that fostering these practices was essential to the development of a cuzqueñista feeling and identity. The wealth of music and dances in the different rural and urban sectors of cuzqueño society, the renewed interest in Peru and abroad in the celebration of "native" or "vernacular" values as the basis of a national identity, plus the belief that Cuzco, as the heartland of the Inca, was meant to play a key role in the development of this identity—all of this inspired the people who established the Centro.

At first most of the members of this institution came from the middle and upper classes in Cuzco, and most were prominent because of their educations either in music or in the university. Juan de Dios Aguirre, Baltazar Zegarra, and Roberto Ojeda, who were all well known for their compositions and arrangements, began their musical training at an early age (Ojeda 1987). Their intense artistic and educational efforts earned them the title—along with Francisco González Gamarra—the Big Four of Cuzco Music in 1959.[26] The founding members also included Humberto Vidal Unda, who, as we shall see, was to become in the following two decades a major promoter of cuzqueñismo and cultural and tourist activities in the city through his work with several institutions. Finally, we must mention Luis

Ochoa and Julio Rouvirós, renowned personalities in the Incaic theater and the stage directors of the misión, who were also among the founding members of the Centro.

The enthusiasm of its founders apparently did not suffice for the immediate consolidation of the institution. In March 1927 a newspaper in Cuzco noted that it was essential to reactivate the "Centro Musical Cuzco," in whose establishment and short life "masters" who had "won recognition in the country [Peru] and abroad" had participated; it was therefore crucial to "return to the work done, to the appreciation attained in Bolivia, Argentina and Uruguay."[27] According to this article, rivalries among the members and the desire to stand out had led to stagnation, but it was essential to revitalize the Centro as Cuzco was being overshadowed by what was taking place in other Peruvian cities.[28] In fact, intellectuals, politicians, and other members of the middle and upper classes throughout Peru were becoming ever more interested in revaluing the festive practices, especially music and dance, of the popular peasant and urban sectors, which in the past had often been the target of critiques and repression from different perspectives. Folklore contests were one of the most effective channels though which this revaluing occurred at the national and cuzqueño levels; in these contests the members of the Centro Musical Cuzco actively participated, as did members of other cuzqueño groups that emerged over time and artists from various social sectors in Cuzco.

THE FIRST CONTEST IN THE PAMPA DE AMANCAES AND ITS IMPACT IN CUZCO

The Concurso de Música y Bailes Nacionales (National Music and Dance Contest), which was organized in Lima in 1927 at the Pampa de Amancaes in the Rímac district, was one of the major incentives for the production and popularization of the regional styles that were developing in different parts of Peru. Throughout the second half of his eleven-year rule, President Leguía had actively sponsored this contest as part of the religious celebrations honoring Saint John. The promotion of this kind of event was a part of the populist and pro-Indian rhetoric adopted by Leguía as part of his modernizing project called the Patria Nueva. It was apparently noted in 1925–26 that migrants were participating in this traditional celebration, which had earlier been considered "for Limeños alone." . . . Now there were "regional music

4. Luis Esquivel receiving an award from President Augusto B. Leguía after his triumph in the Pampa de Amancaes contest. (COURTESY OF THE ESQUIVEL FAMILY.)

and dances, with resident migrants wearing a visibly stylized attire adapted for the occasion" (Vivanco 1973, 33). In response, Juan Ríos, the district mayor, together with President Leguía, channeled the participation of the highland population through a contest, which surpassed the expectations of its organizers from the very beginning.

Some fifty thousand spectators attended the first event according to Vivanco (1973), and from that time onward President Leguía and other national officials regularly attended the contests (34–39). The government provided financial support for this event from the beginning by establishing several awards, including the main one, which was called President of the Republic. The first of the trophies went to a trio of Cuzco musicians living in Lima who "played yaravíes, huaynos and war dances with quenas and piano, formed by Señores Andrés Izquierdo, Justo Morales, and Luis F. Esquivel" (34) (see fig. 4).

By the following year the contest had acquired such a countrywide scope that qualifying rounds had to be held. It seems that mostly provincial migrants living in Lima had attended the first contest. By the second year there was much greater participation by delegations from several coastal and highland departments. Although more studies are required regarding this point, some evidence suggests that people from the provinces who lived in

Lima directly stimulated the establishment and participation of these delegations.[29] This was likewise suggested by the mayor of the Rímac district. In a speech delivered at the 1928 contest, he noted, "This year, unlike the preceding one, the fertile outgrowths of this contest have spread throughout the Republic thanks to the efficacious support you have given them, thus making it possible for very many artistic delegations to come to the capital as representatives of all of the departments of Peru" (*La Crónica* [Lima], June 25, 1928, cited in Vivanco 1973, 36).

It was in this second year of the contest, after the Centro Musical Cuzco had been revitalized, that it organized one of the delegations that represented Cuzco in Amancaes. The other Cuzco representative was the Conjunto Acomayo, which had been established and was headed by the musician, composer, and student of cuzqueño music Policarpo Caballero Farfán, who had been born in Acomayo. The group organized by the Centro Musical, which went under the name of Misión Cuzqueña de Arte Incaico, received the official support and economic sponsorship of the municipality of the city of Cuzco and represented the department on this occasion.

The idea of holding contests in order to promote the practices of the peasantry and popular-urban groups that were being categorized as folkloric—with a positive connotation—had likewise appeared among the cuzqueños before the first contest was held at Amancaes. In January 1927 we find two newspaper articles written by Carlos Ríos Pagaza, a cuzqueño intellectual. In a harsh critique of the attempted suppression of dances at a feast held for the patron saint of the district by the parish priest of San Sebastián, Ríos suggested that these practices should be channeled through contests. In one of the newspaper items he declared, "Once regional dances properly channeled are allowed in all towns in the highlands not just once or twice a year; and once contests are sponsored in the capitals of the departments, then we shall really have done something in terms of strengthening our faded identity."[30]

At the time, the conviction that the best way to develop a real national cultural base was to follow the example set by nations perceived as more advanced, and to "channel"—that is, to polish and elaborate—the "folkloric," "vernacular," aboriginal," or "indigenous" practices (these were some of the terms commonly used), gained strength among the intellectuals of Cuzco and all of Peru. For instance, in the article just cited, Ríos Pagaza claimed that only degenerate minds would try to extirpate the "vernacular dances when more cultivated peoples than ours, such as the Mexicans, perform them for their enormous historical, social, and educational value."[31] Cuzco's intellectuals obviously had gotten wind that the new nationalist and indigenista project in Mexico had found the source of a national culture in living indigenous cultures (López 2004, 2006). By 1921, intellectuals and artists in Mexico had organized a series of public events, sponsored by the government, wherein different types of arts, customs, music, and dances perceived as "authentic" or "indigenous" were elaborated and presented as the source of *mexicanidad* (Mexicanness; López 2004).

In the same line, Antonio Garland, an art director in Lima and a sponsor of the development of national styles, discussed the success attained by the first contest held in Amancaes in a newspaper article and suggested that such events showed that in Peru it was indeed possible to do what had been done by "the famed group of the 'five' Russian authors, [who ran] the musical gamut of their people to harmonize it with such verism and mastery that they set an insurmountable beat in the history of world music."[32] At the time, the examples set by Russia and Mexico were also in the minds of artists and intellectuals in other South American countries, including Argentina, where the interest shown in the performances of the Misión Peruana was directly connected with the designs some had for the development of an American identity based on what was autochthonous.[33] In Cuzco, many of the artists and intellectuals who disseminated the indigenista—and later neo-indianist—ideas sympathized with the political and social transformations that were being undertaken as a result of the Mexican and the Russian Revolutions. Individuals such as Luis Valcárcel, Humberto Vidal Unda, and José Uriel García supported the ideas and political projects the political opposition was developing all over Peru throughout the 1920s, which coalesced in the rise of the Alianza Popular Revolucionaria Americana (APRA), an anti-imperialist party founded by Haya de la Torre in 1924 while he was in Mexico, and the Partido Socialista del Perú, founded by José Carlos Mariátegui in 1927. In 1933 José Uriel García was imprisoned on the island of Taquile in Puno because of his political ideas (Avendaño 1995, 336).

The first contest held in Amancaes influenced the renewal of the activities of the institution still known as the Centro Musical Cuzco. In October 1927 the Centro announced a "departmental contest of traditional, regional music" to be held on the occasion of the festival of the Día de la Raza (October 12). The leaders of this institution stated that organizing this type of activity was one of the major goals laid down at its establishment: to "collect, study, and make known the traditional regional music from pre-Hispanic and colonial times, particularly that which still survives in different parts of the department."[34] The rationale behind the contest apparently was to make the music and dances presented as cuzqueño or Inca draw more heavily on the existing popular urban and rural traditions than had been the case in the first Amancaes contest or in the performances given by the misión. The leaders of the Centro Musical mentioned certain considerations, which had been taken into account while making the decision to organize this regional contest:[35] "Despite the success attained, the performances lately given in the capital of the republic, as well as the artistic manifestations of the same genre previously performed in the country and abroad, were not complete . . . Despite everything that has thus far been done, there is still much unpublished music with a strong autochthonous flavor, which it has proved impossible to appreciate due to the lack of opportunities and means."[36]

The day after this announcement was made, a newspaper comment published in Cuzco—as always with the illusion in mind that Cuzco should represent the nation abroad—hinted that the most outstanding repertoires and interpreters in the contest the Centro was organizing should form the core of the cuzqueño delegation to the 1929 world's fair in Seville, which would "faithfully [show] one of the essential aspects of the Peruvian Andean indigenous soul."[37] In Cuzco there was also a clear idea of the significance the world's fairs had had since the mid-nineteenth century for the definition of national and ethnic identities, as well as for the promotion of a country as a place of interest for European or American visitors (Kirshenblatt-Gimblett 1998). The leaders of the Centro Musical organized its first contest through the Concejo Provincial del Cercado del Cuzco and called on the officials in the local and provincial municipalities to send their representatives. From the comments made when the contest was announced, it is clear that the members of the Centro expected that the contestants would avoid as far as possible following a pattern of regional or national standardization. It is possible that these organizers were aware that the cultural developments that had taken place in the city of Cuzco, which were already being popularized in Peru and abroad as "Incaic and/or typically cuzqueño," were well known in other parts of the department. In trying to use the contest as a way to incorporate new local artistic traditions in the construction of an emerging cuzqueño regional style, the organizers had to be explicit about the need to preserve the local characteristics of these practices and to avoid all modifications in order for them to be considered valid forms. The announcement emphasized that the municipalities should send "remarkable practitioners of indigenous music, with preference of course given to individuals who are indigenous; to music that has the same nature; that the instruments they play be the ones they presently use, without any motif at all [and should] preferably be of their own making no matter how rustic they look; and that, as far as possible, their garb should not be modified so that the group may be considered more ancient."[38]

Although it is clear that what was being sought was the "indigenous," we must not forget that the same document mentions that practices from both the pre-Columbian and the colonial periods were acceptable in the cuzqueño tradition. Having more ancient characteristics—which in this context meant being closer to what had been Inca or pre-Columbian—was not necessarily a prerequisite for something to be considered typically cuzqueño. However, things that were rustic or not too elaborate were desirable in the performances of the participants in the contest, particularly if the delegations or individuals wanted to depict what was indigenous (see fig. 5). The emphasis placed on the indigenous element as having a rustic nature would be retained as a major pillar in the criteria laid down for the folkloric contests held in Cuzco throughout the twentieth century and up to the present day.[39]

The contest's design shows an attempt by the members of the Centro Musical to distance themselves from the Inca or pre-Columbian theme as the center of the cuzqueño identity. This attempt included two trends. The first was to gradually reject the consideration of *indigenous* and *pre-Columbian* or *Inca* as synonyms, a trend that implied that nonnative genres and instruments were an integral part of the traditions considered indigenous. The second trend sought to include the musical practices and dances of artists belonging to the same social milieu as the organizers of the contest in the consolidation of this cuzqueño tradition; since these musical practices and dances were more elaborate and included nonnative instruments and genres, they could not be considered indigenous forms. Among these practices we

5. A folkloric ensemble from Combapata, Canchis (Sacsayhuamán, ca. 1920–30). (PHOTO BY THE CABRERA BROTHERS, FOTOTECA ANDINA ARCHIVE, CENTRO BARTOLOMÉ DE LAS CASAS, CUZCO.)

may include the creations and arrangements that were part of the misión and the *marineras.*[40]

But this incipient attempt to distance themselves from the Incaic thematic does not seem to have been free of contradictions. If, on the one hand, it was stated that the participants considered indigenous should not try to make their performances correspond to stereotyped pre-Hispanic forms, on the other hand the contest imposed two major categories: Incan and criollo forms. This once again matched what was indigenous with the Inca. The Inca music included the "harauis, huancas, pastoral songs, kcashuas, the music from traditional dances (kkachampas, chuncho, etc.)" while colonial music comprised "criollo [music], religious songs, and marineras."[41]

It is likewise worth noting that within the context of this contest both the Incan and the colonial were directly opposed to "notoriously foreign and modern" music, which was completely excluded. It was clear that in Cuzco at the time, as in the capital city of Lima, the calls made to elaborate and sponsor regional and national styles were made within the context of the perceived threat posed by the foreign trends that were being popularized through the new means of communication.[42] In this way, both the typically coastal and criollo style of the capital city, which was being consolidated as a national style, and the "Inca" and/or "Andean" styles became a national art in the minds of the sponsors vis-à-vis the perceived menace posed by foreign music. This was evident in the second Amancaes contest in Lima, where competitions were held for the composers of unpublished pieces in the categories "Inca, Andean, and criollo styles" (Vivanco 1973, 35).

Another element that is clearly present in the contest organized by the Centro Musical is that its members were aware that the musical repertoire considered indigenous or popular was closely connected with dances. The announcement of the contest explicitly stated that the music could be supplemented with "the dances (*bailes y danzas*) of the same nature and meaning [that] are quite common in our highlands."[43] The music and dances performed by groups or couples of "natives" or "aboriginals" had, as was shown in the previous chapter, been part of the Misión Peruana, and this helped give its presentations a greater degree of authenticity in the eyes of the foreign press. This first cuzqueño contest, however, seems to have placed greater emphasis on the significance of dances as a major element of the regional tradition.

The reasons for the participation of self-educated artists in this contest are not easily discerned. It is clear, however, that the organizers of the event believed it had the potential to help them select new elements from Cuzco's rural or popular urban traditions that could be incorporated into the process of consolidation of the cuzqueño regional tradition, which the Centro wanted to lead. According to its members, the Centro would be in charge of spreading this regional "tradition in development" outside Cuzco. According to the announcement of the contest, "Once the contest is over, the Centro, which founded and organized it, will appropriate all of the artistic material that receives an award and will be in charge of its preservation and opportune publication and will likewise select the staff [and] the repertoire should [the talent] be the most genuine and authorized expression of typical cuzqueño music."[44]

The various auditions that took place before and after the contest in the city of Cuzco thus became new spaces where the repertoire and the artists already established in this city, in Lima, and abroad could meet those from the different rural and popular urban sectors of Cuzco. A group formed by three members of the Centro Musical, two members of the Provincial Municipal Council, one from the Centro Nacional de Arte e Historia (National Center of Art and History), and two from the local press were to judge the contestants.[45] In succeeding events the judges of the contests held in Cuzco, who were the most renowned artists and intellectuals, gradually established the criteria by which the pieces were to be considered indigenous and authentic or mestizo, as well as the ideas informing the ways in which this authenticity could be defined. Although, as we shall see, for the cuzqueño intellectuals and artists who were elaborating these criteria, the relative importance of the Incan past for defining the present culture as traditional or indigenous varied according to how strongly they identified with neo-Indianist ideas, what is clear is that more and more often they identified the indigenous with what was most remote from the city of Cuzco and its modernizing influences.

The press did not record the final positions in this contest, nor did it say how many contestants there were, but it did provide descriptions of the presentations that were later held in the city of Cuzco. Although it is not known whether all of the numbers and interpreters who received prizes (*recibieron honores*) in the contest participated in successive auditions, these recitals do seem to have combined numbers and artists already famous in Cuzco and outside the region with new elements of a rural or popular-urban extraction. It is known that the contestants who had been classified as "outstanding" during the competition participated in the first of these auditions.[46]

THE REPERTOIRE OF THE PERFORMANCES AFTER THE CONTEST

A close examination of the repertoire and the participants in these auditions gives a better idea of this space as a point of encounter and consolidation of what was gradually to become known as quintessentially cuzqueño. Manuel Pillco took part in these presentations (*veladas*), as did Cosme Licuona, the musician with whom Manuel had learned to play the harp in the context of Andean church music.

The first audition after the contest included fourteen numbers. Of these, the ones that were clearly considered "successes" of the Misión Peruana were the overture to the Inti Raymi tableau and the *danza de la flecha*, both composed by Roberto Ojeda, and Juan de Dios Aguirre's *Ccoscco llaqta*, which was performed by a choir. A second category comprises the musical compositions and dances that were not presented as either traditional or indigenous but as the creations of a well-known artist interpreted by artists from the middle and upper classes, some of whom had participated in the Misión Peruana and/or were members of the Centro Musical. This category included a piece called *aires chumbivilcanos* (tunes from chumbivilcas) performed on guitar and piano by Alberto Negrón, a leader of the Centro Musical, and by Víctor Guzmán, a former member of the Misión Peruana. Other pieces in this category were a solo sung in Quechua that had been composed by Juan de Dios Aguirre and was interpreted by Etelvina Campero (a member of the Misión Peruana), and two compositions by Luis Pareja, a "mestizo dance" entitled *ccori ñusta* (golden Inca princess) and a musical piece honoring the cuzqueño pioneer of Peruvian aviation, Alejandro Velasco Astete, entitled *despedida a Velasco* (farewell to Velasco).[47] The last two pieces were performed by an *estudiantina* (a musical group formed by students) named after Velasco, which included guitars, violins, mandolins, and quenas, along with the participation of the composer himself.[48]

A third category, in which most of the pieces were placed, included five that were listed in the program as traditional and/or Inca and had no known composer. It is possible that the performers of these pieces had excelled in the contest organized by the Centro Musical. Even so, it must be noted that at least one dance and three of these interpreters had taken part in the Misión Peruana in the "indigenous" contingent. This dance was called *saccsampillo,* and the musicians were Manuel Pillco, Benigno Ttito, and Ciprián Jarandilla.

The program listed the *saccsampillo* as a "dance from Inca folklore" the music of which was performed by the "traditional ensemble from Quiquijana" (a district in the province of Quispicanchis) comprised of a harp and a violin played by the "indígenas" Benigno Ttito and Luis Meza.[49] The same group performed another dance, called *mamala,* that was listed as a huayno dance.[50] Next on the program was a "colonial yaraví and huayno" performed by a "traditional Cuzco ensemble" comprised of a harp, quenas, and tinyas played by Manuel Pillco, Aniceto Villafuerte, González (I was unable to establish his first name), and Ciprián Jarandilla.[51] Finally, there were two pieces performed by a "traditional ensemble" from the district of Huarocondo, in the province of Anta, which, according to the program, was comprised of a "harp, a bandore (*bandurria*), and a violin [an instrument of local manufacture]" played by Víctor Garrido, Néstor Canal, and Angelino Quispe.[52] The musical pieces, which were probably accompanied by dances, were *huachatuya,* a "*harawi* and *kashua* from Inca folklore," and *Casapalca,* a "huayno kashua."[53] The fact that the program had to explain that the violin—a nonnative instrument—used by the Anta musicians was of local manufacture confirms that rusticity had to be maintained in order to ascertain indigenous authenticity before the urban artists.

Finally, the first audition held after the contest also included two pieces of another type among the fourteen chosen ones, a speech by Luis Velasco Aragón—who had also been in charge of the speeches given on the tour conducted by the Misión Peruana—and the recital of a poem written by Miguel Ángel Delgado called *las vírgenes del sol,* which was accompanied by a yaraví and huayno.[54]

We know that after the first recital there was at least one other, which was discussed in *El Comercio* of Cuzco by Carlos Ríos Pagaza, the intellectual who early in the year had defended in that same newspaper the traditional dances performed at the festival of the district of San Sebastián and had made a first call for the implementation of regional contests. When using the discussion of Ríos Pagaza as a source we must bear in mind that his position vis-à-vis the artistic output of peasant and popular-urban groups was clear: these were "precious gems in the rough" on the basis of which cuzqueños would be able to compose symphonies and orchestral music for operas, as had already been done in Russia and Mexico.[55] This intellectual argued that the cuzqueño artists who had thus far used these materials in their own arrangements and compositions had not yet developed these "jewels of native art" to their proper level due to a lack of "study" and "musical technique"; for him, the same was true of the dances.[56]

We should recall that, like Ríos Pagaza, some critics took a similar position regarding the compositions and arrangements of Juan de Dios Aguirre, Roberto Ojeda, and Baltazar Zegarra—that they were too close to the folkloric materials in which they had found their inspiration and were lacking in technical and musical development (Pinilla 1988, 143). In his comment on the second recital held after the contest, Ríos Pagaza said he hoped that artists trained in the erudite techniques would participate so that the creation of a regionalist and nationalist repertoire could "progress." He wrote,

"The only thing that consoles us is that one day other artists—not those of today, who lack study—after many years of arduous and diligent study and prodigious inspiration, will give shape [to this repertoire], availing themselves of the massive resources of musical technique and the dances."[57]

It is interesting to note that just one year before the recital was held and this comment was written, Armando Guevara Ochoa had been born. He was to become the most renowned cuzqueño composer and conductor both in Peru and abroad precisely because of his intensive use of composition techniques considered erudite, his "systematic use of popular melodies," and his creation of "themes of folkloric nature" (Pinilla 1988, 177).[58] It is worth pointing out here that this musician, whose main instrument was always the violin, was a disciple of Manuel Pillco, from whom, according to his own testimony, he learned much about Cuzco's popular music (see fig. 14 on page 145).[59]

Both recitals were apparently successful and were attended by cuzqueños from various social sectors. According to Ríos Pagaza, who reported on the second recital, an event that apparently exceeded the capacity of the Excelsior Theatre, "All Cuzco social classes, all the component parts of the different strata that form our society were in this hall, avid to listen to native tunes and to turn their eyes and hearts to what is our own, authentic, strong."[60]

Although the pieces in this second recital may also be placed in three categories, only the first category remained the same. This was because the criteria used to establish the other two categories in the first recital were mixed in several of the numbers presented in the second recital. Furthermore, the division into three categories can only be established in terms of a higher or lower degree of acknowledged popularity (both of the piece and of the composer), of the participation of musicians of rural and popular-urban extraction, and of the use of instruments and genres considered indigenous, as well as the degree of elaboration or stylization.

The first category would still clearly be comprised of the pieces made famous by the misión, including Roberto Ojeda's *Yahuar Huaccac,* the *danza de la flecha, Suray Surita* (arranged by Ojeda), and the *himno al sol* by Daniel Alomía Robles. In the second category we can include what apparently was a different version (or at least one with additional performers and instruments) of *aires chumbivilcanos,* in which there first appeared a musician of rural popular extraction who would eventually become a major symbol of

Cuzco folklore: Francisco Gómez Negrón (see fig. 7 on page 89). Francisco (better known as Pancho) Gómez and Alberto Negrón, whom we recall was the leader of the Centro Musical, were the guitarists of the group, which was completed by the quena player Ricardo Flórez (see fig. 10 on page 131).[61] This group played another number simply called marinera and huayno, which I also include in this category.[62]

The comments of Ríos Pagaza show that even at the time of these recitals the romanticized image of the male inhabitants of the high-altitude provinces as "Andean *gauchos,*" "*llaneros,*" or "younger brothers of the Far West [cowboys]" was strong in Cuzco's music and dance tradition. As Ríos wrote of the performance of the marinera and huayno, "The performers appeared in typical garb: curbed-brim hat, long heavy boots, and the so-called carahuatanas [chaps], large roweled spurs, the classic lasso use to rope steers, [and] the '*lihui*' used to tackle ferocious bulls with the poncho rolled up across the wide chest."[63]

This image of the virile Chumbivilcas men would gain even more strength with the national and international popularity of Francisco "Pancho" Gómez Negrón, who will be discussed in chapter 4. However, it is worth pointing out here that this image of the men from Chumbivilcas was considered something authentically cuzqueño, though at the same time it was an image that was obviously mestizo and not Inca or pre-Hispanic.

Another number that can be included in this second category is a dance that cannot be placed in the first category because it had recently been created. Ríos's description, however, leads one to think that, because of its level of stylization, this dance was similar to the *danza de la flecha* or the *danza de la honda,* which the misión had popularized. This number was simply called "huayno-música, canto y baile," and Ríos noted the following about its performance:

> This was the number that received the warmest applause from the public, its huayno, its costume, which had character and was ornamented similarly to those still used by the Indians . . . [in some places]. [The huayno] was performed by Pedro Campero and Etelvina Campero, who danced it in a stylized fashion without any abrupt movement, without excessive swaying of the hips, with no gestures that would suggest the flames of lubricity—with rhythm really exquisite. A choir of Indians and mestizos, our own types, accompanied the dancers, [along with] an ensemble of harps, quenas, and other instruments."[64]

Though stylized, this number seems to have exemplified the contemporary popular culture of the countryside, leaving aside all allusions to the Incas. Its genre was the huayno, which was danced at the time both by the peasantry and by mestizos, and the dress tried to imitate the garb of contemporary peasants. The music was played by what was believed to be a "traditional ensemble," as it included harps and quenas. Although we do not know for certain what criteria Ríos used in his classifications, he distinguished Indians and mestizos in the choir. Finally, it must be noted that the dancers were considered to be mestizos from the city of Cuzco because both had been members of the misión in the group said to be composed of "ladies and gentlemen."

It is possible that to produce this piece the members of the Centro Musical adapted and put together numbers and artists that participated in the contest. It seems that this was so because toward the end of his comment, Ríos points out that "of the singers, the one with a pleasant voice of high clear tones was a mestizo no more than twelve years old, who must have been with one of the *murgas* [bands of street musicians] participating in the contest."[65] This use of the participants in the contest to present something more elaborate would be consistent with what had been explicitly stated by the organizers regarding the right they reserved to select the best of the contest in order to take charge of its dissemination.

A musical number that would soon become a classical piece in the cuzqueño repertoire—*punchainiquipi* (on your day), which was composed in 1925 by Baltazar Zegarra—can be included in this second category.[66] The compositions of this cuzqueño, who would be acknowledged as one of the Big Four of Cuzco Music, characteristically focus on national mestizo genres such as the yaraví and the waltz. The former, as already explained, strongly represents the Andean identity, whereas the second genre is identified with the coastal culture. Zegarra, a saxophonist, spent many years of his childhood and youth in Lima, where he studied music and also practiced as a member of an army band. On returning to his homeland, Zegarra dedicated himself to teaching music and composing; his contribution to the development of the "Cuzco waltz"—the genre to which *punchainiquipi* belongs—would prove crucial (Ojeda 1987, 74). For Ojeda, *punchainiquipi* began a new musical genre wherein "the indigenous [element] absorbed the criollo waltz and thus gave rise to a new solemn genre, rich in melodic and harmonic resources" (74).

Ríos Pagaza does not say much about *punchainiquipi,* of which he did not seem to hold a high opinion. This judgment does not seem to have been necessarily based on the quality of the composition itself but rather on the musical group performing it, which he called an "attempted ensemble from Maras." Maras is a district in the province of Urubamba, and it is possible that this musical group was one of the participants in the contest, as its members were not listed. Although he was also critical of another group whose numbers can also be included in this category, Ríos had a better disposition toward the quality of its performance. This was the "Velasco" orchestra, an estudiantina that had also played in the first recital and now performed a yaraví and one of Alberto Negrón's compositions. Ríos criticized the former because, among other things, "we are not seduced by its mestizaje." Judging by this and other comments, this intellectual clearly had a somewhat purist attitude regarding mestizo genres and at the same time believed that in order to represent something really invaluable indigenous music had to be polished. I believe this purist attitude, which was perhaps prevalent among the artists who had dominated the urban scene in Cuzco in previous years, was now giving way to a better valuation of the great variety of artistic elements with an obviously strong presence in the rural and urban areas of Cuzco.

Finally, the second audition included a third category that, though close to the third category established for the first contest, was still somewhat different as it included some elements that obviously could not be presented as indigenous, Inca, or typical. This category includes a marinera called *cachi-cachi,* which was performed by a group from the San Sebastián district. Another piece, called *yana-simi,* which Ríos thought had the "air of an indigenous dance," was performed by Cosme Licuona on the harmonium, accompanied by a harp, two quenas, and a mandolin, which, according to Ríos, were played by "other music amateurs."[67] Here we must recall that Manuel Pillco learned how to play the harp in religious contexts with Licuona from San Sebastián, and it is possible that the harp that accompanied Licuona was that of Mr. Pillco. Finally, this category also included the dance called *saccsampillo* and a number called "*huanca* and *cacharpari*" performed by the same group from Quiquijana that had participated in the first recital, as well as a piece called "Andean song and huayno" played by the group from Huaroccondo, which had likewise taken part in the first recital.

This contest, as has already been suggested, was in many ways meant to provide resources that the members of the Centro would be able to use to form an adequate representative group, as well as a new repertoire that would represent Cuzco in the Amancaes contest the following year. This is how things actually turned out, as the members of the Centro were joined by many of the artists who had participated in the contest. However, as has also been noted, a second group—the Conjunto Acomayo—was formed under the leadership of the brothers Andrés Avelino and Policarpo Caballero Farfán, who also wanted to represent Cuzco. Policarpo had become a scholar of Andean music, which he called "Inca."

THE REPRESENTATIVES OF CUZCO IN LIMA IN 1928: LA MISIÓN CUZQUEÑA AND THE CONJUNTO ACOMAYO IN THE AMANCAES CONTEST

Amancaes contest went nationwide in its second year, with the participation of delegations from different provinces. But, as Núñez and Lloréns (1981) point out, in those early years "the participation of Limeño music, and of coastal music in general, was still bigger" (55). These scholars, and others, have noted that it was only between 1939 and 1945 that this event was dominated by the Andean presence (a change that coincided with the massive migration of highlanders to Lima); this was also the time when the non-Cuzco highland groups stopped presenting themselves as Inca groups (Núñez and Lloréns 1981, 55; Vivanco 1973, 38; Romero 2001, 160).[68] In this regard we must recall that by the contest's second year three categories had been established in which to place the contestants: criollo, Inca, and Andean. Although it is by no means clear what type of music was classified as Andean but not Inca, it seems obvious that the Inca category carried a great weight in determining the major prizes, at least during the early years of the contest.

Three groups represented Cuzco this second year. As in the previous year, the first group was formed by cuzqueños living in Lima and was led by the pianist Luis Esquivel. The second group was the Conjunto Acomayo, and the third was the "official" cuzqueño representative, called the Misión Cuzqueña de Arte Incaico (Cuzco Mission of Inca Art), sponsored by the municipal government of Cuzco. The latter group had in fact been formed based on the group of artists who had gathered together under the name of the Centro Musical Cuzco, which in turn was based on the experience of the Misión

Peruana de Arte Incaico. Both the group and the repertoire of the Misión Cuzqueña had in turn been expanded thanks to the contest and the auditions the Centro Musical had held the previous year. The Conjunto Acomayo, on the other hand, was mostly formed by peasant artists unknown in the urban milieu independent of the Centro Musical and was under the direction of Policarpo Caballero Farfán and his brother, Andrés Avelino.

The association between the Misión Peruana de Arte Incaico, which had been acclaimed abroad in 1923–24, and the Misión Cuzqueña de Arte Incaico, which had participated at Amancaes, was quite clear, at least for the press in Cuzco and Lima.[69] This drew a critique from at least one observer in Lima, who believed that it was unfair that such an experienced group should participate at Amancaes while the remaining participants had less experience.[70] Besides the similarity between the names of both groups, there was also the fact that the two directors of the Misión Cuzqueña had the same role in the Misión Peruana alongside other individuals, while nine of the approximately twenty-two members of the group had also been part of the Misión Peruana.[71] The Misión Cuzqueña included both new composers and artists who were making themselves known in the urban milieu of Cuzco, some of whom had been outstanding in the contest organized by the Centro Musical or had joined the Centro. Among them were Baltazar Zegarra and two of the musicians, members of the group that played *aires chumbivilcanos* in the second audition held after the contest: Francisco Gómez Negrón and Ricardo Flórez.[72]

As for the repertoire performed, we know that it included numbers popularized by the Misión Peruana such as *Surai Surita, awajkuna, pariwana,* and *mosoq punchai* (tableaux showing peasants at work). The new numbers included the *pajonal chumbivilcano* and *Inkachu* (see fig. 6).[73] Although on this occasion the melody of the first of these two pieces, which is usually known simply as *pajonal,* was presented as a Roberto Ojeda composition, the theme is actually one of several whose authorship is disputed, probably because it is based on a popular anonymous melody.[74] For instance, *pajonal* is also attributed to Alberto Negrón, who was also a member of the Misión Cuzqueña and a leader of the Centro Musical.[75] It is not clear whether the *pajonal chumbivilcano* was performed with dancers, but *Inkachu* was and still is essentially a dance. This dance, whose collection seems to be attributed to Roberto Ojeda almost without dispute, depicts a love

6. A group (probably from the Asociación Folklórica Kosko) performing the dance *Inkachu* (Cuzco, 1940s). (PHOTO BY EULOGIO NISHIAMA, FOTOTECA ANDINA ARCHIVE, CENTRO BARTOLOMÉ DE LAS CASAS, CUZCO.)

scene between peasants wherein the young males must pass several tests of strength and skill in order to win the love of their ladies. This dance apparently was the one that most caught the attention of the public, as it is the dance that the Misión Cuzqueña performed in the ceremony in which the prizes were presented.[76]

Like the Misión Peruana abroad, the Misión Cuzqueña was highly successful in Lima and won the first prize awarded to a music and dance group—the Presidente Leguía Award. It is also known that a special prize given by the "supremo gobierno" (Supreme Government) was awarded to Teodoro Valcárcel, a Puno musician and composer, and that another thirty-seven prizes were also awarded.[77] The Conjunto Acomayo was also among those who were extremely successful and received prizes; according to one account, it won "the first prize in its class" (Ttupa 1988, 18).

This Cuzco group differed from the Misión Cuzqueña in various ways, which were noted by the Lima press. Although it was acknowledged to be under the direction of "a man of musical technique, who has collected autochthonous melodies in their places of origin," the group itself was believed to be composed of "authentic Indians."[78] Although we know more of Policarpo Caballero Farfán, the group's acknowledged director, it should be noted that his brother Andrés Avelino apparently had a significant role in its establishment. It was Policarpo, however, who attracted the most attention due to the recognition he was already receiving not just as a composer and a musical educator in his homeland but also because of the studies he was undertaking of Andean and cuzqueño music.

Policarpo Caballero was born in 1894 in the town of Pomacanchi in the province of Acomayo. After developing his music in his homeland, Caballero left for Cuzco while young and there studied the mandolin with Leandro Alviña, a pioneer of cuzqueño regionalist and nationalist music. Caballero continued to study the violin, as well as composition, choreography, and musical pedagogy, in Lima, Tucumán, and Buenos Aires. On his return to Cuzco he dedicated himself to the study of what he called "Inca music" and instructed self-taught popular musicians in the violin and harp free of charge. It was on the basis of this experience that he formed the Conjunto Acomayo, in which he took part as a violinist alongside Mariano Nuray and Luciano Gallegos, who were also violinists; the harpists Bruno Machuca, Isidoro Ticuña, and Fermín Yauri; and the flutist José Domingo Rado.[79] Except for Rado, who apparently was somewhat well known, these artists were not a part of the artistic circles of the city of Cuzco.

Little is known of the repertoire the Conjunto Acomayo performed in the Amancaes contest, but we do know that the materials played in Lima included three of Caballero's compositions and arrangements,[80] *Condemayta, iskay urpi* (two doves), and *la despedida* (the farewell).[81] *Condemayta,* a piece that was considered a "ronda incaica" and had been composed in honor of Tomasa Condemayta, the female indigenous leader of Acos (Acomayo province) and a martyr in the Tupac Amaru II revolt, became, along with *taqekuy,*[82] one of his most famous compositions and a classic piece of the cuzqueño repertoire.

There is not a single comment about the presence of a dance troupe accompanying the Conjunto, so it seems to have been comprised of musicians alone. We do know that after the group's successful participation in the Amancaes contest, Caballero formed the Compañía Lírica Inkaika, based on the Conjunto, which included dances and traveled to various cities in Peru, Bolivia, and northern Argentina (Ttupa 1988, 20). This Compañía Lírica does not seem to have been long-lived, but what did persist up to about the mid-1950s was the Conjunto Acomayo, albeit inactively during some periods. Dances seem to have become an integral part of the Conjunto after the second Amancaes contest, and throughout its final stage they even became the group's central activity.[83]

One of the best-remembered achievements of this group is its successful participation in the celebrations held for the fourth centennial of the Spanish founding of Cuzco in March 1934, where it was awarded "the first five prizes, as well as the grand award, 'Presidente Mariscal Oscar R. Benavides.'" It also took part in the following year in the Fourth Centennial of the Spanish founding of Lima, where it won a gold medal and a diploma (Ttupa 1988, 20).[84] The group apparently experienced its first period of decline in the late 1930s, when Caballero dedicated himself more intensely to his musicological research and traveled extensively in Argentina.

Once they had won and received recognition through their participation in the Amancaes contest, neither the Conjunto Acomayo nor the Centro Musical Cuzco participated in this event. The contest itself declined a few years later with the downfall of Leguía and only gained new strength in 1939–45. Although the Andean presence at this event was massive throughout this period, the contest itself was no longer the major venue for artistic expression among provincial migrants and visitors to Lima because alternative locations began to appear such as the *coliseos* and radio programs.[85] It was also in the 1930s that new spaces for artistic expression began to appear in Cuzco, where the Centro Musical—which became the Centro Qosqo de Arte Nativo in 1933—and the Conjunto Acomayo took part. It was also in this decade that the neo-Indianist or new Indian ideology developed and gained strength among Cuzco's intellectuals and artists. This ideology, whose principles were summarized in the book *El Nuevo Indio* (*The New Indian,* 1930) by José Uriel García, gave a stronger impetus to the trend, already present among cuzqueño artists, that revalued the mestizo and the cholo element in their artistic output and moved even farther away from the Inca thematic. All of this was clearly mixed with the fact that Cuzco, which had been named the archaeological capital of South America in 1933, gradually became a focus of touristic interest.

3

. . .

TOURISTIC CUZCO, ITS MONUMENTS, AND ITS FOLKLORE

> The inner struggle between both souls—the autochthonous and the Hispanic, to dislodge one another—has already had its concretion (*concreción*) in art and folklore, in plastic arts and in customs, in form and in language. Form triumphed on the side of the invasive element; the expressive language was an achievement of the Andean soul—but not of the Inca soul because the Inca is a mere accident that gave rise to a period and no more than a period. Art and folklore, form and language—they are the fusion of the new Andean world.
> JOSÉ URIEL GARCÍA

> The historical and artistic significance of its monuments is no longer under discussion. The stamp of an unequivocal and general admiration has established it. The point now is to stress it, reaffirm it, and say it out loud to the world over, and also particularly to all of Peru, so that the flow of studies and tourists on occasion of the Fourth Centennial of the Spanish founding of this fountainhead of history is abundant and worthy of the city that is now inaugurated as the archaeological capital city of South America. JOSÉ GABRIEL COSIO

A new intellectual and cultural movement began developing in the city of Cuzco in the late 1920s at the same time that cuzqueño artists from various social sectors were creating a repertoire that would gradually become known as "folkloric" (even though the authors of some pieces were known) and "typical" or "traditional" of Cuzco, at both the national and the regional levels. This movement—which, as was explained in the introduction, was more commonly known as the neo-Indianist or New Indian movement, after the title of a book written by José Uriel García (1930), its main ideologue—rejected several conceptions prevalent among the members of the previous phase in the indigenista movement led by Luis Valcárcel. One major difference, at least with respect to the way Andean cultural elements were understood, is that García strove to do away with the idea that contemporary Andeans should be seen as an Incan survival.[1] Andeanness had to be essentially conceived as a fusion of autochthonous and Hispanic elements, as is shown in the first passage that opens this chapter. This passage likewise shows that for García the best example of this fusion was found in music and the so-called folkloric dances that were widespread all over the Cuzco region and were becoming ever more popular in the capital cities of Cuzco and Peru. Although it cannot be denied that José Uriel García and the other members of this movement were influenced both by foreign nationalist ideologies, which claimed that mestizaje was a way of attaining nationalism, and by modernist ideas, which valued cultural innovation, I here posit that the undeniable fusion of the elements and traditions found in the folkloric practices that were developing at the time provided García, as well as other intellectuals, with the materials that inspired them to propose their new ideas forcefully.[2]

Paradoxically those who proposed and developed the new regional and nationalist ideology, which valued everything mestizo and cholo, became direct promoters of the touristic potential of Cuzco, and this reinforced the image of the region as a national and international symbol of the glorious Incan past. Men such as José Uriel García and Humberto Vidal Unda—the founder and driving force behind *La Hora del Charango* (The Charango Hour), a major site of the artistic-folkloric output studied in chapter 4—dedicated many of their efforts to turning Cuzco into a national and international tourist center and at the same time promoted spaces for the cultural practices that were considered folkloric. It was in the period 1920–50 that the perception of Cuzco as a tourist center became significant in the activities of the intellectuals and artists in the city of Cuzco who were promoting folkloric activities, even though it was not until after a major earthquake hit the city in 1950 that it began to emerge as a center dedicated to the attraction of international tourism, and it was only in the early 1970s that the tourist industry became significant for the economy of Cuzco.

The relationship established in Cuzco between the promotion of artistic-folkloric performances and the desire to make its archaeological monuments a focus of interest for both Peru and the world is not unique to this region. This is a strategy used by other developing countries, which hold spectacles that try—as a way of proving their modernity and to outline national identities—to establish a continuity between the past and what is believed to be a living cultural heritage, either in international events or in their places of origin (Kirshenblatt-Gimblett 1998). These spectacles, which try to simplify for the tourist—and therefore present in concentrated fashion—the otherwise complicated task of deciphering the intricacies of the everyday life of culture the tourists are approaching (59), are essentially an attempt to establish what Kirshenblatt-Gimblett calls a "touristic realism" in order to convey the illusion that these are nonmediated events (8). Clearly the artists who took part in the folkloric creation in Cuzco in the early twentieth century and performed their art were driven by the growing interest their region had as a major national and international tourist center, which in turn supported the significance of Cuzco and its culture as a source of Peru's national identity. This chapter shows that the activities of the American Albert Giesecke, along with the "discovery" of Machu Picchu by Hiram Bingham, were decisive for the insertion of Cuzco into the world's tourist circuit, particularly the North American circuit.

MACHU PICCHU AND TOURISM ENTER THE SCENE

There is no question that a new era began for Cuzco with the so-called "scientific discovery of Machu Picchu" in 1911 in terms of the place this region would hold in the Peruvian and international *imaginaire.* Although the site is mentioned in eighteenth- and nineteenth-century documents, and was not unknown to the people living in the area, it was to a great extent thanks to the efforts of two American citizens, Hiram Bingham and Albert Giesecke, that Machu Picchu became a major focus of regional, national, and international interest.[3] As was pointed out by Mariana Mould de Pease (2000), and is shown by the correspondence between these two individuals,[4] from his position at the University of Cuzco (Universidad Nacional San Antonio Abad del Cuzco or UNSAAC) Giesecke "had an instrumental role in consolidating the 'scientific discovery' of Machu Picchu" (136), even though his name usually does not appear when the discovery is discussed. The significant role of Giesecke in the social, cultural, and intellectual development of Cuzco has been widely acknowledged both by his disciples and by students of indigenismo. His role as a major actor in the development of tourism in Cuzco and Peru is not conspicuous, however. The following discussion highlights some aspects of Giesecke's role, though it deserves a study of its own.[5]

Although several critiques point out that Bingham manipulated events and data in various ways in order to claim for himself alone the grandiose feat of discovering Machu Picchu, it is clear that his enthusiasm and personal drive greatly helped "to impregnate [the] Western imagination forever [with this site] when he presented Machu Picchu lucidly and quite early as the foremost place in the New World to explore in solitude" (Mould de Pease 2000, 136).[6] Mould de Pease likewise notes that Bingham was "set on being a major figure in the international sphere" (135), a goal he attained not just through his academic activities and as an explorer but also through politics as a governor and senator of Connecticut, as well as through his role in his country's military aviation in 1917–18.[7] Even José Gabriel Cosio—a major Cuzco intellectual in the first half of the twentieth century who was one of the early explorers of this archaeological site and criticized the extolling of Bingham as the "discoverer" of Machu Picchu—admitted as much, writing, "It is not true that Doctor Bingham was the discoverer of these remains; he gave them [instead] a life of fame and [made them] of archaeological interest. Machu Picchu was known by many people, but its renown is due to Bingham."[8]

Bingham received the help and support of Albert Giesecke, with whom he had remained in close contact since 1909, when he carried out his first explorations from Cuzco to Lima in search of the last capital of the Incas established by Manco Inca, which appeared in some colonial chronicles under the name of Vilcabamba. In this first exploration Bingham had visited the ruins of Choquequirao on the border between Cuzco and Apurímac, a site that had been pointed out as the capital city he was looking for. Bingham rejected this theory because he believed the buildings at this archaeological site did not have the Inca architectural features found in Cuzco and because he had news of another possible site called Vitcos in Cuzco.[9]

Having formed the "Yale-Peru Expedition," Bingham was received in 1911 by Giesecke, who offered him logistical support and above all invaluable data that would lead him to the famed "scientific discovery." Let us examine some passages written by Giesecke in which he describes the help he gave to Bingham.

I received Hiram Bingham and the members of the Expedition. In the following days they busied themselves buying mules, getting muleteers, acquiring more provisions and preparing the baggage. In the afternoons Hiram Bingham came to my house, sometimes accompanied by several members of the Expedition, to discuss the purpose of their journey and particularly his desire to find the site where the last Inca had lived when he established his Capital at a place called Vitcos. I sometimes invited some professors from the university (particularly Doctors José Gabriel Cosio and Romualdo Aguilar) to the meetings.

My information was the most detailed and proved to be reliable, as a few months before I had been fortunate enough to acquire them on the journey to the Hacienda Echarate with my great friend, congressman Braulio Polo y la Borda. This information of course [included] the account given by Arteaga, the warden of the San Miguel bridge, and the scant importance he attributed to the ruins, [which were] hidden by the forest in the site of Machu Picchu.

Hiram Bingham set out in mid July. . . . Arteaga took Hiram Bingham and Sergeant Carrasco to the site of the ruins.[10]

The following year Bingham organized a second scientific expedition in order "to clear and preserve Machu Picchu" with the support of Yale University and the National Geographic Society in Washington, D.C., which in 1913 devoted a whole issue of its magazine to showcasing the findings of the second expedition.[11] Cuzco scholars and intellectuals launched at least two other expeditions in the same year as Bingham's second, one of which included Giesecke and a group of students from UNSAAC (Tamayo Herrera 1981, 115).

It was only around 1934, after work was carried out by the Commission for the Fourth Centennial of the Spanish Foundation of Cuzco, and particularly after a zigzag road from the Urubamba River to the archaeological site was built in 1948, that a larger number of tourists had access to Machu Picchu. Flores Nájar (1994) points out, however, that from the 1920s on there were handbooks meant to guide the tourist during his or her stay in Cuzco, and this indicates that the possibility of turning Cuzco into a center of national, and above all international, tourism was already being seriously considered. *El Cuzco y sus Monumentos: Guía del Viajero,* one of the first guidebooks, written by the R. F. Rosario Zárate, was printed in Lima in 1921 and was clearly aimed at the international public because it included an English summary (Flores Nájar 1994, 209). The author wrote, "We do not 'intend to present a full study of all that is remarkable and worth seeing in this grandiose and classical city, and even less illustrate this with abundant and wearisome detail; all that we aim at is to provide the traveler with some brief indications of the major sites in the city from the Inca, colonial and historical-archaeological viewpoint, the knowledge of which mainly attracts tourists, be they national or foreign" (quoted in Flores Nájar 1994, 210).

In 1924 José Gabriel Cosio published *El Cuzco Histórico y Monumental.* This tourist guide, written "to help the traveler become easily and rapidly acquainted with the city of Cuzco, to which he has been brought by the curiosity of visiting and informing himself of the archaeological and historical treasures held by the city," included ample data on archaeological and colonial sites outside the city of Cuzco, including Machu Picchu (quoted in Flores Nájar 1994, 10). In 1925 José Uriel García published *Guía Histórico-Artística del Cuzco* with the editorial collaboration of Albert Giesecke, and this, as Flores Nájar points out, "can be considered an abbreviated and simplified version of *La Ciudad de los Incas,* [written] to be used by the tourists, who were already a part of the urban landscape of the lethargic city of Cuzco in the 1920s" (213). This same author points out that lodgings, meals, and guides to the archaeological monuments for tourists were already being advertised in 1928 in the *Guía Comercial, Profesional, e Industrial del Cuzco,* which was printed in 1928 (209).

In the 1930s and 1940s the cuzqueños clearly continued developing the path that would turn Cuzco into a tourist center of Peruvian, but above all foreign, interest, with some governmental and foreign support, driven by a strong desire to consolidate their regional identity and their proposals regarding the national identity. The following two chapters examine new institutions and local spaces besides the Centro Qosqo, such as the Instituto Americano de Arte de Cuzco (American Art Institute of Cuzco) and the Hora del Charango, which sponsored the artistic-folkloric output but at the same time played a significant role in the promotion of the image of Cuzco as a center of cultural and historical interest through its monuments and living culture. Even so, it must be acknowledged that Alberto Giesecke played a key role in connecting Cuzco quite early on with Peru's central government and the United States and Europe, as well as in channeling and promoting the interest in Cuzco and the provision of services.

GIESECKE AND CUZCO

A detailed study of Albert Giesecke's significant role in the intellectual, social, economic, and cultural development of Cuzco throughout his fruitful life is a study in itself. Although here I emphasize his activities regarding the development and promotion of Cuzco as a center of touristic interest, Giesecke, both in Cuzco in 1910–23 and in Lima from that time until his demise in 1968, undeniably participated in and promoted several aspects of cuzqueño life to those living in the region, as well as those established in Lima.

Born in Philadelphia in 1883, Giesecke studied economics, education, philosophy, and law at Harvard University as well as in Berlin, London, and Paris. He was teaching at the University of Pennsylvania when Francisco García Calderón called on him on behalf of the Peruvian minister of education (Avendaño 1995, 345; *Revista Universitaria* 1960, 24).[12] The Peruvian government was looking for a specialist in economics and university management to reform Peru's universities and high schools (25). After he had been working in Lima for seven months preparing his recommendations for reform, President Augusto B. Leguía, in Giesecke's words, "surprised" him by offering him the position of president of UNSAAC, which was soon to be reopened after having been shut down by a student strike. Giesecke accepted the position after dispelling his initial misgivings (25).

Manuel Jesús Aparicio notes that "the successful rectorship of Alberto A. Giesecke has been quite adequately called the 'Golden Age of the Universidad de San Antonio Abad' in the Republican period; Giesecke made himself the standard bearer [of reform] and made all [parties] join in the modernization of the University and of Cuzco, giving rise to a current for revaluing Cuzco" (2000, 102). During his stay in Cuzco as president of the university from 1910 to 1923, Giesecke was also a city alderman and mayor three times. The intellectuals and politicians who interacted with him always acknowledged his invaluable role in setting new courses in the social and cultural life of Cuzco. So it was with Luis Valcárcel, who explicitly did so several times, for instance, in the account he gave of his friendship with José Uriel García and the strike that preceded Giesecke's arrival.

> Uriel García and I were good friends since our first years of college life. In 1909 we had already fought together in the first strike ever in America over student

demands. Our [demands] were very radical. . . . Thanks to the strong campaign we made we managed to have the university reopen in 1910 with an entirely new staff, [and] a young director who was our foremost friend. We respected and loved him throughout the fourteen years he held his position. Don Alberto Giesecke was this great director who taught us to know our country; with him we learned to study and behave as responsible people" (1986, 17).

Besides his role in the university, Giesecke is known for having headed the census of Cuzco in 1912, opening the road that leads to Sacsayhuamán, paving several streets, building the slaughterhouse and market, organizing the Archaeological Museum, and in general establishing a connection between the university and the social and economic life of Cuzco. Giesecke's role in promoting the study of the archaeological and historical riches of Cuzco was also acknowledged by his contemporaries, who more than once paid him homage and clearly saw him as someone "who made all of the scientific and archaeological value of Cuzco known both in the U.S. and Europe."[13] His "invaluable" intervention "on occasion of the earthquake . . . conveying the help of the American people to Cuzco at the time that this misfortune struck," was also widely acknowledged.[14]

As already noted, Giesecke was a key figure in providing Cuzco with a new place in both the Peruvian and the international imaginaire through his help with the exploration and "discovery" of Machu Picchu. But due to the positions he held in Lima, his role in channeling attention and resources to Cuzco and Peru through foreign and Peruvian touristic interest in this region was even more important. After establishing a family with a cuzqueño lady, Esther Matto Usandivaras, Giesecke moved to Lima first with a position in the Ministry of Education, which he held until the late 1940s, after which he served as civil attaché in the American embassy. In these two positions, he played a key role in Peru's cultural, scientific, social, and touristic relations, having already undertaken a political role as a commissioner who collaborated with the Tacna and Arica Plebiscite in 1925.[15] His letters show that he took part in, or was aware of, each and every major project of archaeological and scientific research undertaken in Peru, as well as every private or state-led effort made from the 1930s onward to channel foreign tourism into the country.[16] This was demonstrated, for instance, when the Peruvian government entrusted him in 1936, through the Ministry of Foreign Affairs, with the touristic promotion of Peru abroad. This role is best summarized by Giesecke himself in a passage from the "Report" he presented that year to the incumbent minister or foreign affairs, Dr. Alberto Ulloa Sotomayor.

> I am honored to enclose the report I prepared as a result of my visit to the United States of America, where in compliance with the Supreme Decree (Resolución Suprema) given by this Office dated March 11th 1936, I studied the major and most indispensable phases for the organization of a tourist [flow] to Peru.
>
> I am ready to orally expand the present report with further details in regard to some of the points included therein should you so desire. I am naturally ready to continue with the task of organizing all that is related to the desire the Government of Peru has of facilitating or promoting the coming of tourists from the United States of America.
>
> I want to hereby make note that I carried out this assignment without spending a cent from the Governmental Treasury. In this same disinterested spirit I gave conferences on Peru, particularly illustrated conferences on Cuzco, before well-educated entities and in universities.[17]

Although the report was essentially about all of Peru, Giesecke stressed that the promotion of tourism in the country should emphasize Cuzco with the argument that "this is the greatest point of attraction for tourists."[18] A few years before Giesecke prepared this report, the Peruvian government had begun to take some interest in the promotion of tourism to Cuzco after the city had been awarded the title of Archaeological Capital City of South America. This proclamation was made as preparations for the celebration of the Fourth Centennial of the Spanish founding of Cuzco (which I will refer to as the Fourth Centennial) were beginning. Both events combined to give rise to a new touristic interest in Cuzco.

CUZCO, THE ARCHAEOLOGICAL CAPITAL CITY OF SOUTH AMERICA: A NEW INSPIRATION FOR ARTISTIC-FOLKLORIC CREATIONS

Echoing a resolution recently passed by the Fifteenth Congress of Americanists, held in La Plata, Argentina, and in reply to the congressional initiative headed by the representative for Cuzco, Félix Cosio, on January 23, 1933, the Peruvian government issued law no. 7688, which recognized Cuzco as the Archaeological Capital City of South America. As the passage by José Gabriel

Cosio that opens this chapter shows, this acknowledgment was another opportunity for promoting the image of Cuzco as the major Peruvian center for tourism, an opportunity for the study of Andean history and archaeology, and a crucial element in developing a national identity. As already noted, with this acknowledgment came the celebrations of the city's Fourth Centennial, which enabled the cuzqueños to attract the interest of the government and the country, as well as interest abroad.

The Peruvian government supported several projects that sought to consolidate the nature of the city as a tourist center and a focus of archaeological and historical studies through laws and supreme decrees sponsored by cuzqueño politicians and intellectuals. For instance, we find, among other things, that Cuzco was declared the future site of the National Museum of Archaeology; permission was given to open a department of American history and archaeology in the University of Cuzco; and resources were provided to improve the roads that led to the archaeological sites of Machu Picchu and Pisac, to repair these sites and the old governmental palace, to undertake urban sanitation works, and to open a "bureau for archaeological popularization and the organization of tourism."[19] This office apparently was not established before 1936.[20] However, a year after the law providing for the celebration of the Fourth Centennial was passed, the finance secretary decided to establish in the city of Cuzco a Central Commission for Publicity and Tourism, which would "work without pay, using all possible means available, to prepare the publicity required for the celebration of the Fourth Centennial . . . and channel the flow of tourists which for this reason should be heading to Cuzco."[21] The first individual who appears in this document as a member of this commission was Dr. Albert Giesecke, followed by Drs. Fortunato Herrera, Manuel Velasco, Atilio Sivirichi, and Julio Velarde and Señor Francisco González Gamarra (the latter an artist and musician included among the Big Four of Cuzco music). Although the members of the commission were not paid, the government did provide funds for their task.[22]

Despite these efforts, in the late 1930s the state of the infrastructure meant to receive tourists in Cuzco was not encouraging. For instance, the February 1937 issue of the magazine *Turismo*, which was published in Lima, pointed out that Cuzco "should be the major tourist center of Peru, but all the facilities for tourism must be improved."[23] A newspaper article published that same year, discussing a new tax that was to be paid on entering the ruins of Machu Picchu, gives an idea of the lack of facilities for visitors.

> Under our noses we have the wonders of Machupijcho, but instead of building a good highway, of establishing an acceptable hotel or inn in the ruins, [or] of keeping the city of stone clean and presentable, it is abandoned and left to the tropical vegetation [which] invades it and continues destroying the marvelous ruins; there is a hotel by name only, where one can get neither a bed nor even a fork. And, on top of it all, a tax of one golden sol [Peruvian currency] must be paid to see Machupijcho. . . . The tourist has to make a tiresome journey of half a day by train, [endure] the inconvenience of climbing three kilometers uphill on foot or on pack animals, and worse still part with a sol [just] to have the pleasure of contemplating the megalithic city.[24]

The improvement of the infrastructure and the organization for tourism would continue until the late 1960s, albeit at a slow pace. In the mid-1960s, Albert Giesecke was still working and advocating—at the head of the by then established Corporación de Turismo del Perú (Peruvian Tourism Corporation)—for the construction of a tourist hotel at Machu Picchu to replace the inadequate lodgings.[25] Even so, it cannot be denied that both events—the declaration of Cuzco as the Archaeological Capital City of South America and the celebrations held for the city's Fourth Centennial—jointly stimulated regional and a nationwide interest in Cuzco as a touristic and cultural center. At this time we also find a new incentive for the institutions based in the city of Cuzco to promote artistic-folkloric creations and practices. For instance, a "departmental contest" was organized by the Centro Qosqo a few months after the first of the aforementioned events.

Here, as in other regional and national folkloric events discussed in this and other chapters, and as in the case of folkloric festivals held in other parts of the world, we find a convergence of various motivations and interests on the part of the organizers and the participant groups, as well as the influence of several other factors of a historical, social, and technological nature (Cantwell 1992, 295). These interests and factors determined the shape of the folkloric events and the variant effects they had on Peruvian and cuzqueño society throughout the first half of the twentieth century. As Cantwell has suggested, the folkloric performances and contests held in Cuzco and Lima may be understood as events wherein "folk culture and official culture embrace[d] one another: the one to win honor from the attention of cultural institutions allied with education, science, commerce, or government, the other to disseminate the influences of folk culture into the popular imagination and, by way of advocating and sustaining it, into the commercial marketplace or public policy" (1992, 263).

Thus, in the first half of the twentieth century in Cuzco, the archaeological finds; the promotion of tourism; the intellectual and political desire to sustain and promote a regional and a national identity; the desire of the organizers of the contests and the participants to make the peasant and popular urban practices known and appreciated by cuzqueños, Peruvians, and foreign tourists; the rise of the study of folklore; the coming of radio; the examples of state support for folkloric art set by countries such as Russia and Mexico; and the ideas regarding modernity circulating at the time—these, among other factors, came together to materialize the folkloric events of the time. These events helped crystallize a folkloric repertoire that would gradually be known as typically or traditionally cuzqueño and at the same time inspired and underpinned the significant regionalist and nationalist proposals made by the neo-Indianists.

OF CONTESTS AND CELEBRATIONS: A CLOSER LOOK AT CONTEMPORARY REALITY

The year 1933 is also most meaningful for the history of the Centro Qosqo, as it was in this year that the Centro became officially known—through Supreme Decree 149—as the first "folkloric institution" in Peru.[26] But before this official recognition, the Centro Qosqo, with its recently acquired name, had already organized the above-mentioned contest, stimulated by the recent recognition its city had received. When the contest was convened it was explicitly noted that "this goal of a high cultural significance deserves the support of all the authorities and institutions, all the more so since Cuzco is the Archaeological Capital City of South America [and] the center in which the vernacular art must most intensively be cultivated."[27] In the announcement the Centro Qosqo depicted the contest much as it had the one it had organized in 1927, still under the name of the Centro Musical Cuzco. Not only were both contests responding to the recognition Cuzco had been given at the national level—desiring in the former case not only to retain the first place attained by Cuzco in the Amancaes contest but also to improve the standards of performance and in the latter to show that the "vernacular" or "aboriginal art" (the name used in the 1933 contest) was on a par with Cuzco's archeological monuments—but both had similar goals, guidelines, and organizations. In the nationalist and traditionalist spirit that drove the organizers of the second contest, as in 1927, it was established that it would include only the "purely national and historical art" and exclude all "foreign and modern" works.[28] It was likewise noted, in exactly the same terms as in 1927, that the Centro Qosqo would use the occasion to increase the repertoire it was promoting as traditionally cuzqueño, as well as to incorporate new artists into the institution.[29]

Even so, some differences in the way these two events were announced in the press indicate two points worth emphasizing. On the one hand, in the 1933 contest the significance of the promotion of the "native" culture was based not so much on the fact that it was a survival of the (Inca or colonial) past but on the existence of a rich contemporary repertoire that had to be recognized as art. On the other hand, it can be surmised that by 1933 the appeal of participating in this type of event for people outside the city and the province of Cuzco had grown, as had the number of groups performing music or dances acknowledged to be folkloric.

In relation to the first point, whereas for the 1927 contest the members of the Centro Musical had based its organization on the fact that "one of its major goals [of the Centro] is to collect, study, and make known the typical regional music, particularly that which still survives from pre-Hispanic and colonial times in different parts of the department,"[30] by 1933 this same institution, now known as the Centro Qosqo, supported the event, arguing that "one of the major goals of its establishment was to disseminate and reveal Peruvian art[, that] . . . in all parts of the department there are artistic groups and artists [who are] almost anonymous and are not valued due to the lack of adequate opportunities[, and that] there is a pressing need to organize artistic contests so as to stimulate and convey such fertile and meaningfully suggestive motifs."[31]

As for the second point, we find that the 1933 contest had to limit the number of participants per group and in general the number of groups participating. The help of the Provincial Municipal Council of Cuzco was sought, just as in the first contest, both financially and to summon the participants through their respective municipal councils. But, whereas in the former case no mention was made of a limit set on the number or the preliminary rounds, now it was requested that all "artistic delegations" be "authorized by the municipal council of each province, which will send a single delegation with a maximum number of ten individuals after the previous process of elimination in their respective provinces, with the exception of Cuzco, which can be represented by [as many] groups as there are."[32] Once in Cuzco, the groups selected would have to participate in a second qualifying round, this time with the same type of judges as in the first contest: members of the Centro Qosqo, the City Council, the university, and the local press. It must also be noted that at the time the organization of contests was not limited to groups of artists and intellectuals connected with the Centro Qosqo, as this initiative had also been taken by institutions formed by cuzqueños of popular extraction such as the Workers' Sports Center of the Pachacutec Soccer Club (Centro Deportivo Obrero del Pachacutec), which organized a contest of "native, criollo music" in 1931.[33] This supports the idea that interest in organizing these contests and participating in them was spreading to other sectors of Cuzco's society.

Besides the two major points noted above, which indicate that the dances and music of the rural and the popular-urban sectors were being increasingly perceived by middle- and upper-class cuzqueño intellectuals and artists as a form of contemporary art (and not as a vestige of Inca or colonial art) worthy of being reappraised and that by 1933 the appeal of participating in the events or contests sponsored by the city of Cuzco had grown, there also are two new elements in the second contest that have to be pointed out. These elements are connected with the various names given to these contests. The names of the 1927 contest that appeared in the press focused on "music," and it was at times called a contest of "aboriginal music," "Inca music," or "autochthonous music." The 1933 contest, however, was more inclusively labeled "Aboriginal Art."

So, whereas the first contest called for the participation of "musicians" and pointed out that their performances could be supplemented with "dances (*bailes y danzas*) of the same type,"[34] the second contest called for the participation of dances as a separate category but retained the "typical dance music" category.[35] This means that the organizers were becoming more interested in the dances practiced in the various provinces of Cuzco, which were not choreographic inventions of the type composed by the members of the Misión Peruana (e.g., the *danza de la flecha* or the *danza de la honda*). In fact, dances of this type, such as the *k'achampa, sijlla, saccsampillo, mamala,* and others, were already part of the Misión Peruana de Arte Incaico and appeared in the 1927 contest, as well as in the recitals that followed it. It is therefore highly likely that the organizers provided dance an independent space due to the fact that, on the one hand, music and dance were closely connected for the musicians from the rural and popular-urban sectors and, on the other hand, that this practice was becoming ever more popular among the middle and upper sectors of Cuzqueño society to which the organizers belonged.[36]

The second of the new elements is that the space for certain forms of expression, which until then had been limited to the middle and upper sectors of urban society, now expanded to include the participation of all sectors in Cuzco society in "traditional tableaux . . . , choirs, and the other regional motifs."[37] This is connected to the development of a new tradition in Cuzco drama—the costumbrista theater—and to the popularization of the Incaic theater, as these "traditional tableaux" and "regional motifs" were above all dramatizations. It was noted in chapter 1 that César Itier had shown that by 1920 Incaic theater had become popularized, that is, it had begun to be appropriated by the "popular urban and semiurban classes," not just in Cuzco but also in other Quechua-speaking regions (2000, 63). Popular sectors were taking up these types of representations just as the intellectuals and members of the upper classes at the regional and the national levels were losing interest in them. In fact, elites harshly criticized these popular groups.[38] In the 1930s we find several companies formed by humble individuals from the provinces of Cuzco who were writing and performing Inca dramas.[39]

At the same time that this was happening around 1930, Itier says, "the confluence of the Quechua drama tradition and the interest in popular [culture]" gave rise to the genre known as the "costumbrista comedy" or "costumbrista drama" (2000, 82). Both established directors and actors in Incaic theater, such as Julio Rouvirós and Luis Ochoa, and new artists from the rising neo-Indianist movement, such as Andrés Alencastre, dedicated their efforts to writing and staging plays inspired by the social, cultural, and political life of contemporary Cuzco. These plays tried to depict not just very common, everyday ritual customs such as the *kurus belakuy* (about the vigil of the cross), the *chukcha rutukuy* (a haircut), and the *rimaykukuy* (asking for someone's hand in marriage) but also the clashes between landowners and peasants, which had been particularly bloody in the previous decade.[40] Luis Ochoa, for instance, staged the play *Qosqo qawarina* (Contemplating Cuzco), in which he showed the conflict between an Indian and his boss, while Andrés Alencastre, who will be discussed at length in the following chapter, wrote and staged plays such as *challakuy*, in which he showed the pursuit of some Indians who had murdered a landowner (*gamonal*) due to the abuses the latter had inflicted on them.

By this time we also find that the music and the dances were gradually moving to the forefront in these costumbrista plays, as well as in those that still retained the Inca theme. Such was the case of the performance of the Conjunto Acomayo during the celebrations of the Fourth Centennial; this group, headed by Policarpo and Avelino Caballero, had been acclaimed in the 1928 national contest held at Amancaes. They performed the Quechua zarzuela (operetta) *T'itu Q'usñipa*, which the press described as "an Inca drama [that was] all song," with a cast "of close to fifty people, with a large, traditional ensemble,"[41] with the Inca interpreted by an "indigenous dancer" thanks to his skill in dancing the "difficult warrior dance of the Pomacanchis."[42] The biography of Policarpo Caballero claims that the performance of the zarzuela on this occasion won for the group "the first five prizes, as well as the main 'Presidente Mariscal Oscar R. Benavides' prize, which was a beautiful silver cup with Inka decorations" (Ttupa 1988, 20).

The Fourth Centennial celebrations clearly gave rise to spaces for the promotion of artistic-folkloric presentations. Just as in the public works undertaken for this occasion, these activities were promoted and led by intellectuals, artists, and politicians both cuzqueño and cuzqueñistas (such as Albert Giesecke), and the government responded by passing a law that provided funds for the organization of a "historical, artistic and cultural contest."[43] Itier points out that this celebration marked "an abrupt, albeit short-lived, rebirth of Quechua drama in all of its manifestations" in which not just the established directors and actors from the city of Cuzco participated but also groups from the provinces and at least one composed of workers.[44]

The following year the same kind of celebrations, now held in Lima, provided both the Centro Qosqo and the Conjunto Acomayo an opportunity to attain more recognition as representatives of Cuzco at the national level. These were the celebrations held for the Fourth Centennial of the Spanish Foundation of Lima. This time the performance given by the Conjunto Acomayo apparently drew more applause than that of the Centro Qosqo, at least at the national contest held on this occasion, where the Conjunto was accorded a higher position and received a bigger cash prize.[45]

Besides participating in this contest, both groups took advantage of the opportunity to hold other presentations in Lima and—in the case of the Centro Qosqo—other provinces. For example, the Lima press recorded that the Conjunto Acomayo performed in honor of the "Minister of England, his wife and the British colony," a performance that was apparently a success.[46] Just as in the 1928 Amancaes contest, the group was still perceived as more indigenous and authentic than the Centro Qosqo—or at least it was presented as such by the press. This was explicitly stated by the cuzqueño intellectual Antonio de la Torre, who claimed in a speech transcribed in the press that "all they sing, all they play, all they dance, is purely, genuinely, and unquestionably aboriginal, with a Quechuaness (*quechuismo*) that will not easily be equaled or surpassed by any other manifestation of the vernacular art."[47]

By now the Centro Qosqo was no longer acknowledged by the cuzqueños themselves as an indigenous or aboriginal group. In fact, in the program of a performance held in Lima's Teatro Municipal, the group admitted that its work was stylized. In order to stress the group's professionalism and artistic experience, the program indicated that it was "the same [group] that had made a triumphal tour of Buenos Aires and Montevideo, and had won the First National Prize in the 1928 Amancaes contest."[48] Nevertheless, although a few members of the recently established Centro Qosqo had indeed participated in both events, the groups referred to in the program actually were the Misión Peruana de Arte Incaico and the Misión Cuzqueña de Arte Incaico. More to the point, of the twenty-four artists in the delegation the Centro Qosqo sent to Lima in 1935, only Roberto Ojeda and Manuel Pillco had participated in the Misión Peruana de Arte Incaico, and they, as well as Baltazar Zegarra, had also appeared in the performances of the Misión Cuzqueña de Arte Incaico.[49]

One last point that must be made is that both groups, in different ways, had not fully left behind allusions to the Inca period as part of the cuzqueño and Peruvian identities. But whereas the Centro Qosqo continued the trend that glorified the Inca empire, the Conjunto Acomayo presented a more rebellious image and was critical of both the Inca and the colonial rulers. In the speech cited above, Antonio de la Torre made the following comment regarding the identities of the Conjunto's members:

> The native artists who form the "Conjunto Acomayo" are legitimate heirs of those brave and sentimental Indians whose rebellious and sublime art astounded the court of the Inka, the Child of the Sun, when the K'osñipas from Sayhua and Ranchi raised the banner of rebellion against the magnificent Huayna Ccapac. . . . These are also virtuous and modest artists, the descendants of Doña Ana Ttito Cunsimayta [*sic*], that intrepid warrior and cacique [Indian chief] who, in complicity with the illustrious Tupac Amaru, rallied the Indian masses of Canas, Acomayo, and Chumbivilcas against the outrages committed by the Spanish elites and authorities.[50]

Although de la Torre was an intellectual outside the group, it is possible that this type of presentation was influenced by the image the leaders of the Conjunto wanted to project. We must also remember that in the celebrations for the Fourth Centennial the zarzuela performed by the Conjunto Acomayo showed the rebellion of the people of Acomayo against Inca rule.[51]

Although there is little information regarding the repertoire performed by the Conjunto Acomayo, we do know something about the pieces the Centro Qosqo included in its performance in Lima's Teatro Municipal, which gives us some idea of the themes and images that were being consolidated in this institution's repertoire. This repertoire is consistent with the trends seen in the departmental contest this institution had organized just two years before, and it is highly likely that it included some of the elements present in that event, as the Centro itself had stated in the rules.

THE CENTRO QOSQO IN LIMA: A NEW REPERTOIRE CRYSTALLIZES

Several newspaper accounts indicate that the Centro Qosqo's expedition to Lima on occasion of the Fourth Centennial of the Spanish founding of the city was controversial. Some cuzqueño intellectuals and artists were not convinced that the Centro would be able to adequately represent Cuzco, and there were disagreements within the institution as well. In a letter sent to the

Cuzco press by Humberto Vidal Unda, the secretary of the Centro Qosqo at the time and the leader of the group that went to Lima, he stated that, despite the opinion of some "interested parties" in Cuzco, who had carried out an "odious campaign" against the tour, it had been a success.[52]

The critiques apparently arose due in part to the exclusion of some artists who were renowned in Peru and abroad and had not been included in the delegation despite being members of the Centro. For the critics this questioned the "artistic value" of the group because they felt Cuzco should be represented by its most accomplished instrumentalists and composers.[53] The delegation, however, had been limited to twenty-four artists following an order given by the mayor of Cuzco. It was more concerned with including acknowledged artists of "native art"—because the program they would perform was "of a purely vernacular nature [far] removed from classic or foreign influences"—than famed orchestra musicians, as it was "easy to complete the delegation with famed masters in the places where they had to perform."[54] What is indeed striking in relation to the statement made by Vidal Unda is that Pancho Gómez Negrón, who was just then becoming a major symbol of cuzqueño "folklore" personifying the image of the *ccori lazo*, which was an image included in the Centro Qosqo's program, was not included. Gómez Negrón had gone to Lima in 1928 as a member of the Misión Cuzqueña after excelling in the auditions held after the 1927 contest.

Vidal Unda complained that on reaching Lima, after having first performed in Arequipa and Mollendo, the Centro Qosqo had not found a state-run, well-organized national contest but one that had been auctioned off to a private firm, which was exploiting the groups from the provinces by forcing them to "perform in all kinds of scenarios, even low-class ones." The members of the Centro opposed this "out of respect for the group, as well as for the department" they were representing.[55] This comment brings to mind two important points regarding the place of provincial folklore at the national level. The first is that at this time the government was not overly interested in organizing these folkloric contests or other kinds of events and entrusted them to commercial firms. The second is that by this time the performances of this kind of group had a significant audience, and this is consistent, as other scholars have noted, with migration from the provinces to Lima and the subsequent appearance of new spaces for the practice of folklore: the so-called coliseos (coliseums) (Núñez and Lloréns 1981; Romero 2001, 93). These coliseos, which were actually humble and rustic places sometimes even roofed with a circus tent, were managed by private entrepreneurs who benefited from the desire of people of various extractions born in the provinces to share a space where they could hear their favorite artists (Romero 2001, 93).

To return to the performance given by the Centro Qosqo in Lima's Teatro Municipal, "Judging by the applause, the numbers repeated, and the congratulations received from major intellectuals, it was an all-out artistic triumph," according to Vidal Unda.[56] A close look at the numbers the group performed gives an idea of some of the images and ideas that were then coalescing within this institution to represent the cuzqueño and Peruvian identities. I have shown elsewhere (Mendoza 1998, 2000, 2001) that ever since the cuzqueño delegations performed abroad with the Misión Peruana de Arte Incaico, and in Peru at the Amancaes contest, three sets of characteristics had distinguished the composition and the re-creation of the pieces these groups performed under the general headings of the lives of the Incas and the lives of contemporary peasants. The first characteristic is the aggressive warrior spirit of the past that still survived, particularly in some provinces far removed from the city of Cuzco. The second is the bucolic and at the same time lethargic and productive life of the contemporary peasantry and its Inca forebears. The third is the festive and licentious spirit that arose during celebrations, especially those of a carnivalesque kind. Cutting across these three characteristics were the sentimental themes of nostalgia and love for both the homeland and one's beloved, themes that are prominent in several pieces. Although some numbers may be more clearly placed in one of the categories, they often combine elements from two or all of them.

Although the Inca theme was losing ground in the artistic-folkloric elaborations in the city of Cuzco, we must not forget that the celebrations held the previous year had sparked a brief rebirth of interest in this subject. It therefore comes as no surprise to find that the Inca theme was still present in this performance of the Centro Qosqo. The program announced that "the Conjunto presents restorations and stylizations of Inca, colonial, and contemporary tableaux, customs, music, songs, and dances, faithfully reproducing the rites, dress, and lavish decorations."[57] Besides emphasizing the fact that these presentations were elaborate and stylized, as well as recalling the ancient glories of the cuzqueño groups associated with the Centro, the program ascribed equal importance to Inca, colonial, and contemporary times. But the program, which had fourteen numbers, only included two that were explicitly presented as Inca: an (unidentified) "Inca melody" performed by "the Orchestra" (i.e., the symphonic orchestra); and "the weavers" (more commonly known as the *awajkuna*), performed as an "Inca costumbrista tableau,"[58] although it was in fact one of the compositions of Roberto Ojeda that had been acclaimed in the tour of the Misión Peruana de Arte Incaico.

Besides its explicit presentation as Inca, "the weavers" can be included in the second set of characteristics listed above because it depicts the Inca past and contemporary Andean life through bucolic images that praise productivity and manual skill (see fig. 2 on page 29). Some of these characteristics were explicitly stated in the descriptions of the tableau given in the programs of the performances held in the 1930s and 1940s. The following is a characteristic example of the way this tableau was presented.

> While Mancu Khápaq taught the men of the Kosko people how to use the bow, the *makana* [war club] and the *warakas* [slings], [as well as how to] cultivate maize and shape stones, Mama Ojllo—Peru's first great historical woman—taught her women how to spin and weave, a skill that is innate among the aboriginals of Peru; nowadays men and women spin while walking on their long journeys, when they take a break from plowing the land, or simply when they stir the fire. When their work does not draw them far away from home they weave their clothes with their own hands or gather as if at a party, forming quaint and picturesque groups of weavers just like in this scene, which is precisely called "Awajkuna" (The Weavers). (Paúkar 1947, 26; see also fig. 2 on page 29)

The program then lists two numbers explicitly presented as warrior dances, which can therefore be included in the first set of characteristics. These are *wifala,* which appears in the program as a "triumphant war dance," and *wajra pukara,* which is simply listed as a "war dance."[59] Although it is not mentioned in the program of the 1935 performance of the Centro Qosqo, the former is usually acknowledged to be a dance "gathered from folklore" that was arranged by either Roberto Ojeda or some other member of the Centro Qosqo (Paúkar 1947, 27). The second dance was based on a composition of the cuzqueño musician Andrés Izquierdo, who was also a member of the Centro Qosqo. Unfortunately there is no description of *wajra pukara,* but, thanks to a list of the artists who danced it in subsequent performances in Cuzco, we know that it was an all-male dance (27). For *wifala* we do have abundant descriptions, as it is a dance that is often performed even today in all kinds of festive events in Cuzco. This dance can also be easily included in the second and third sets of characteristics because it depicts both a festive spirit and a bucolic image. One program from the mid-1940s connects *wifala* with the Inca military past—although this may not have been the case in the performance of the Centro in Lima in 1935—and describes it as "a warrior dance that has been preserved unchanged since Inca times. It represents the joy of victory. With a graceful and rhythmic dance the *ñustas* [princesses] wave pennants and join the brave soldiers of Kosko, who have given victory to the Inca banners and extended the span of the empire, perhaps defeating the *aukas* [enemies] who threatened the sovereignty of the Children of the Sun. The Indians dance carrying large pennants and covered with winglike mantles, white as the pennants" (27).

To continue with the repertoire of the performance given in the Teatro Municipal of Lima in 1935, the "Grand Orchestra" (which probably was a symphonic orchestra, although there is no description of the instruments it contained) that accompanied the Centro Qosqo interpreted another piece besides the "Inca Melody." This was one of the yaravies that are still regarded as classic pieces in the repertoire of Cuzco music: *al despertar* (on awakening), a piece composed by Baltazar Zegarra, one of the Big Four of Cuzco Music.[60] As was noted in chapter 2, although the yaraví in its various forms is known as an essentially mestizo genre among the highland traditions, it inherited from the pre-Hispanic harawi its evocative and nostalgic nature. The lyrics that sometimes accompany this yaraví, which were also written by Baltazar Zegarra, confirm the nostalgic nature of this piece because they refer to a love lost: "Que amargo es para mí vivir sin tu amor, tan solo el recuerdo de aquella mujer que antes me quería. Por eso no quiero despertar jamás porque no la encuentro" (How bitter it is for me to live without your love, with just the remembrance of the woman who once loved me. That is why I do not ever want to wake up, because I cannot find her").[61] The "sad and nostalgic" tone in connection with love is likewise present in another piece performed by the Centro Qosqo, which had also been part of the repertoire of the Misión Peruana de Arte Incaico: *pariwana*.[62] In the 1935 concert the piece was performed as a female solo sung by Aída Medrano and was listed in the program as a "pastoral song," so it can be included in the second set of characteristics.[63]

The subject of an amorous deception present in *al despertar* also appears in two of the other pieces in this program in huayno (wayno or waynu) rhythm that would likewise become classic pieces in the repertoire of cuzqueño music: *picaflor* (hummingbird) and *ingrata* (ungrateful woman). The first piece was presented in the program as a "duo of song and dance" performed by a man and a woman and the second as a "criollo tableau with choir and dance."[64] In Cuzco, both pieces are considered "popular huaynos" or "folklore," that is, their authors are unknown, but some do credit Roberto Ojeda as the person who first collected *picaflor* (which is known in other parts of Peru as *quisiera ser picaflor* [I would like to be a hummingbird]) in the 1930s (Ojeda 1987, 71). It was around this time that these two huaynos were first seen as examples of the emergent "cholo" or "mestizo" spirit, as is shown in the following description:

> They are cholo waynus that denote the jovial spirit that agitates the love life of the new Peruvian Indian (the mestizo). Their merry and melancholic music, as in a contradiction, articulates in both [songs] the mischievous disdain both the cholos and the cholas pretend to have for each other when courting. The beau says in song that there are others like her beloved who yearn for his wooing, while she reciprocates and claims that many and better suitors want her favor. In these waynus, we cuzqueños cede our presumptuous wish to disdain those who are disdainful of us. So it is, and so it will always be, and the cholo bard expressed in his songs the passion the beloved chola stirs in us (Paúkar 1947, 28).[65]

The 1935 program likewise notes that *ingrata* was accompanied by the "traditional orchestra" that accompanied the pieces performed by the Centro Qosqo, along with an "estudiantina" and a "grand orchestra." It has already been suggested that this last term refers to a symphonic orchestra similar to that which accompanied the Misión Peruana, and which was based on the few musicians the Centro had brought, as noted by Vidal Unda in the letter cited above, supplemented with musicians living in the places the Centro visited. Although there is no information on the instruments played by the estudiantina and the typical ensemble that performed with the Centro, at the time the former usually comprised a set of string instruments that above all included guitars and mandolins, and sometimes charangos, whereas the traditional ensembles included a harp, at least a violin and a quena (sometimes more of each), a drum, perhaps a guitar or a mandolin, and sometimes a *pampapiano* [harmonium] too. The traditional ensemble that accompanied *ingrata* and *picaflor* also played two independent musical pieces as part of the program, and quite likely accompanied most of the dances.

The program included two more dances acknowledged as folklore that would become part of the traditional cuzqueño repertoire and the prototypes for the invention of similar dances: the *ccori lazo* (described in the program as a "costumbrista dance and dress from Chumbivilcas") and the *llamero* ("llama herder," described as a "pastoral dance").[66] I will return in the following chapter to the significant role of the image of the *ccori lazo* in the construction of a mestizo identity in Cuzco, but we must bear in mind that this image, which exalted the virile and fierce men from Chumbivilcas, had already appeared in Cuzco's contests and stages from at least 1927 and in Lima from 1928, embodied by Francisco Gómez Negrón (see fig. 7). *Wayna chura* is one of the dances that took shape in these years as an incarnation of the spirit of the *ccori lazo*, and it retains this fame today.[67] To give an idea of the romantic image of the brave bandit and Chumbivilcano lover depicted by this type of dance, all we need do is quote the explanation a program from the 1940s provided.

> The "korilaso" (golden lasso), rustles cattle with unparalleled mastery in much the same way as he steals hearts wherever his luck takes him, like a "sailor in every port." He is undeterred by the guns of the police nor by the harsh and stubborn grumbling of the gamonal. With manly poise and arrogant strength he takes it all, both good and evil. When he abandons his inborn attitude as a brigand it is only to flirt [with] the cholas he seduces; for them he gives up everything, [including his] courage and audacity. (Paúkar 1947, 29)

The different dances to which the image of the indomitable Chumbivilcano and his romances gave rise (besides the ones mentioned above there are others, including like *chumbivilcana* and *Barbarita*) combined the three sets of characteristics in various ways. They show the valiant and aggressive spirit of the people in provinces far removed from the city of Cuzco within a romantic image of the cuzqueño countryside and at the same time prominently depict the festive and licentious side of the relations between men and women in this region.

7. Pancho Gómez Negrón (Cuzco, 1930s). (PHOTO BY MARTÍN CHAMBI, MARTÍN CHAMBI PHOTOGRAPHIC ARCHIVE.)

I have noted elsewhere (Mendoza 1999; 2000, chap. 5; 2001, chap. 5) that the *llameros* and similar dances must be understood as part of an image that is quite common in the Peruvian Andes and alludes to the important commercial and social role played by the people from the *puna* (the highest and most arid plateaus of the highlands, normally more than 3,500 meters above sea level), who carried goods through a vast and rugged land on their llamas, connecting the puna with the valleys. These popular depictions, which apparently go back to pre-Hispanic times and are at present personified by a popular cuzqueño dance, the *qollas,* emphasize the close connection that exists between these individuals and their pack animals by establishing a metonymic relationship with the animals (imitating the llamas) through the costumes and the choreography (Mendoza 2000, 168–69; 2001, 252–54). Nowadays this is one of the dances the cuzqueños use to explore the paradoxes and contradictions of the "indigenous" identity (Mendoza 1999; 2000, chap. 5; 2001, chap. 5). *Llameros* is an arrangement made for the stage of an image that was quite popular in Andean towns in the 1930s and 1940s and may be included in the second set of characteristics, which emphasizes the bucolic image of the Andean natives. This is exemplified by the following description of the dance:

> Across valleys and ranges of mountains, through cliffs and fields of straw, the Indians cover the vast expanses of the fatherland, defying the weather and the distance, the north wind, rain, snow, sunstroke, the elements and hunger, following their llamas loaded with maize or coca, *charki* or *chuñu*,[68] and on their journeys they rest from their labors as conspicuous walkers enlivening their "*pascanas*" [stops when the cargo is unloaded] with dancing and singing. For the Indian, the llama is the most generous animal nature has provided for him; the llama gives him the succulent meat that will allay his hunger, the warm wool that will clothe his nakedness, the fuel that enlivens his home, and the pack animal that carries his provisions. Indian ideology has stereotyped this conception in the dance "The Llameros." (Paúkar 1947, 28.)

The program the Centro Qosqo performed at the Teatro Municipal ended with *Ccoscco piris*, a number performed with a "choir accompanied by the traditional ensemble," and a "huaino accompanied by guitar and charango" entitled *agüita de puna* (water from the puna).[69] The former piece was part of the repertoire performed by the Misión Peruana, and is a "traditional cuzqueño song" (a term used in the Misión's programs) or folklore. Although during the tour this song was connected to the Inca past, referring to the "settler who departs following the imperial command to populate other lands," above all it focuses on the image of the *piris* (a small and quite strong chili pepper from Cuzco) in quite a poetic way, "with exquisite and truly untranslatable verses" (Valcárcel 1924, 82), on romantic disappointments, and on being far away from the land where one belongs.

Qosqo piris kútuykuska	A bite of Cuzco piris
Maras kachiwan t'inkuska	Mixed with salt from Maras
pitañataq misk'ishanki	who are you sweetening
ñoqata hayarqowaspa	after having deceived me or [having burned me strongly]

noqan kani haqay rumi	I am that stone
qaqamanta thunimuni	I have pried myself loose from the rock
mana piqpa alau nisqan	with no one loving me
chiri wairata muchuni	suffering the cold and the wind[70]

Finally, as regards the accompaniment of the huayno *agüita de puna,* it must be noted that the charango was gaining importance in major performances that presented the cuzqueño identity on Peruvian stages. This instrument, which Andean peasants had used for at least two centuries, soon became the central symbol in the emerging identity of the "new Indian" or mestizo, which was taking shape among the intellectuals and artists in the city of Cuzco. The *Hora del Charango,* a radio program examined in the following chapter, was the main site of interaction between artists from the various sectors of Cuzco's society. Some of these artists dedicated themselves to innovation in playing this instrument.

Thus, by the mid-1930s we find in Cuzco a repertoire that had developed under the guiding principle that Cuzco was becoming a Mecca of international tourism and a source of nationhood; this repertoire included the prototypes of what in subsequent years would be presented as typically or traditionally cuzqueño in shows staged for various kinds of spectators, from Peruvian and foreign tourists to intellectuals in Lima. The themes and images the pieces in this repertoire used tended to be influenced by the three sets of characteristics, but the rich artistic-folkloric output of the following decades, both on the stage and as part of religious festivals, went beyond these prototypes and reformulated them. Things became even more complex as the repertoire of the so-called mestizo dances grew and the practice of these forms was gradually accepted by social sectors that had previously refrained from practicing traditions that were considered indigenous. The adoption of the practice of the charango, and the subsequent transformation of its style, clearly illustrates this process.

4

. . .

LA HORA DEL CHARANGO: THE CHOLO FEELING, CUZQUEÑONESS, AND PERUVIANNESS

> The name of the charango, that small guitar the cholos—who comprise the national majority—carry on their backs every day [in order] to pour out their feelings, to cry out their pain, or to shout the Eureka of their joy, has been chosen as the symbol of these broadcasts. Another name could of course have been chosen, such as the Peruvian hour, the hour of Cuzco, or something along those lines, but *the charango was preferred because it is humbler and perhaps more cholo.* To feel *the immense flow of emotions this small instrument can produce* one must have been born on Peruvian soil, have fed on its sap, and [have] felt its needs and problems. HUMBERTO VIDAL UNDA, EMPHASIS ADDED

> I learned in Huarocondo by chance, [when] I heard some [people] playing. . . . [Don Julio says that after settling in the city of Cuzco,] in school I also played. I carried [my charango with me] because I liked it . . . ; I remember that *the music teacher punished me for taking my charango [to school] because at that time the charango had no prestige at all. . . .* Whoever played the charango was criticized; they believed he had come out of a *chicheria* [pub] or a tea shop.
> JULIO BENAVENTE DÍAZ, EMPHASIS ADDED

Delia Vidal de Milla recalls that, "charged with emotion," Cuzco intellectuals and artists launched the radio program *La Hora del Charango,* which galvanized cusqueñista, Peruvianist, and Americanist feelings in the region around the cholo or mestizo identity.[1] This program, which local artists and intellectuals remember and value as one of the major landmarks in the cultural transformations of Cuzco at the time,[2] made a definite contribution to the reappraisal and transformation of an Andean tradition hitherto scorned—a tradition that, as Don Julio Benavente Díaz, one of the major charango performers in Cuzco, recalls, was associated above all with people of peasant or lower-class urban extraction.[3] Artists from the various social sectors in Cuzco used this program to create new repertoires and styles that could be shared by all these sectors, while intellectuals used it to present major ideological proposals that sought to find specific images with which to develop a cuzqueño and Peruvian identity.

A closer look at the kind of interactions this radio program generated allows us to move beyond the idea that it was a conduit through which "the new intellectual elites [the neo-Indianists] implemented a hierarchical representation of regional identity" (De la Cadena 2000, 150). Careful study shows instead that it was thanks to this program, which allowed the introduction of the physical and sonorous charango into areas where it had been heretofore violently excluded, that a new aesthetic arose with a sentimental drive that would be shared by various rural and urban sectors of Cuzco.

In her study of Cuzco photography, Deborah Poole points out that the notion of an "Andean emotion," strongly nourished by the philosophical and aesthetic values of intuition and feeling was a key tenet of the neo-Indianist movement (1997, 195–196). This feeling or emotion, which was bursting with nostalgia and love and was best articulated by music, had its roots in the strong connection of the people to the land where they had been born and raised. This land and its mountainous landscape furnished a common element for all the cuzqueños who had the same aesthetic sensitivity and felt that they formed part of a community going beyond all ethnic-social differences and by definition excluding "the forms of European mimicry that the cuzqueños believed had undermined Lima's spirit and authenticity" (178).

The significance of being rooted in the land in order to feel the strength of the cuzqueñista and the Peruvianist feelings evoked by the music played on the charango is prominent in the words of Vidal Unda that open this chapter. With his reference to "Peruvian soil," Vidal Unda, the creator and main driving force behind the radio program, shows the central tenet of his thinking and action that was shared by other artists and intellectuals of the time, that is, that the community of what is "our own" (*lo nuestro*) was not limited to what was cuzqueño but included all that was Peruvian. What many of these artists and intellectuals wanted was to provide the rest of the nation with specific referents, based on highland traditions such as the music of the charango, that would embody the national identity. This proposal of national identity was nourished by the perceived invasion of foreign cultural elements that was becoming ever more blatant in Peru thanks to the development of technologies such as the phonograph, radio, and cinema. The cuzqueños, in turn, were trying to challenge the cultural proposal of *criollismo* as the source of national identity that was gaining strength at the time on the Peruvian coast and particularly in Lima. This criollo tradition, which was gradually incorporating the music and dances of the Afro-Peruvian populations and was beginning to make its presence felt in the mass media (Lloréns 1983, 35–94), was in fact in a strong position to claim to be representative of the entire nation.

Through radio, which was spreading all over Peru, the cuzqueño artists and intellectuals launched their proposal for a cuzqueñista national identity with charango music as its core symbol. This proposal often brought with it the need to continue fostering fraternity among American peoples through elements that could bring them together. But, whereas this proposal of an Americanist fraternity, between Peru and Argentina, for instance, had been sought during the tour of the Misión Peruana de Arte Incaico in the images of the pre-Hispanic Indian and the autochthonous element (see chapter 1), the so-called neo-Indianists, like their contemporary intellectual counterparts in other parts of America, endeavored to find this same Americanism in mestizo traditions such as the charango, which made clear the convergence of the pre-Hispanic and colonial traditions in contemporary Andean culture.

The charango likewise gained its strength as a symbol in the neo-Indianist proposal from its condition as a major accessory in the idealized image of the brave and romantic cattle rustler—an image that had surfaced in the music and dances of Cuzco in the figure of the *ccori lazo* or *qorilazo*. The *walaychu* is an image that incorporates the qorilazo and sometimes is even considered identical to it. As Deborah Poole points out, many of the ideals advocated by the neo-Indianists were best articulated with the image of the walaychu, the Andean bohemian who "replaces his family and community tradition with a deeply sentimental attachment to the land . . . to a province, region, or landscape . . . [which becomes] the source of the walaychu's heightened artistic and musical sensibilities" (1997, 177–78). This image had crystallized in Cuzco in the person of the legendary Pancho Gómez Negrón, who had taken part in musical events in Lima and Cuzco in the late 1920s. This man, who bore the nickname "*saqra* charango" (the charango devil) due to his "unique playing" (Valencia 1994, 155–56), was hailed by José Uriel García as "the true manifestation of the new Peruvian Indian, [and] a concrete example [of him]." By this time Gómez Negrón had for some years been making this instrument fundamental to the creation of new repertoires and styles in the cuzqueño tradition (see fig. 7 on page 89).

It is clear, however, that with the stimuli it provided and the debates arising from it the radio program *La Hora del Charango* had a lasting impact on the place of this instrument within the urban musical tradition of Cuzco. The program also included several pieces and musical styles that did not belong to the charango tradition, and it provided a new stimulus for artistic-folkloric creation in which various sectors of cuzqueño society were involved.

CHARANGO AND ROMANCE IN THE ANDEAN TRADITION

With my charango, my faithful friend
I laugh hard at life.

And because of the wickedness of this life
I take the world as my *montera* [hat].[4]

That is why you're my rebellious *maqt'a*[5]
the moaning chords of the *cholada*

Because with the mermaid[6]
you sing the Andean lament ironically

I am glad I have stolen
the heart (*el corazoncito*) of my dear Maria

I am glad I've stolen
the heart of my dear Alicia

She moaning and I singing
We will love each other tonight

HUAYNO COMPOSED BY JULIO BENAVENTE DÍAZ[7]

When the charango musical tradition entered urban Cuzco in force in the 1930s, it clearly retained a long Andean tradition that identified this instrument with romance. Although much of this direct association had faded away in urban Cuzco by the late twentieth century, partly because this instrument had traveled all over the world as part of the repertoire of a music that is generally known as "Latin American" or "Andean,"[8] the connection between the charango and romance that still survives today, particularly in the rural areas of the Cuzco-Puno region, was still strong at the time that *La Hora del Charango* appeared. Since charango music included both Andean and European elements and was associated with love and nostalgia, it provided a concrete element that fused both the "cholo" ideal contemporary cuzqueño intellectuals were trying to foster as the symbol of Peru and the brave and enamored walaychu that, as Poole (1997) points out, was also a central element of the neo-Indianist feeling.

Scholars agree that the presence of this "small guitar" (*guitarrico* is what Vidal Unda called it) is recorded in the colonial period, at least in 1700, in what was then known as Alto Peru (Upper Peru, i.e., Peru and Bolivia) (Turino 1984, 255; Parejo 1988, 9). Its size and the materials used for its strings, its sound box, frets, and pegs vary according to the area and groups using it, but it is clear that the relatively small size of the sound box (ranging from 10 x 7 to 6 x 4 inches) gives the characteristic high-pitched sound to this instrument (Turino 1984, 267). The type of sound produced by the charango is consistent with one of the strongest pre-Hispanic aesthetic preferences in the Andean tradition—the preference for high-pitched sounds (Romero 1988, 234). It is likely that this aesthetic preference, along with its ease of transportation and perhaps even the fact that it could be "hidden inside the poncho—as Don Julio claims—so that it would not be seen by the Spaniards as [this instrument] was forbidden," all contributed to the development of the small charango.[9]

Many believe that the *vihuela,* a Spanish stringed instrument that appeared in the sixteenth century and had five rows of strings, was the probable inspiration for the charango.[10] But, despite the evident Spanish influence in the development of this instrument—there were no stringed instruments in the pre-Columbian Andes—the charango has been closely associated with the Indian and peasant identity from at least the early nineteenth century. This instrument, which is traditionally played only by men, became directly associated in the Andean region with the process of courting and falling in love and more specifically with the power of the charango to seduce the desired woman.

In his study of the romantic side of the practice of charango, Thomas Turino (1983) explains in depth that in the southern Peruvian Andes there is a strong association between the image of the mermaid and the seductive power of the charango player. We have, for instance, the explicit mention of a mermaid in the huayno composed by Don Julio Benavente quoted above. It is worth noting, like Turino (1983), that in some parts of the provinces of Canas and Chumbivilcas in Cuzco, as well as in the rural areas of Puno, where the charango has a central role in the courting process, this instrument is not for specialists and is really considered a key element in winning the heart of one's beloved. Among these young people there are several rites that are meant to help the charango attain the seductive power one desires, and the most prominent of these rites are those that try to acquire the supernatural power of the mermaids, who, according to the oral tradition, live in the springs, rivers, waterfalls, or lakes close to the villages (96–101).

The most popular style of charango playing in these rural areas has traditionally been that of strumming, "whereby a single-line melody is made to vibrate among the majority of open-sounding strings" (Turino 1984, 259). This style, along with other characteristics of the peasant charango that were popular at the time this instrument began to be revalued by the artists and intellectuals in the city of Cuzco, was despised by some members of the elite, for whom it was a "monotonous strumming, lacking in sweetness and expressiveness."[11]

This revaluing of the charango in urban and bohemian Cuzco, which was to a great extent fostered by *La Hora del Charango,* caused the devotees of this instrument to develop other techniques such as the *t'ipi* ("pinch" in Quechua). This type of plucking made with the nails allows the harmonic and melodic lines to be clearly distinguished, an aesthetic preference that, as Turino points out (1984), was assumed by "mestizo" artists (260). Turino likewise notes that this new style was "further characterized by the systematic juxtaposition of t'ipi and strummed sections" (261). Don Julio César Benavente Díaz (see fig. 8) was the most renowned practitioner of the t'ipi technique and in general the driving force behind the new style that developed in urban Cuzco with the initial stimulus given by *La Hora del Charango.*

Besides the feelings of love with which the practice of the charango was traditionally associated, the music of this instrument also inspired in the

8. Julio César Benavente Díaz (Cuzco, 1978). (BENAVENTE FAMILY ARCHIVE.)

artists and intellectuals of the city of Cuzco a love for the land, the landscape, and their cultural heritage (both colonial and pre-Hispanic), as well as a certain degree of rebelliousness against the established social order and the pursuit of a rapport with the Andean majority, which was identified as cholo or mestizo. Known as either a "rebellious maqt'a" (as in the huayno by Don Julio) or an "insolent cholo . . . proletarian songbook, [and] people's operetta" (in the words of Edmundo Delgado Vivanco),[12] the charango also acquired a dissenting spirit and was identified with the exploited majority. This comes through clearly in a passage by José Uriel García, who writes that "with the birth of the Charango, its strings completely transformed the huayno, cleansing it of all that was archaic. The peasant love and the poetic imagination of the mestizo endowed it with the passions of the dregs of society, [and] of the exploited class. . . . [It thus] moves forward imperiously through the fairgrounds, stirs with enthusiasm the chichería and the celebration of the farm laborer and the artisan, [and] celebrates the festival of the patron saint. . . . Its sounds correlate with popular passions" (Uriel García 1949, 110–11).

By identifying the charango with the cuzqueño and Peruvian majorities, the artists and intellectuals who promoted this radio program were linking cuzqueñoness and Peruvianness with the mestizo and cholo identity leaving behind their identification with the "archaic" element. As noted, a key image in this neo-Indianist proposal of a regional and a national identity was that of the rebellious and bohemian qorilazo or walaychu, whose artistic skills, closely connected to the landscape and the land, were worthy of admiration and imitation. This was what transformed individuals such as Pancho Gómez Negrón into symbols of a regional and national identity for intellectuals such as José Uriel García, who considered Negrón a "true expression of the new Peruvian Indian" (Valencia 1994, 155). Although it has not been established whether Pancho Gómez ever performed on *La Hora del Charango,* there is no question that his playing was an inspiration to many, including Don Julio Benavente, who developed their art and discourse with this instrument.

PANCHO GÓMEZ NEGRÓN: THE SAQRA CHARANGO

I also listened somewhat to the way Pancho Gómez Negrón, a renowned man from Chumbivilcas, played, particularly the stuff pertaining to his Chumbivilcas way; [he] rode his horse, had his charango slung across his back, he rode through the streets of Cuzco just like that, with his *qarawatana* [chaps] and now and then strumming his charango to the sound of his thunderous singing voice. JULIO BENAVENTE

Around the 1920s to the 1950s [Pancho Gómez Negrón] made the Andes vibrate with joy and nostalgia with his popular songs and his waynos, which the people still sing. Pancho Gómez Negrón was thus a living demonstration that music, like no other artistic manifestation, provides mankind with one of the greatest pleasures in life, reaching the innermost corners of the heart, and producing feelings of love, nostalgia, passion, anguish, fervor, etc. ABRAHAM VALENCIA ESPINOZA

The legendary Pancho Gómez Negrón was born on March 2, 1908, in the village of Colquemarca, province of Chumbivilcas, where his parents had also been born.[13] Valencia (1994) writes that as a child Pancho Gómez showed a "passion for native music, which led him to sing popular songs with peasant children" and motivated him to learn how to play the harp when he was around thirteen (154). A self-taught musician, like Manuel Pillco, Gómez Negrón came from a humble provincial family. His first socializing experience in Cuzco came at a later age than Pillco's, but, unlike Pillco, he did manage to take some high school courses in the city, after which he returned to his homeland until he was sixteen, when he finally settled in the city of Cuzco (154). By then Gómez Negrón had taught himself how to play his favorite instrument, the *kirkinchu* (a charango made out of an armadillo shell), as well as the guitar, mandolin, piano, melodeon (or *pampapiano*), harp, *waka waqra* (a trumpet made out of bull's horns), and different types of *pinkuyllu* (a vertical flute with the reed made out of *huarango* wood that has six holes and is a meter long). He played these instruments both in the homes of local affluent families and at peasant festivities (154).

Pancho Gómez Negrón, like Manuel Pillco, mingled with artists, bohemians, and intellectuals in the city of Cuzco, among whom he acquired quite a name and was in demand thanks to his musical talent. We saw in chapter 2 that he participated in the recitals held in the city after the 1927 contest organized by the then Centro Musical (renamed the Centro Qosqo in 1933). By then he was already embodying the romantic image of the Chumbivilcano qorilazo and being hailed by the local press. A year after this performance, he joined the Cuzco delegation that triumphed in the Amancaes contest in Lima. Apparently it was after this last performance as part of a group that Gómez Negrón decided, in accordance with the freewheeling and independent spirit of the walaychu, to follow an individual artistic path for a long time. This changed around 1942 when shortly after marrying he began to tour with his wife, who was a singer, and with whom he once went as far as the northern border with Ecuador. It is known that between his performance in Lima in 1928 and a tragic accident in 1944 that seriously impaired his health and led to his early death, Gómez Negrón traveled extensively throughout Peru and even performed in Bolivia and perhaps in Argentina and Chile.[14] The recognition he received as an artist did not bring about his financial well-being, and he suffered financial hardships right up to his death. This not only limited his ability to tour outside Peru and purchase the medicines he needed, but it also left his widow and children destitute after his premature death.[15]

It is worth pointing out here, along with Romero (2001), that Pancho Gómez appeared as a major figure at a moment when two closely connected trends were developing within the Andean musical tradition. The first was the ever-greater recognition accorded to individual authors and composers, and the second was the increasing popularity of individual singers. Both trends were connected to the development of new sound amplification systems and the artistic spaces that were appearing in the city of Lima for its Andean migrants (113–14). Although these trends increased around 1950 with the coming of the "golden age" of commercial recordings of Andean music and its countrywide "conquest of the radio dial," the popularity of people like Pancho Gómez in the late 1920s and mid-1940s proves that these trends had begun decades earlier.[16] In Cuzco, *La Hora del Charango* in fact marked the moment when the Andean music associated with the popular urban and rural majorities of this region (e.g. the huayno) began to make its presence felt in places where access to it had previously been restricted.

The tragic accident that prostrated Gómez Negrón and led to his death six years later occurred in 1944 during his performance in the first reenactment of the Inti Raymi ceremony, which was held during the first Cuzco Day celebrations.[17] By then Gómez Negrón was quite renowned in the Cuzco region and throughout Peru, and his music, particularly that which he played with the charango, had been recognized as "art" and the prototype for "neo-Indian music." He even gave two concerts in the city of Cuzco during the same month that were described as neo-Indian.[18] A review of his first concert in the Cuzco newspaper *El Sol* makes it clear that by then he was already acknowledged as the representative par excellence of the Peruvian and American identity—the latter based on the Andean or highland element. According to *El Sol*,

> the recital of neo-Indian musical art was given in the Teatro Municipal by the vigorous and renowned *colquemarquino* [native of Colquemarca] artist Francisco Gómez Negrón, the popular "*ccorilazo*," as he is known in artistic circles. . . .
>
> This recital of a purely Peruvian art was attended by a very large public, which filled up the various sections of the theater, avid to hear the performance of the artist who, after long wandering across the lands of the continent and the cities of the Republic, returned to the homeland to help us savor the delights of *our highland, that is, American, art.*[19]

By 1942, then, the charango was already being praised by people from various social sectors in the city of Cuzco. But by 1937, even though in the hands of the saqra charango this instrument had entered the repertoire of the Cuzco music that represented this region in national contests, it cannot be claimed that many members of the Cuzco middle and upper classes had blessed the practice of the charango as an art form worthy of representing the region and the nation. The debates and emotions—and in general the space of artistic production—engendered by *La Hora del Charango* were closely connected to a change in the status of this instrument within the cuzqueño tradition, as well as to the stylistic transformations its practice underwent.

It is likely that Pancho Gómez did not actually participate in *La Hora del Charango* due to his "footloose ways," but the fame the charango acquired in his hands must surely have contributed to its popularity among artists in the city of Cuzco. Although no reference has yet been found showing that Pancho Gómez used the t'ipi technique that would later become popular among the charango players in the city, we do know that he was one of the driving forces behind a practice that is characteristic of the interpreters of Andean music to this day, that of alternating Quechua and Spanish in the songs. Valencia Espinoza (1994, 155) points out that in the performances of Pancho Gómez "the Quechua verses were contrasted with the Spanish ones in a beautiful harmony and rhythm," as can be seen in the huayno "Enfermerita de Antonio Lorena," which he composed after his accident. Here are a few stanzas.

Saqsaywaman fiestaman haykuni machay qapariq, hobero potropi.	I entered the feast of Saqsaywaman Riding a gold-colored horse to instill fear.
Mi corazón está de luto Por el porrazo de un caballo bruto.	My heart mourns Because a rough horse knocked me over.
Mejoral carro, maytan apawanki; Mejoral carro— Hospitalmanchu, presidiomanchu, Imaynallataq vidayllari kanqa.	Mejoral car—and where are you a-taking me?[20]— Is it to the hospital or jail? And what will become of me?
Enfermerita de Antonio Lorena	Sweet li'l nurse of Antonio Lorena Hospital,

Ponme una almohada de pura lana	Give me a pillow of pure wool,
De esta manera soñar contigo	This way I'll dream of you,
De otra manera soñar con otra	Otherwise I'll dream of someone else.[21]

In this huayno we find that even when dealing with his misfortune Pancho Gómez did not stop evoking his nature as an "outlaw (and womanizing) walaychu" by flirting with the nurse at the Antonio Lorena Hospital to whom he dedicated this song. When stressing the bohemian and womanizing nature embodied by Pancho Gómez Negrón, one cannot avoid bringing up a cuzqueño oral tradition that is widespread, particularly in the city of Cuzco, and was already known in the early twentieth century. This is the story of "Juan the Bandit," which seems to have been particularly well known and popular among the artists in that city.[22] Briefly, the various accounts of this story emphasize the womanizing and bohemian aspects of the main character, who was likewise skilled at playing stringed instruments such as the guitar, charango, or mandolin. At a given moment Juan the Bandit is threatened by the devil, who wants to take him to hell because of the misdeeds Juan was used to carrying out. He is saved by a cross and subsequently leaves his wicked ways behind.[23] Although a detailed analysis of the various accounts of this tradition are needed to establish the messages it was trying to impart to those who retold and/or listened to it, the essential point here is that in early-twentieth-century urban Cuzco there already was a strong association between the womanizing bohemian individual and his music, which was played on stringed instruments, the charango in particular.

Pancho Gómez died when he was forty-two. "A crowd of fellow countrymen and admirers bade the artist farewell," Valencia Espinoza recounts, "sorrowfully singing his songs" (1994, 160). This artist clearly played a major role in the introduction of the charango tradition into the urban cuzqueño environment by embodying neo-Indianist, cuzqueñista, Peruvianist, and Americanist ideals and feelings. These ideals and feelings took shape and were forcefully disseminated through *La Hora del Charango.*

LISTENING TO OUR OWN: THE HUAYNO AND THE CHARANGO AS OPPOSED TO FOREIGN MUSIC

Listeners:

A grave responsibility weighs on us, those who inhabit this legendary land known as Cuzco, this land generously endowed with traditions and archaeological riches, as well as with *an enormous artistic trove that is sadly fading away, absorbed by the invasion of an art that is not ours.* And our responsibility is precisely to safeguard and uplift Peruvian art *so we will be able to present ourselves with a defined personality, just like other peoples, . . .* Cusco must present itself as great as it is through radio; it must transmit its culture and its artistic trove *far removed from being a slavish imitator of other peoples who arrogantly transmit their folkloric riches.* HUMBERTO VIDAL UNDA, EMPHASIS ADDED[24]

When the government decided to present several cities in this country with radio receivers and loudspeakers, it was surely in the belief that it was making this gift to the popular majorities who, naturally, do not have the means to purchase on their own *these modern instruments that are already irreplaceable in social life. . . .*

Since the municipality had the good idea of placing the loudspeakers that the government had presented to the people of Cuzco in the main square, *we have witnessed a tremendous reality—so tremendous [in fact] that only the blind and the deaf can deny it. The greatest influx of people to the programs broadcast through those loudspeakers takes place on Monday nights, when Radio* OAX 7A *broadcasts the famed* La Hora del Charango.
AMARU, EMPHASIS ADDED

Using the modern technology at his disposal, Humberto Vidal Unda headed a process whereby the sonorous presence of the music and the instruments associated with the rural and urban majorities could no longer be evaded by those who did not acknowledge these traditions as theirs.[25] In an effort to reverse the trend among the most affluent social groups in the Cuzco region and throughout Peru, the cuzqueño artists and intellectuals used the radio to oppose the alien musical fashions with music that could be considered both Peruvian and cuzqueño. Radio, which had only reached Cuzco in 1936, enabled cuzqueños to spread their music and the region's image as a center of archaeological and touristic interest through the *La Hora del Charango,* ultimately to any part of the world where a receiver could pick up the sound waves.

Many of the comments made by intellectuals and artists during *La Hora del Charango* explicitly denounced the so-called invasion (the words are Vidal Unda's) of foreign musical fashions, which were to be fought by presenting specific examples of what was called "our own" (*lo nuestro*). When these individuals used the concept of what was "our own," as opposed to what was alien, they often did so using it as a synonym for what was cuzqueño and Peruvian in an effort to place their "art" at the forefront of the nation's attention. This perceived threat was not exclusive to the cuzqueños, or to the people in other Andean cities, but it was also found among the representatives of the so-called tradition of criollo music, which had developed mainly in Lima (Lloréns 1983, 44–61).

Just as in other parts of Latin America, the different musical traditions that were developing in the Andean cities, as well as in Lima, had until then incorporated some elements derived from foreign fashions that somehow enabled them to adapt their repertoire to the new tastes (Lloréns 1983, 35–61). Although even in Lima before 1920, as Lloréns points out, "the phonograph does not seem to have reached beyond a small public that was limited to the well-off classes and to the sectors that lived tuned to the technical novelties of the international market," there is no denying that the industrial production of this technology in the early twentieth century marked "the beginning of a whole new era in the diffusion of music" that certainly had an impact on the production of music in several cities in Peru (36–37). In 1920–40, when the presence of the phonograph, radio, and talking movies began to spread foreign musical fashions even faster, particularly those from the United States, musical creations within the "Andean" and the criollo genres found themselves ever more influenced by these fashions, and this led, for instance, to the "Inca fox " (or "Inca fox-trot"), the "Inca jazz" and the "Inca camel-trot," the first two of which were included in the concerts of *La Hora del Charango.*[26]

Still we find that in the late 1930s, and as the influence of the new mass media continued to grow, the artists and intellectuals in the criollo tradition, as well as the one emerging in the city of Cuzco, developed an ever more explicit concern over this perceived invasion. It became urgent to clearly define what was properly Peruvian, either in the criollo or the cuzqueño proposal, so that it could be spread through the same media.[27] As Lloréns points out, "Peruvian music was hardly ever recorded on records during the first three decades of the [twentieth] century," so most of the recorded music that was listened to in Peru at that time was foreign, and particularly from the U.S. (1983, 37–38). Criollo music began to spread nationwide via the airwaves in the mid-1930s, something Andean music did not achieve until the early 1950s.

As Lloréns points out in relation to the rapid growth of the Andean population in the city of Lima, while this reaction vis-à-vis foreign music was taking place in both the Lima and the Cuzco regions, the criollo tradition, having already incorporated Afro-Peruvian traditions from the coast, began to be adopted by "middle-class urban groups and the dominant class of Peruvian society" as *the* national music (1983, 77–78). The proposal of criollismo as *lo nacional* (the national essence) had been actively promoted since the 1930s by the centros sociales y musicales (social and musical clubs) in Lima, partly as a response to the perceived foreign invasion; this campaign was stepped up around 1940 and even inspired the Peruvian state to issue a supreme decree establishing the Día de la Canción Criolla (Criollo Song Day) in 1944 (76).

When *La Hora del Charango* debuted in 1937, its promoters wanted their music to attain the status of "national music" just like their criollo counterpart—a wish that was unfortunately not fulfilled despite the fact that the representatives of Cuzco music and dances persisted in their efforts for several more decades. Faced with the growing presence of Andean people in the city of Lima, it proved difficult for the upper classes in Peru to accept the proposals the mestizos in the Andean cities made for nationhood, and they chose the criollo proposal, which embraced the cultural and artistic tradition of an idealized black race. As Lloréns points out, "The Andean (*Lo andino*) was thus pushed to the background as a sort of prenationhood or a 'second-class nationality'" to which the adjectives *vernacular* or *folkloric* were applied, whereas the criollo (*lo criollo*) was acknowledged as the popular (*lo popular*) music (1983, 78–79).

Paradoxically, in the late 1930s the cuzqueño artists and intellectuals found themselves competing both inside and outside Peru with musical traditions that were identified with Afro-American populations (see fig. 9). From the very inception of *La Hora del Charango*, the comments made on this program and in the press denounced the preference of those with access to the emerging mass media for foreign "black" music such as jazz. For example:

9. A group of Cuzco intellectuals and artists, including Rafael Yepez, Julio Gutiérrez, José Uriel García, Manuel Pillco, José Domingo Rado, Ricardo Flórez, and Martín Chambi (Cuzco, 1940s). (PHOTO BY MARTÍN CHAMBI, MARTÍN CHAMBI PHOTOGRAPHIC ARCHIVE.)

> Good for the group that has begun the Charango Day, and let us hope that it will be the cornerstone (*piedra angular*), that January 1 will lay down the foundations for an institution devoid of selfishness, conventionalisms, or presumptuousness, which later will yield the fruit of a spiritual and artistic entity that interprets the desires of the race, and *manages to recover the artistic credit that has been ruined by the cannibals of harmony, who, driven mad by that black music, only feel their nerves vibrate to the sensuous rhythm of jazz.*[28]

> It is with the charango, with the indigenous and mestizo choreography and song, with popular paintings and plastic arts, that we, the men of today, want to dignify and assert the sense of our nationality against the foreign colonialist invasion that begins *with jazz, black music, Yankee fashion, [and] the indecent cinema,* to finish by devouring our most precious riches.[29]

In the discourse of contemporary cuzqueño artists and intellectuals we find the Cuban rumba and the Argentinean tango as invaders along with jazz, two musical and dance genres of Latin American origin that had become very popular in Europe and the United States in the 1930s (Daniels 1995, 20). Although Julio C. Gutiérrez, whose words are quoted above, did not explicitly mention the rumba, it is possible that his reference to "black" music did include this genre. It is worth pointing out that the origins of the tango are closely connected to the music and dances of the black population of the River Plate—a fact that is not usually acknowledged even in Argentina itself (Savigliano 1995, 32–33). Finally, it is possible that by "black music," this cuzqueño intellectual had in mind the Afro-Peruvian traditions that were attaining a nationwide presence as part of the criollo tradition.

The promoters of *La Hora del Charango* thus used charango music and the genres that were recognized as being truly Andean, such as the huayno and the yaraví, to counteract foreign influences and define Peruvianness as mestizo and Andean. But, whereas this campaign obviously proved successful both among the popular majority of the city of Cuzco, which jammed its main square to listen to the program, and among the musicians of rural and popular urban origins who participated in its concerts, the men who promoted the program had to face the critiques and resistance of some members of cuzqueño society, who questioned the quality of the charango and many of the broadcast performances that were presented as representative of Cuzqueñoness and Peruvianness. One example of the kind of debate that this radio program gave rise to is an exchange between Humberto Vidal Unda and Alberto Yábar Palacio, which took place both on the program and in the local press.

THE YÁBAR PALACIO–VIDAL UNDA DEBATE: CRITIQUE AND DEFENSE OF "LO NUESTRO"

> The number of people who listen to us grows daily. This reassures us and obliges us to continue with this task. *The bilious critique of the dandy gentleman* (*caballerito fifi*) who is ashamed of the huayno and believes himself to be a superman whenever he hums a tango is of no importance. These children have a slave psychology, believing that all that pertains to the master is better and all that is one's own is something to be ashamed of.
>
> HUMBERTO VIDAL UNDA, EMPHASIS ADDED

The public debate between two prominent figures of the city of Cuzco's cultural scene—Humberto Vidal Unda, the creator of the *La Hora del Charango*,[30] and Alberto Yábar Palacio, an art critic for the newspaper *El Sol*—in early June 1937, just slightly over two months after the radio program was first broadcast, illustrates some of the tensions the program raised among members of the middle and upper classes in the city vis-à-vis the depiction of Cuzqueñoness and Peruvianness. The debate became public with an article written by Yábar Palacio—whom Vidal Unda called a "dandy gentleman," implying that he belonged to Cuzco's upper class—in which he expressed his opinion regarding the quality of the radio program.[31] The discussion apparently had begun before the first newspaper article by Yábar Palacio, for he made reference to previous conversations with one of the organizers of the program, perhaps Vidal Unda himself, whom he claimed had responded negatively to his comments and had called him "dandy."[32]

In his article, Yábar Palacio seriously questioned the quality of charango music, the huayno, and the yaraví as they were presented in the program, which was the way in which the popular musicians performed them in the different festive milieus of Cuzco. For instance, Yábar Palacio claimed that "musically, the charango is a veritable disaster. A monotonous strumming lacking in sweetness and expression. Our music in general is very tiresome and boring. A huayno is far too similar to all other huaynos, a *triste* [a music genre that means 'sad'] to other tristes, a yaraví to all other yaravíes. They are a weeping music, languid and dormant. The proof is that it has not been accepted anywhere else and is not heard [anywhere] except for some parts of Peru and Bolivia. What is not accepted proves to be no good."[33]

This critic based his written comments on two closely related arguments: the fact that this music had to be improved and perfected if one was to present a good image of Peruvian music to the rest of the world, and the fact that many individuals who were of the same opinion as the writer had asked him to voice these critiques for them. These individuals had told him that they "disliked our music, particularly that of the charango," and suggested that the program "should at most last for fifteen minutes and instead of [being broadcast] every week should be monthly or every two weeks" because "the same pieces [were repeated too often] each time, the [only] difference being that sometimes their performance is worse than others." However, these individuals did not admit this to their artist friends to avoid attracting their "enmity" and "antipathy."[34]

Vidal Unda replied in another newspaper just a few days after the first article by Yábar Palacio appeared, in which he clearly expounded his position vis-à-vis those who in his opinion were devoid of "the feelings," "emotions," and "needs" of "the great Peruvian masses" and thus did not understand the true meaning of the "nationalist" and "artistic movement" that he was sponsoring through *La Hora del Charango.* What mattered for Vidal Unda and other contemporary artists and intellectuals who promoted cuzqueñismo and nationalism was the creation of an art that would attract an aesthetic and emotional community that would include all sectors of society, enabling them to share a moment of solace.[35] The technical development of this art was a secondary matter. As Vidal Unda argued, "It must be pointed out that technique is not the goal of art, just its auxiliary media. The aim of Art is to articulate that entire world of feelings and emotions that seethe inside us, to socialize them and to convey them to other people. . . . How many times have we seen intuitive artists that manage to convey all the immense tide of their pains and joys through their intermittent and awkward notes?"[36]

It may well be that the head-on defense of the "intuitive artists" in this and other writings of Vidal Unda are related to his own artistic experience. As was noted by his sister Delia, besides being an enthusiastic promoter of the folkloric art of Cuzco and even becoming a dancer and actor in public performances, Humberto Vidal was a "self-educated musician who played the charango, bandore, guitar, the violin, and the piano."[37] Unlike the "intuitive artists" that Vidal Unda probably had in mind when writing the lines cited above, he was a middle-class intellectual from Cuzco with a high level of formal education. The son of a Spaniard who owned a small hacienda close to the district of Combapata, Humberto, who was born in 1906, undertook his primary studies at home and in a school in Sicuani and then enrolled for his high school education in the Colegio Nacional de Ciencias in the city of Cuzco. After graduating as a doctor of philosophy and a teacher, he worked in primary, secondary, and university education until 1947, when he became a full-time professor of metaphysics in the Universidad Nacional San Antonio Abad of Cuzco (Vidal De Milla 1982, 124–25).

Although appealing to the emotions and feelings common among the cuzqueños was more important for Vidal Unda's cuzqueñista and nationalist projects than his concern for the production of a refined and technically accomplished art, this does not mean he was opposed to cuzqueño artists becoming acquainted with, and using, the repertoires and techniques developed in Europe and North America. Quite the contrary: Vidal accepted the use of new technology as "a means by which to best achieve this need to express [oneself and of] transmitting . . . [and] mingling with the rest."[38] This attitude was made clear when he became the first president and chief promoter of the Asociación Orquestal Cuzco (Cuzco Orchestral Association) in 1945. This institution gathered cuzqueño musicians who had been educated with classical Western music, and, in Vidal Unda's words, it sought to "cultivate and disseminate our musical wealth, as well as to make known the great creations of the world's artists, whose works belong to mankind" (Vidal De Milla 1982, 18).

After Vidal Unda's reply to the comments of Yábar Palacio, the latter withdrew in writing some of his previous opinions and acknowledged that he had "generalized disparaging concepts of our music" and enjoyed "our vernacular tunes like anyone else."[39] Even so, Yábar Palacio confirmed his belief that for Cuzco music to be enjoyed by all—he included here people belonging to his social class, all other Peruvians, and foreigners—it had to be perfected with "well-directed rehearsals [and] with discipline and study."[40] This desire for Cuzco music to be developed and perfected using techniques that were not traditional in the Andean world was likewise voiced and shared by several intellectuals and artists who actively supported *La Hora del Charango.*[41]

Some of these followers of the program also voiced their concern over the perceived informality and improvisation in some of the first programs, flaws that seem to have been corrected with the establishment of an organizing committee one year after *La Hora del Charango* was created. This committee likewise facilitated the participation of groups from the provinces, something that the public had apparently requested as it provided variety and originality to the musical repertoire of the programs. *La Hora del Charango* thus became a space where, through the radio, intellectuals and artists of various social, urban, and rural origins interacted and shaped regional music that sought to be recognized as the national music.

THE REPERTOIRE AND THE PARTICIPANTS IN THE PROGRAMS

Charanguito, Charanguito	Little charango, dear charango
aucca runa huaccaycachecc	which makes the enemy cry
chaska ccoillor tutayachecc	which darkens the evening star
rumi sonccocc luluycunan	which softens a man with a stone heart

En las punas silba el viento	In the puna the wind whistles
por no llorar su destino;	so as not to cry its fate;
en el CUZCO canta i sueña	in Cuzco only HUMBERTO VIDAL
solamente HUMBERTO VIDAL	sings and dreams
¡Charanguito, charanguito!	Little charango, dear charango!
no llores más tu pasado	don't mourn your past anymore;
canta i grita como antes	sing and shout as before,
¡ya no vivas en tu dolor!	don't wallow in your pain anymore!
Ccoscco llaccta apu-mama!	Sacred mother of the people of Cuzco
tucuy runacc sonccon kkirecc;	who hurts everybody's heart
huahuallayquita callpachaycuy,	give your son strength
yuyaychaycuy VIDALMI SUTIMPAS	give him wisdom, HIS NAME IS VIDAL

JORGE TORIBIO CÁRDENAS ANDRADE[42]

We sincerely applaud Humberto Vidal, a dynamic and enthusiastic young man to whom we owe the accomplishment of the program mentioned in this chronicle . . . [for] to ennoble the charango, the cholo instrument of Peru, was his idea. At first many souls who cannot see beyond their noses laughed at Vidal and his charango. Now that it has been attained they cannot do anything but applaud Humberto Vidal. JOSÉ URIEL GARCÍA[43]

La Hora del Charango made its debut on March 29, 1937, three months after it had been scheduled to start. Judging by the comments made by the press, it was a complete success. Both this and subsequent programs served as spaces in which musicians from various sectors in the cuzqueño society of the time could interact by forming new musical groups, interpreting pieces and styles that were already being identified as traditional cuzqueño music, and giving rise to new ones, such as the t'ipi, in the practice of the charango. Although this creative process had already been set in motion by the stimuli discussed in previous chapters, the fact that the radio had an impact both nationwide and abroad gave this program a special significance. Those who lived in or were passing through the city of Cuzco who did not have a radio set (the majority), clustered around the loudspeakers placed in the main square and around the radios in some stores in downtown Cuzco in order to listen to the shows.

La Hora del Charango was not a strictly musical program; speeches, poems, and melopoeia were also essential components, as were advertisements, which, as one article put it, contributed to "the campaign [being waged] to attract the inflow of tourism in which all cuzqueños are engaged."[44] The program, which, as we have seen, was not free of criticism, incorporated stylized musical pieces that had already achieved recognition outside of Cuzco, as well as pieces popular among the cuzqueño majority that were neither polished nor perfected but had great power to evoke emotions. Deliberately setting aside the "athletic" conception of music production developed in Europe and the United States, wherein music is valued for the complexity and technical perfection of the pieces (Nettl 1997, 258), Vidal Unda met with other self-educated musicians in order to create cuzqueñoness and Peruvianness through the charango and other stringed instruments. Vidal Unda played the charango, guitar, and other instruments from the very first program alongside other musicians of popular extraction such as Manuel Pillco, and he played the musical accompaniment to melopoeia composed for the program by renowned intellectuals. For instance, during the opening program Vidal Unda performed a charango and harp duet with Manuel Pillco of the huayno *esos tus dos ojos* (those two eyes of yours); played in a trio comprised of charango, harp, and violin with Pillco and the renowned Roberto Ojeda the Ayacucho huayno *yau yau fulana* (hey, hey, you); and accompanied with his charango the melopoeia *visión andina* (andean vision) composed by Víctor Navarro del Águila, a local intellectual.[45]

As could be expected, the first programs included mostly musicians who lived in the city of Cuzco. The gamut went from musicians of rural origin and popular extraction who frequently visited the city's bohemian circles, such as Manuel Pillco, to well-to-do musicians who had been born in the city and educated in classical music such as Armando Guevara Ochoa. Although in the early days the participation of musical groups from the provinces was not missing altogether, a greater effort was made to ensure their participation during the second year, when the organizing committee had been established. We also find that from the beginning the repertoire performed was not limited to Cuzco music but also included the music of Arequipa, Apurímac, Puno, and Ayacucho, played either by cuzqueño musicians (as in the case of the huayno performed by Pillco, Ojeda, and Vidal Unda in the first program) or by musicians from those regions who were visiting Cuzco.

Along with the inaugural speech by José Uriel García, the melopoeia of

Navarro accompanied by Vidal's charango, and the huaynos the latter performed with other musicians, the first program included *despedida* (farewell), a huayno played as a charango and guitar duet by Nicanor Abarca and Eulogio Salinas; *los vendavales* (strong winds), an arequipeño yaraví performed by Timoteo Abarca and Emilio Valdivia; *puneñita* (dear woman from Puno), an "Aymara huayno"; *himno a Manco* (hymn to Manco), a "Quechua-Aymara composition," performed by the Cuarteto Puno headed by José M. Torres Pacheco; *el toro pinto* (spotted bull), which was classified as a criollo huayno and performed by Abarca and Valdivia; *chicha fuerte* (strong corn beer), a huayno performed by the Conjunto Leandro Alviña; *bolero,* a guitar duet performed by Constantino Zamalloa and Ernesto Corvacho; *marinera y huayno,* played on the guitar by Constantino Zamalloa; "Cuculí," a huayno played as a charango solo by Timoteo Abarca; the yaraví *el volcán* (the volcano) and the huayno *mayo rata-rata* (the river that follows me), sung by the sisters Irma and Olinda Ramos Guevara; a huayno Chumbivilcano sung by Luis Vidal (a brother of Humberto); *Alaucho,* a huayno played on a bandore by Edmundo Delgado Vivanco; *quejas* (complaints), an arequipeño yaraví performed by two artists from that department;[46] *el paco y el auqui* (the diviner and the spirit of the mountain), a "Quechua melopoeia" by Andrés Alencastre (who was better known under his nom de plume, Killco Huarak'a); *poema Indio* (Indian poem), by the poet Luis de Rodrigo; and finally a speech by Humberto Vidal.[47]

A journalist at the newspaper *El Sol* assessed this "art session . . . as one of the best and that has most genuinely expressed regional, popular cuzqueño or Peruvian music, as one sees fit to call it."[48] Although the comment claimed that all the performances were worthy of praise, the writer emphasized that in the musical section the huaynos played by the Ramos Guevara sisters and above all the performance given by the Conjunto Leandro Alviña had captivated the audience. The latter group, which had apparently been recently formed, included at the time Fortunato Ugarte and Killco Huarak'a as quena players, José Castillo and Julio Galdo as guitarists, and the mandolin duo of Eduardo Pacheco and D. Álvarez.[49] This group would frequently appear on *La Hora del Charango,* with some of its members changing over time.[50] Andrés Alencastre (Killco Huarak'a) apparently was one of the musicians who did not remain long in the group because at the time he was already standing out as a composer and a singer of huaynos, accompanied by his *chillador* ("squealer," a small charango), as a poet, and above all as a stage director in the flourishing costumbrista theater of the time (see chapters 1 and 3).

Andrés Alencastre Gutiérrez, one of the most active and renowned artists in 1930–50, was born in 1909 in the district of Layo, province of Canas. The son of a *hacendado*, Leopoldo Alencastre, who was murdered in 1921 during a peasant uprising, Andrés obtained most of his formal education in Cuzco city.[51] Killco Huarak'a had founded an artistic group called K'ana Layu Llaqtay some years before the *La Hora del Charango* went on the air, performing "tableaux of 'aboriginal' customs accompanied by dances, music and poems" and "his costumbrista Quechua comedy El *pongo Killito*" in the city of Cuzco (Itier 2000, 84).[52] Along with his group of "Indians and mestizos," Alencastre performed this, his first "costumbrista-sarcastic piece," in the main squares and schools of various provinces of Cuzco (Gonzales 1999, 12). In 1939 Killco Huarak'a's play *challakuy* was a great success within the context of the contests organized by the Instituto Americano de Arte, which will be discussed in the following chapter. Paradoxically, this play presented the case of a gamonal murdered by the peasants and at the same time denounced the abuses the landowners inflicted on the peasantry.

Having already attained artistic recognition, in 1940 Killco Huarak'a entered the Universidad Nacional San Antonio Abad del Cuzco (UNSAAC), where he received his teaching degree and much later, in the 1970s, received a doctorate in education (Gonzales 1999, 12–14; Avendaño 1995, 51). After teaching in schools in Sicuani and Cuzco city, Alencastre took over the chair of Quechua in the UNSAAC (Gonzáles 1999, 12–14; Avendaño 1995, 468). His greatest recognition in Peru and abroad was as a Quechua poet and a student and promoter of the colloquial use of this native language.[53] His poems and melopoeia read on *La Hora del Charango* certainly were some of the pieces most discussed and appreciated by the press.

La Hora del Charango stimulated the formation of musical groups in the city of Cuzco that were anxious to join in Vidal Unda's proposal for a regional and national identity. One of these groups was *La Lira Cienciana*, which was formed by the enthusiastic senior students of the Colegio de Ciencias Faustino Valencia, Bernabé Grajeda, Luis Ochoa, Julio Miranda, and Manuel Gamarra, who wanted to "show their enthusiasm in this way."[54] Another group that participated in the early shows was the Conjunto Baltazar Zegarra, which in 1938 paid homage to this Cuzco composer and musician on *La Hora del Charango* by changing its original name, Conjunto Beethoven.[55]

The names of the groups that came from the provinces generally did not appear in the press and were often given the common labels "traditional groups" or "indigenous groups." A certain romanticization of these groups, and a kind of disdain for "popular" musicians, that is, those who were self-educated and lived in the city of Cuzco, can be perceived among some journalists. For instance, one article praised the participation of traditional groups from Acomayo, Quiquijana, and Tinta, "formed mostly by genuinely indigenous artists" who had brought along "unknown and highly original motifs," particularly the third one.[56] This same article, however, criticized other numbers in the program, writing, "We are against the inclusion of such improvisations in a program that is not only becoming popular but is even gaining prestige outside the departmental boundaries, which is why the organizers of the weekly folkloric hour are bound to ever more rigorously refine and select the numbers. *A shrillness that is loathed by the very artistic instinct of the people, and which shows us in a very bad light, cannot be accepted under the pretense of popularity.*"[57]

There was thus a conflict between those who shared some of the concerns voiced by Yábar Palacio and wanted the perceived informality and scant sophistication of the numbers—apparently those performed by self-educated or amateur musicians—to be limited or expunged from the program and others, such as Vidal Unda himself, who valued this type of performance because it represented the real practice and feeling of the majority. Vidal Unda made an effort to ensure that all who felt inspired and wanted to participate in the program would be able to do so. We thus find that the melopoeia and poems read on the program included those by well-known poets such as Andrés Alencastre, Luis Nieto Miranda, and Luis Ángel Aragón and those by inspired amateurs who wanted to express the admiration they felt for the work undertaken by Vidal Unda. Such was the case of Jorge Toribio Cárdenas Andrade, the composer of the above-cited huayno who dedicated a melopoeia to Vidal Unda just a few months after the program first aired without ever having met him in person. The following are just seven of the thirteen stanzas illustrating the recurrent themes of the "rebellious" charango (a metaphor often used to depict Andean music in general), which represents the feeling of the downtrodden and forgotten Andean majorities and of Humberto Vidal Unda as a great promoter of respect for this musical tradition.

> Cry charango! Cry your melodies
> bleed out the pain of your wounds,
> of those old wounds eaten away
> by time and your own rebelliousness.
>
> Your bold silence is now centuries old,
> and the remembrance alone is painful
> due to the vile forgetfulness it characterizes:
> disloyalty to the race with scorn.
>
> Only a humble heart recalls
> your symbolic vibrations of yore,
> lost in the fog of deceit,
> and only now you return to the crusade.
>
> The unvanquished man who yearns for you,
> is your precursor HUMBERTO VIDAL,
> nerve (*nervio*) and root of vital importance,[58]
> unique genius and visionary soul.
>
> Charango! Now that you have a new life,
> sprout forth like a mushroom from the soil,
> unleash your moans and banish forgetfulness
> so you arise dashingly and with felt warmth
>
> Charango! Break the fatal silence
> and may the gentle rhythm of your notes,
> burst into wandering hearts
> riding the sonorous ETHER of space.
>
> Charango! Play your notes with new life,
> More vigorously, and with more force
> because only in you remains the hope
> that your notes will forever LIVE.[59]

In response to calls for better organization of the program, which was actually gaining a nationwide presence, the organizers established an organizing committee just slightly over a year after *La Hora del Charango*'s first broadcast. The main goals of this committee, whose members were Vidal Unda (chairman), Julio Gutiérrez, Constantino Zúñiga, Gerardo Aragón, Víctor Navarro del Águila, Miguel Ángel Delgado, Teófilo Huaihuaca Saldívar, and Ernesto Vidal, were to "attain a greater literary and musical attraction," to "try to include in all programs the participation of groups from the provinces," and to "undertake intense labor for the reinstatement of the prestige of our great musical artists, who undeservedly sink into oblivion and receive indifference [as their reward], consumed by the apathy of our milieu."[60] This last goal in fact began to be fulfilled slightly after the establishment of the committee with the above-mentioned homage given to the musician and composer Baltazar Zegarra.[61] It is also clear that artists who were still unknown in the urban milieu of the region gradually used this program to join urban artistic circles and make a decisive contribution to the development of the musical traditions of Cuzco. Such was the case of Don Julio Benavente Díaz, who would be recognized throughout Peru and abroad as a major charango player and who developed the t'ipi technique, thus defining what has come to be known as the "Cuzco style" of charango playing. The transformations the charango tradition would undergo in the hands of Julio Benavente contributed to the greater acceptance of this musical tradition among the middle and upper classes of cuzqueño and Peruvian society.

JULIO BENAVENTE DÍAZ, THE "CHARANGO GOD"

I play in the Cuzco style. . . . I have thus loved the charango for many reasons, for the people, for women—MY ANDEAN CHOLO, as I called my charango, "*is a musket that hunts hearts with invisible bullets full of feelings, [of] songs from the Pampas of Anta in Huarocondo, my homeland.*"[62] JULIO BENAVENTE DÍAZ

"The Charango God"—so he was nicknamed in a Lima magazine in 1949—was born in the district of Huarocondo, in the province of Anta, on November 18, 1913 (see fig. 8 on page 99).[63] His father, José Benigno Benavente Velasco, died when Julio was still in primary school in Huaroccondo and Paruro.[64] He began playing the harmonica at the age of seven, an instrument that also brought him fame and success (El Chucchito 1999, 76). Carmen Díaz Reyes, his mother, came from a family of landowners in the Pampa de Anta, and it was perhaps thanks to these resources that Julio was sent to

Cuzco city to attend high school at the Colegio de Ciencias and later education at the UNSAAC.

Benavente Díaz began to play the quena, bandore, and guitar as a teenager, but he developed his true musical talent through the charango, drawing his inspiration not just from the peasants in his homeland but also in the city of Cuzco from the legendary Pancho Gómez Negrón. We have seen how Don Julio explained that in high school he was already passionately in love with the charango and how this caused him to be punished by his school's music teacher because at the time this instrument was still rather despised in certain sectors of Cuzco society (Calvo 1999, 120). He remembered *La Hora del Charango* as the landmark that initiated the acceptance of the charango in the urban milieu of Cuzco, allowing this instrument to become the means of affirming a popular identity that brought together several sectors of society (120). Benavente made himself known in the artistic circles of this city through his participation in the *La Hora del Charango,* and in due course he became a "socio nato" of the Centro Qosqo de Arte Nativo.[65]

Don Julio Benavente's recognition as a solo player both regionally and countrywide began with his performance at the Teatro Segura of Lima in October 1949, where he appeared as part of a group of cuzqueño artists (El Chucchito 1999, 78; Calvo 1999, 121).[66] His success came almost by chance because, as Don Julio himself said "the stage machinery broke down in the Teatro Segura, [and] they got me out in front of the curtains (*a boca de telón*) to entertain the audience. . . . I played a Cuzco huayno, singing with that voice of a cuzqueño cholo. . . . The next day Delfín Fajardo stated in a magazine that Julio Benavente had brought the sweetest huaynos from Cuzco . . . José María Arguedas was also there; he translated the poetry of that same huayno into Spanish in the Sunday paper" (121).

José María Arguedas promoted Don Julio throughout Peru and abroad shortly after this performance and invited him to participate in musical events in the Feria Internacional del Pacífico (International Fair of the Pacific) held in Lima. As Don Julio recalls it, "José María Arguedas also introduced me as an extraordinary charango player; we were there, and at the October fair he placed me as a cultural bumper (*parachoque de cultura*) when the Spanish choir and dances came to the Feria" (Calvo 1999, 121). Romero (2001) points out that between the late 1940s and the 1960s José María Arguedas, a renowned Peruvian writer and anthropologist, was also the major promoter of Andean folklore in Lima and in Peru (97). From his position as chief of the Folklore and Popular Arts Section in the Ministry of Education, and then as the director of the Casa de la Cultura (the institution that preceded the Instituto Nacional de Cultura), Arguedas endeavored to further the knowledge and dissemination of the regional varieties of Andean music and dances as they were practiced in their places of origin, leaving aside previous stylizations and stereotypes made under the Incaic model (97–98). Arguedas, however, was not a "purist" who wanted Andean forms of expression to remain free of change or commercialization but quite the contrary. For instance, he was a great promoter of the first recordings of Andean music in the late 1940s (97–98).

Having already developed the t'ipi technique and combined it with traditional strumming, Don Julio developed what would eventually be known as the Cuzco charango style, in contrast to the styles from Ayacucho or Apurímac. By clearly emphasizing the melodic lines of the song, which had not been an aesthetic preference in the rural charango tradition, Julio Benavente sought to expand the public appreciation of charango music to include members of the Cuzco upper classes, as well as the public in Lima and abroad. He noted, for instance, that he introduced charango music into the elite Club Cuzco (Calvo 1999,122).

Julio Benavente combined his interest in pedagogy and charango music and had international experience that was not common among self-educated cuzqueño artists. After excelling as a teacher,[67] as an official in the Cuzco branch of the Department of Education, and as the author of educational materials, he was awarded scholarships in the late 1950s to resume his graduate studies in New York and Ohio.[68] After his return to Cuzco in 1961 he taught in the education department at the university, and in 1982 he was invested with honors by the city of Cuzco (he was awarded the Palmas Magisteriales in the Amauta degree) (El Chucchito 1999, 77). Along with these professional achievements, Julio Benavente attained artistic recognition both in Peru and abroad and was invited to musical events held in Lima, Bolivia, Ecuador, Argentina, the United States, England, and France, where he recorded his first compact disc in 1988. Benavente received many honors throughout his life that recognized him not just as an extraordinary performer but also as a great promoter of the teaching and playing of the charango in Peru and particularly in Cuzco. In 1972, UNESCO bestowed on him the title Cultural Patrimony of Andean Music, and in 1988 the city of Cuzco awarded him the Gold Medal of the City of Cuzco for his work as a practitioner of Andean music (79).

Don Julio composed many pieces, some only in Quechua, some in Spanish, and some that combined his extraordinary poetic mastery of both languages. This is clear, for instance, in the composition *charango fiel compañero* (Charango, you faithful partner) and one that made him famous throughout Peru in the performance given in the Teatro Segura of Lima: *ripukunay q'asapatapi* (The Mountain Pass through Which I Must Go).[69] He devoted much effort to ensuring that the reappraisal of the charango fostered by *La Hora del Charango* would continue in Cuzco and Peru. To this end he undertook several activities, of which the most outstanding was the establishment of the Centro de Estudios del Charango Peruano (Center of Peruvian Charango Studies) in 1986, which gathers the best Peruvian practitioners of this instrument (Parejo 1988, 12). Some years before, Benavente reorganized a program at Radio Tahuantinsuyo that sought to continue the significant work undertaken by the *La Hora del Charango,* but this time the program would be called *La Hora de Charango y Quena* (The Charango and Quena Hour).[70]

The charango of Don Julio Benavente, as El Chucchito says, embodied for many the "feelings," "love," and "rebelliousness" of the people of Cuzco (1999, 80). His death on November 7, 1995, was greatly felt by these same people, who even today remember him fondly as "El Cholo Benavente" because he and his "Andean cholo," which is what he called his charango, carried out the key task of stirring admiration for, and pride in, the art born in the Andes and the fusion of traditions.

The significance of *La Hora del Charango* for the interaction of artists from different social sectors of Cuzco society declined after about three years of important and intense cultural work in this city. This was perhaps due in part to the creation of new spaces for the promotion of folkloric art brought about by the establishment of the Instituto Americano de Arte de Cuzco on October 1937. The following chapter shows that the contests sponsored by this institution, the development of tourism in Cuzco, the establishment of other new institutions, and the activities Cuzco Day and Cuzco Week gave rise to produced more spaces for this interaction. By 1942 the program had been replaced at the station with another one organized by the Instituto

Americano de Arte, which was called *La Hora Folklórica.* Like *La Hora del Charango,* it was broadcast on Monday nights.[71] It is clear, however, that with the debates, interactions, and styles it produced *La Hora del Charango* marked a crucial moment in the development of the cholo feeling, cuzqueñoness, and Peruvianness.

5

...

CREATIVE EFFERVESCENCE AND THE CONSOLIDATION OF SPACES FOR "FOLKLORE"

> Whoever does not feel beating within him the seeds of the new forms is withdrawing from the major imperative of the historical moment: to create.
>
> ALBERTO DELGADO

> You and the gentlemen from the "Instituto Americano de Arte" understand the extent of a task still humble but of a deeply nationalist orientation; no other institution is called upon to favor and even encourage the cultural manifestations of our artistic milieu, and for these reasons I insist on requesting the effective help of the remarkable institution you direct so well. RICARDO FLÓREZ

The creative artistic-folkloric effervescence of the city of Cuzco in the mid-1920s intensified during the late 1930s and early 1940s. We saw with *La Hora del Charango* that this overflowing creative energy was not just an integral part of the cuzqueñista and Peruvianist ideological and political projects but also inspired and gave them a specific shape. Through art and these projects, and with its capital city as the center, cuzqueño society underwent qualitative transformations that culminated in the notion of "cuzqueñismo," which desired to place not just the highlander element but Cuzco itself at the very center of Peruvianness.

But if the cuzqueñista feeling—cuzqueñismo—that was developing in those decades had as its central tenet the idea of turning Cuzco and its culture into the essence of nationhood, the way in which different individuals and social groups understood this task and the strategies they used to carry it out differed. Intellectuals such as Luis Valcárcel placed a stronger emphasis than others on stimulating this feeling by exalting the glories of the Inca past and establishing its continuity with the present. On the other hand, scholars such as José Uriel García suggested that the essence of cuzqueño culture (*lo cuzqueño*), and of everything Andean in general, could be found in the confluence of the pre-Hispanic and the colonial traditions, that is, in cholo or mestizo culture, and therefore defended it as the basis for this regionalist and nationalist feeling. There were others, such as Albert Giesecke, whose cuzqueñismo stressed the importance of modernizing Cuzco and developing its touristic potential. On the other hand, the peasant and popular-urban artists who participated in the artistic-folkloric creations of the time sought to place their own forms of aesthetic expression at the forefront of public attention in Cuzco, in Peru, and among the tourists. Finally there were those, such as Humberto Vidal Unda, who combined all of these concerns in a unique way and tried through activism to use politics to gain the favor of the national government.

To analytically conceptualize the crucial role that artistic-folkloric activities played in these changes, a theoretical proposal made by Raymond Williams, who understands "thought as felt and feeling as thought," proved useful, as it enabled me to approach what was "actually being lived" (the "practical consciousness") by the cuzqueños who were participating in these major changes (Williams 1977, 131–32). The intellectuals and artists from different social sectors in Cuzco who shared common spaces through the artistic-folkloric practice sought to create, feel, and make something that all cuzqueños and Peruvians could feel and consider their own. Conceptualizing thought and feeling as conjoined helps us understand the inspiration and strength with which these cuzqueño artists and intellectuals carried out their projects. These projects were inspired by the milieus of artistic-folkloric production in which the different sectors of cuzqueño society participated physically, visually, or aurally (in contests and shows, parties and other kinds of private meetings, or radio programs).

The words of the poet Alberto Delgado cited above, which come from the introductory speech at a "Velada de Arte Folklórico" (Evening of Folkloric Art) in honor of the wife of Manuel Prado, the Peruvian president, confirm that *crear* (to create) was imperative at the time. Art would be useful in nourishing and consolidating contemporary politics because, in Delgado's words, "in the domain of aesthetic emotion" one may find "the paradigm and the register [of the] nationalist and democratic feeling."[1] Artists and intellectuals such as Delgado were not satisfied with suggesting that cuzqueño art could be used to create or lay the foundation for Peru's politics and Peruvian nationalism but also proposed that this art should become "the original expression depicting the America envisioned by Americans."[2]

Cuzco's intellectuals and artists sought to attract the attention of the national government from the early decades of the twentieth century so that it would not merely accept the proposal according to which Cuzco and its culture should be placed at the very center of the construction of the nation's identity but also accept responsibility for meeting Cuzco's political and institutional needs, including the need for infrastructure. Throughout his populist administration, President Augusto B. Leguía echoed many of the concerns of these intellectuals and artists. Chapter 3 showed that in order to attain international recognition for its archaeological monuments and the Fourth Centennial celebration of the Spanish foundation of their city, the cuzqueños, with the crucial support of a U.S. citizen, Albert Giesecke, sought state support for several types of improvements in their region. In events such as the one just mentioned honoring the wife of the president, local artists and intellectuals sought to please the incumbent administration and at the same time continue asserting that Cuzco's art was worthy of receiving the state's support as it was the legitimate fountainhead of national identity. We shall see below that some subsidies were obtained for local institutional projects thanks to the steps taken by cuzqueño intellectuals who became senators and congressmen, even though in the long run they did not prove significant. The cultural institution that organized the presentation for the president's wife had already received the first of these subsidies, which had been granted by law almost a year before the event.

In the context of this creative drive, an external stimulus that occurred the same year in which *La Hora del Charango* made its debut led to the establishment of one of the most important cultural institutions of Cuzco: The Instituto Americano de Arte, Sección Peruana, Comité del Cuzco (American Art Institute, Peruvian Section, Cuzco Committee) better known simply as: Instituto Americano de Arte de Cuzco (American Art Institute of Cuzco, henceforth IAAC). Although the initiative for the establishment of this institute was quite clearly derived from a joint effort undertaken by intellectuals and artists from other parts of America—Argentina and Mexico in particular—in order to place "art" or "popular culture," understood in broad terms, at the very center of the construction of their national identities, in Cuzco the IAAC evidently thrived because it took charge of several major tasks that were crying out to be served at the institutional level. These tasks essentially lay within two very closely connected fields: the creativeness derived from the fluid interaction among artists from various social sectors of Cuzco, and touristic development of the region.

As seen in relation to artistic-folkloric production, the Centro Qosqo de Arte Nativo had assumed the institutional mission of promoting this art from the mid-1920s on through contests and performances held in and out of Cuzco. Within the region, the activities sponsored by the members of this institution, as well as by *La Hora del Charango*, were a major contribution to the creation and appreciation of spaces where this art could unfold. At the time when the establishment of the IAAC was proposed, the active promotion of these spaces by the Centro Qosqo had declined (the last contest it had promoted had been held in 1933), and this institution was undergoing an institutional crisis that was evident by 1943 (for this crisis and the definitive restructuring of the institution in 1951, see below). Thus, there was a major institutional vacuum that was filled by the IAAC, whose founders included several founding members of Centro Qosqo.

One point that must be kept in mind is that this vacuum at the level of institutional promotion in no way means that other types of spaces, ones that enabled the confluence and meeting of different individuals, styles, and aesthetic preferences in Cuzco throughout the twentieth century and the early twenty-first, were likewise undergoing a decline. The practice of music at church services, family parties, festive and religious celebrations, and informal gatherings in private houses were—then as now—major spaces for these encounters and the development of new musical styles. The cultural institutions in the city of Cuzco, including the IAAC, have always based their activities on existing networks of artistic and social interaction in Cuzco, thus giving rise to new situations wherein these networks expand and become more complex.

But the artistic creativeness that the IAAC sought to promote at the time was not just limited to the production of music, dance, and theater that came under the folklore label. What was new in this institution was that it meant to stimulate "all the manifestations of modern American art,"[3] including the plastic arts, literature, and photography, as well as the production of music that would promote the knowledge and the use of the world's classical traditions and techniques. For some, the latter would contribute to the development of Peruvian music. This is illustrated by the support given to the establishment and maintenance of the Asociación Orquestal Cuzco (Cuzco Orchestra Association).

With regard to the second area of activities of the IAAC, we have seen in previous chapters how the image of Cuzco as a center of historical, archaeological, and touristic interest, which had been growing in previous decades, received a major stimulus with the proclamation of the city as the Archaeological Capital City of South America in 1933 and the celebrations held for the Fourth Centennial of its Spanish Foundation in that same year. But some isolated efforts to promote tourism in the region notwithstanding, there was as yet no organized institutional activity. We thus find that, although the *finalidades* (goals) of the IAAC made no explicit mention of its mission vis-à-vis the promotion of tourism, it is clear that by including among its major goals the inventory, preservation, and restoration of the "monuments and other objects of ancient art spread throughout the region" (i.e., pre-Columbian and colonial objects and monuments), the members of this institution did feel the pressing need to collaborate in the development of this burgeoning regional activity.[4]

A prolific artistic output and the desire to attract "the greatest possible attention"[5] to the region for its historical significance and its touristic potential were two of the major elements in the cuzqueñismo that the IAAC actively helped to create. It was in this institution that the idea of having day- and weeklong celebrations in honor of Cuzco, as well as the ritual that would become their focus, was conceived: Inti Raymi, a replication of the Inca ritual held for the winter solstice. The celebrations of Cuzco Week gradually became one of the most important contexts for the institutional promotion of artistic-folkloric production in the twentieth century and today.

This chapter shows that, besides placing an Inca symbol at the center of cuzqueñismo, the activities promoted by the IAAC were obviously meant to recognize and provide an ever more important place for the art that was being identified or defined as mestizo. From this moment on, specific mention of the importance of both indigenous and mestizo art would be a constant. It was also around this time that the trend—already present in previous events—of distinguishing what was mestizo from what was indigenous crystallized. This was understood not in terms of a different nature but in relation to the degree of stylization and elaboration of the artistic product, as well as the place of origin of the product or its performers (rural or urban), or the historical period it was related to (pre-Hispanic, colonial, or republican). It will be seen below that, while the artistic-folkloric events used the two categories to distinguish between the participating numbers and groups, at the same time an effort was clearly being made to consider all of them as equivalent within the category of folklore or popular art.

The category of cholo therefore came to play a major role in this context, wherein continuity was being sought at the same time that differences between what was Indian and what was mestizo were being established. Thus, in 1939 the so-called movement of cuzqueño *cholismo* crystallized with the establishment of the Asociación Los Cholos (The Cholos' Association), which was cofounded and encouraged by members of the IAAC such as Humberto Vidal Unda and Luis Felipe Paredes (both persevering intellectuals who sponsored folkloric art) and the poet Luis Nieto Miranda. With this movement, artists and intellectuals endeavored to reject the negative ethnic and racial connotations of the term *cholo* and turn it into a source of "pride, distinction, and authentic cuzqueñoness (*cuzqueñismo*)" (Aparicio 1994, 140). The same term was used at the time, within the context of the contests and folklore performances, to refer to peasant artists who participated in these events, as well as to artists who were of lower-class urban extraction.[6]

Finally, as illustrated by the letter written by Ricardo Flórez quoted earlier, the IAAC was used by many groups of artists—some of which were formed only by self-educated artists while others also included musicians with a formal education or who were already known in the city of Cuzco—to find support for their own projects (see fig. 10). These artists believed that the projects were part of the nationalist effort Cuzco was undertaking at the time, as was explicitly noted by Flórez. The Asociación Folklórica Kosko (Kosko Folklore Association or AFK), which was founded in 1945 with the support of the IAAC, had been essentially organized and promoted by self-educated musicians who wanted to have a major presence in the art scene of the city and to adopt the role of representing a cuzqueño expressive culture to the country and the tourists who were finding their way to Cuzco in ever growing numbers. This group would compete for some years at the regional

10. Ricardo Flórez, first from the left; Manuel Pillco with his harp; and Francisco Flórez, first from the right (Cuzco, 1940s). (PRIVATE ARCHIVE OF THE PILLCO FAMILY.)

and the national levels with another group likewise sponsored by the IAAC, which depended on a state-run entity: the Conjunto Folklórico de la Corporación Nacional de Turismo (Folklore Group of the National Tourism Corporation of Cuzco).

TO DEFEND, PROPAGATE, AND STIMULATE ART: THE BEGINNINGS OF THE CUZCO BRANCH OF THE AMERICAN ART INSTITUTE

Among the Hispanic-American nations, Peru is one of the countries with a great and admirable artistic culture; *it is an art full of suggestions and orientations, with originality and vigor capable of building the greatness of the continent's culture,* comparable to the art and culture of the other continents. What is lacking are centers formed by individuals with technical capacity and devotion for all that has spiritual value as a manifestation of certain peoples and periods, centers that, besides attending to all that was handed down by previous generations, sponsor and stimulate the new creations of the present. In this respect, Peru is not a country stagnated in the culture of bygone ages but a *land where the people who support nationhood have an admirable and undying vigor for constant creation in art as well as other forms of civilized life.* We therefore need associations that sponsor high-culture disciplines as a stimulus for invaluable creations. JOSÉ URIEL GARCÍA, EMPHASIS ADDED

The words of José Uriel García, the leader, founder, and first president of the IAAC,[7] show that for the cuzqueño artists and intellectuals who were the driving force behind this cultural institution the artistic manifestations of the past, present, and future were essential to providing the strength (*fuerza y vigor*) required for the consolidation of the cuzqueño, Peruvian, and American (Hispanic American) identities. By the time the IAAC was established, the efforts to shape nationalism or Americanism (understood as a Hispanic Americanism) using some elements derived from living cultures considered indigenous were not altogether new in Cuzco or other parts of America (Rowe and Schelling 1991; López 2004, 2006). Here, however, the activities the IAAC promoted and the spaces it created are studied in order to take a close look at the way in which, for renowned intellectuals or self-educated musicians, the artistic production within the Cuzco milieu became the best way to inspire and consolidate the cuzqueño, Peruvian, and American identities. A close look at the spheres of interaction on which this institution was built, as well as the ones it engendered or supported, brings us nearer to the complex artistic interaction that was then taking place and eventually gave rise to what is still recognized as traditionally (*típico*) cuzqueño.

After participating in the Second International Congress of American History, held in June and July 1937, as well as in the establishment of the Instituto Americano de Arte in Buenos Aires in July, José Uriel García returned to Peru with the task of opening branches of this institution that would "carry out a parallel work on behalf of the enrichment of American art" in tandem with the main office (the *central*).[8] The first of these branches was established shortly thereafter in Cuzco, on October 7, 1937, with the participation of renowned artists and intellectuals from the city of Cuzco, who agreed to "defend, propagate, and stimulate Art."[9] For García, what was required besides the obvious need to "stimulate our artists in the various phases of art," was a defense of "the artistic riches" of the region, which were being "destroyed, exported, or at least altered," as well as their dissemination. He wrote that "since Cuzco is an inexhaustible source of artistic riches and motifs for art, [it is] essential that their knowledge be spread."[10]

In succeeding months the bylaws and objectives of this cuzqueño institution were gradually defined and slightly modified, but at the core it was always emphasized that the art it advocated (understood in broad terms) belonged both to the past and the present, with the idea that both would be used "to create a continental aesthetic consciousness, [and] particularly a Peruvian consciousness."[11] It seems, however, that throughout the period when the Centro Qosqo left a vacuum with regard to institutional support for the development of folkloric art in the city, the IAAC placed a particular emphasis on this area, as its goals stressed that it would foster the study and development of the music and dances included within the category of folklore due to the "outstanding conditions of its traditions."[12] The activities undertaken by the IAAC would refocus on other areas of art after the Centro Qosqo had been revived and several other private and governmental institutions had been established in the 1950s, 1960s, and 1970s.

Although the IAAC was clearly established thanks to academic and intellectual stimuli derived from other Latin American nations, this institute thrived in the cuzqueño milieu thanks to its connection with the creative strength and inspiration of the time and so developed its own characteristics. In a retrospective reflection on the activities carried out by this institution during its first ten years, Roberto Latorre, a respected journalist and political Marxist activist, noted some of the differences between the activities undertaken by the IAAC and those of similar institutions in Argentina and Mexico, showing the emphasis the members of the first placed on interacting with so-called popular artists. In the hope of stimulating the establishment of a similar institution in La Paz, Bolivia, Latorre pointed out the following in a letter to his friend and "comrade" Álvaro Bedregal, who lived in that city: "The institutes in Argentina and Mexico became councils of academic debates that I find irrelevant. They never reached the popular masses, [and] they never did anything on behalf of the popular artists that are so scorned in our world. The Cuzco Institute had no time for debates. No one was interested in attaining wisdom, nor in showing off his capacities and knowledge. We dedicated ourselves to stimulating the popular artists and the others to work, promising them small remunerations under the guise of prizes."[13]

As soon as this institute was established, its members began their promotional activities by organizing the first Popular Plastic Arts Contest that same month of December, which still takes place within the context of the traditional Christmas handicraft fair known as the *santurantikuy* (literally, "the purchase of saints"). The initial intent was to organize at the same time a

Popular Music and Choreography Contest culminating "in a great evening of art" on the thirty-first of that same month.[14] The contest, however, was not held until the following year at Carnival time.

It was by extolling the cuzqueño plastic arts, which obviously showed the conjunction of cultural heritages in the Andean world, that the organizers of the contest sought to "vindicate the despised mestizo people, make them aware of their weight in the social scale," and thus "set a path in the future [for] popular art, which is the only real [art]."[15] Defining what is "popular" is no easy task, and so it proved for the members of the IAAC when they began their promotional activities. For these artists and intellectuals it was clear that "popular art" should be defined at the level of the artistic product and the artists who made it. It was only in the rules of the first *santurantikuy* contest that the organizers explicitly defined popular artists as those who could not be considered professionals in their respective fields.[16]

The definition was quite broad in relation to the artistic product, as it defined "regional popular art" as that which was "inspired, crafted, and made with our themes, motifs, and materials."[17] The contests and the exhibits included from the beginning various types of plastic arts such as toys, figures depicting the people of Cuzco, and/or the regional environment, paintings, commercial emblems, banners or posters, engravings, drawings, and sculpture, among others. The members of the IAAC purchased the pieces they considered most valuable from the very first contest with the intention that they would someday become part of a Museum of Popular Art. This dream came true in 1963, when the museum opened its doors.

Besides its central role in organizing the events held for Cuzco Day and Cuzco Week from 1944 onward, during its first decade the IAAC organized ten plastic arts contests held within the context of the *santurantikuy,* one for the whole department of Cuzco in 1942, one for "Popular Music and Dance" alone, three for "Popular Music, Dance, and Theater," one for "Literature, Painting, and Music," and one for "Native Music." In addition, there were seven contests for painting, two for sculpture, three for drawing and painting for schoolchildren, and two for banners for chicherías. In turn, from April 1942 onwards the institute sponsored a weekly *La Hora Folklórica Peruana* radio program, which continued the tradition of the legendary *La Hora del Charango.* The program was sponsored by artists and intellectuals such as Vidal Unda and Roberto Ojeda, who had supported the original program and now continued their efforts to give Cuzco music a national and international presence through radio within this new institution.

Far more space than these brief pages would be needed to explain the importance and impact of the activities of the IAAC in the period 1937–50. Reference must be made, however, to some of the other spaces promoted by this institution, which had a major impact on the artistic and intellectual life of Cuzco at the time. According to an account given by Latorre, in its first ten years the premises of the IAAC housed "twenty-three exhibits of painting, three of photography, [and] almost forty lectures on art and education [were given]."[18] Latorre likewise recalls that the IAAC was able to make "the government pass laws defending the artistic riches of Cuzco and promoting respect for the architectural style of this land" and also organized the Academy of Plastic Arts.[19] It is also known that the premises of the IAAC housed institutions such as the Asociación Orquestal Cuzco (founded in 1945), the Asociación Folklórica Kosko (1945), and the Conjunto Folklórico of the Corporación Nacional de Turismo (1947) during their early days and that the institute organized and often sponsored performances of music, dance, and theater such as the above-mentioned "Velada de Arte Folklórico" in honor of the wife of President Manuel Prado.

All of the promotional activities carried out by this institute, the contests in particular, obviously required financial resources. Despite its having sought government funding, in its first three years the IAAC was almost entirely supported with resources derived from the artistic shows the institute organized to raise money and by donations from commercial and entertainment firms such as the Empresa del Cine Italia (Italian Cinema Company), which almost financed in full the first contest of "Popular Music and Dance" in 1938.[20] For this and subsequent events, the members of the institute also requested the help of local transportation and communications enterprises to provide transportation for the contestants who came from the provinces and to publicize the events.

Thanks to José Uriel García, who was then a senator,[21] and other political representatives of Cuzco in Lima, such as Francisco Tamayo, the representative for Urubamba, the Peruvian government officially recognized the IAAC and its mission in 1940 and awarded it a monthly subsidy to help support its promotional activities. Although the subsidy continued for several decades, it was always uncertain, and the members of the IAAC had to constantly pressure politicians to keep it or to have the original sum restored after it was cut. Although in time this subsidy was more symbolic than useful, it did provide significant help in the early years. For instance, the subsidy comprised almost 60 percent of the income in the 1943 budget.[22] The artistic performances held to raise funds and the help given by commercial firms and institutions such as the Chamber of Commerce, Industry, Agriculture, and Livestock Raising of Cuzco would continue as major sources of income in succeeding decades.

Although it is a point that requires more research and analysis, it must be noted that many of the events sponsored by the IAAC in its first decade included significant female participation. In 1947 Latorre wrote to his friend Bedregal that the institute had twenty-five male members and a female section with the same number of members.[23] When this committee was dissolved in the 1960s its female members acquired the same status as the male ones joining the executive boards that managed the institution.

Finally, it must be stressed that the first attempts to collect, record, and catalogue some aspects of the contemporary culture that were considered "folklore" were made in this institution in collaboration with the local university. For instance, in 1938 the first serious attempt to collect, record, and catalogue what was then known as "popular literature," which included "legends, tales, sayings, ballads, verses, fables, [and] traditions," among other elements that local people considered important in their tradition, was jointly carried out in cooperation with the "Peruvian literature program at the university."[24] In 1941 the institute included in its budget "a heading for the collection and cataloguing [of] musical folklore."[25] This task was finally entrusted to Roberto Ojeda and Juan de Dios Aguirre in 1942, who by April of that year had presented to the members of the IAAC the first volume of the "Catálogo del Folklore Musical del Cuzco" (Catalogue of Cuzco's Musical Folklore).[26] The budget for the following year still included resources for the continuation of the musical catalogue, and for the preparation of a "Fichero Folklórico" (Folklore Card Index).[27] A folklore program was established the same year at the university, validating even more the artistic and intellectual activities in this field.

The idea of preparing complete folklore index files and calendars of festivals in the region gradually took hold of more intellectuals and artists in the city of Cuzco who moved between the university and other cultural institutions of the city. For instance, Humberto Vidal Unda fostered the collection of files (*fichas*) with information on festivals, music, and dance in the Folklore Section (established in 1947) of the National Tourism Corporation (Corporación Nacional de Turismo). He also organized this corporation's "conjunto." By then Víctor Navarro del Águila, a member of the IAAC and professor of folklore at the university, had already published in the institute's journal, in 1944, the first detailed "Calendar of Popular Festivals in the Department of Cuzco" (Navarro del Aguila 1944).[28] Since its inception in 1942, this journal publicized the various activities carried out by the artists and intellectuals who belonged to the IAAC. As mentioned, the collection of folkloric traditions, their staging, the pursuit of a national identity based on an idealized past, and the promotion of tourism have often gone hand in hand not just in Cuzco but also in various other parts of the world (Herzfeld 1986; Kirshenblatt-Gimblett 1998).

Contests that sought to stimulate the creation of folkloric or popular music, theater, and dance had a prominent place among the promotional activities carried out in the early years. These contests placed an even stronger emphasis on the participation of both "indigenous" and "aboriginal" art, as well as that which was considered "mestizo."

THE STIMULUS OF COMPETITION: MUSIC, DANCE, AND POPULAR THEATER

As we see, the contest organized by the Instituto Americano de Arte has raised a great enthusiasm and a fertile creative activity among the popular artists. *EL COMERCIO*

The members of the IAAC organized four regional contests of dance, music, and theater (except for the first, which did not include the latter) between 1938 and 1941, convinced by previous experiences that contests, resulting in the series of public performances in the city of Cuzco, were one of the best ways to promote and disseminate popular cuzqueño art.[29] These contests also encouraged the participation of artists from the neighboring departments of Puno and Apurímac, but only contestants from the first of these two departments arrived for the second event. Beginning with the first event, the organizers made an explicit effort to invite practitioners of both mestizo and indigenous or aboriginal art by including them in the category of popular or folkloric art. In this new effort of neo-Indianist inspiration, all of this was expected to give shape to a national identity.

When defining its "themes," the guidelines of the contest proposed that they would be "related to Carnival, [and] be inspired by indigenous or mestizo customs from various provinces and peoples in the department and the southern Peruvian region."[30] The rules for the second of these contests, in 1939, likewise established that "the compositions, musical pieces, or creations of a choreographic or theatrical nature must preferably be original [and] based on indigenous and mestizo folklore, the subject being of free choice."[31]

However, in practice these artistic events and the pieces and performers included in them could not so easily be classified within one category or another, nor was it necessary owing to the way in which the rules and the criteria for participation had been laid out. Whenever these rules and criteria were listed an effort was made—albeit not always explicitly—to include individuals and artistic practices that could be taken to lie closer to the pre-Hispanic past and were from provinces other than Cuzco (those that were believed to be more Indian or authentic), as well as those that came from the vicinity or inside the city of Cuzco and evinced some stylization and European influence (those taken to be mestizo). The term *indigenous* was explicitly used whenever there was a need to emphasize that individuals (their provenance and attire), their instruments, or the style of music they practiced had to fall within the first category. If it were possible that the art and the people who practiced it came from both ends of the classificatory spectrum, the word *indigenous* was explicitly used in some cases (if the intention was to show a preference for or to encourage the participation of those who could be included within this category), but it was sometimes left open. Finally, no ethnic/racial classification was supplied when it was clear that the art and its practitioners could be classified as mestizo. For example, in the first contest the rules state the following:

> *Music Groups.* The following may participate in the contest: (a) flute ensembles (fifes); of these ensembles, those formed by Indians of either sex will be given preference. (b) estudiantinas with stringed and wind instruments. (c) bands of indigenous musicians. (d) melodeon. (e) harp and violin, preferably indigenous. (f) Popular songs, individual and collective.
>
> *Choreographic and Pantomime Groups.* (a) huaynos. (b) marineras. (c) Carnival kashuas. (c) tableaux showing dances, pantomimes, village celebrations, parties, binges (*jaranas*), etc.[32]

One thing that shows the organizers were not just interested in promoting what was considered more authentic or pure (and in many cases was synonymous with indigenous) but also in helping folkloric art develop its repertoire and techniques in order to lead to new creations is what the rules explicitly considered under the heading of "themes." These could be "taken wholly from popular folklore—folkloric reproductions—or [could be] original compositions inspired by this same folklore," that is, the jury would consider, on the one hand, "pure folkloric art" and, on the other, the "original creations based on folklore."[33]

The first two contests organized by the IAAC were successful in convening groups from both the province and city of Cuzco, as well as from other provinces (see figs. 11 and 12). Each contest had six preliminary rounds and a final. Although the rules did use the classificatory categories of indigenous and mestizo (albeit not always explicitly so in the latter case) to invite the participation of all Cuzco people and to establish the criteria for participation, when it came to judging it was clear that the artistic reality was far more complex than these two categories implied.[34] This was even clearer in the second contest because, although the rules solicited the participation of different types of groups, some of which carried the label indigenous, when the prizes were awarded only three general categories were considered: dance, theater, and music.[35] For the final decision no attempt was made to differentiate between the categories resorting to ethnic/racial terms, as had been done in the first contest.

Some newspaper comments regarding these artistic-folkloric performances hint at how arbitrary or ambiguous classifying a group of artists and/or their art within the mestizo or indigenous category sometimes proved to be. Some comments are, for instance, available for the group headed by Manuel Pillco, which participated in both contests. After its performance in the first contest it was noted that "the good *indigenous group* headed by the popular harpist Manuel Pillco performed well-chosen numbers. The yaraví, the huayno, and finally the marinera, danced and sung by couples of children in *traditional Indian garb,* won the unanimous support of the public. . . . The quena and the piano players in Pillco's group were worthy of note, [and] both showed good taste and feeling in their performances."[36]

11. A folkloric group from Quiquijana (1930s). (PHOTO BY MARTÍN CHAMBI, MARTÍN CHAMBI PHOTOGRAPHIC ARCHIVE.)

Manuel Pillco's group was given the prize for second place in the category "traditional indigenous ensembles," while the first place was declared void in this category.[37] The category for which the group was awarded a prize is interesting as one of the genres the ensemble performed was the marinera, a music and dance genre that, though widespread in the region for decades, was actually of coastal origin and had only crystallized in the late nineteenth century (Romero 1988). The yaraví, of course, is also a mestizo genre of colonial origin, but it had long been identified with the indigenous or highland population. Also the piano this group included is quite removed from what can be considered indigenous.

The fact that the judges had trouble awarding the prizes for the categories originally established is corroborated by the fact that several were declared void and several were ignored when judging the contestants. It apparently proved easier for the judges to award the individual prizes, which did not have to fall into any category. In the end, ten individual and ten group prizes were awarded. Although Pillco's group was unable to win the first prize for a "traditional indigenous ensemble," perhaps due to the problems encountered in classifying it as such, Clemente Qawana,[38] its quena player, did win one of the individual prizes and the boy who danced the marinera won an honorable mention.[39]

12. A folkloric group from Pisac in the 1930s or 1940s. (PHOTO BY MARTÍN CHAMBI, MARTÍN CHAMBI PHOTOGRAPHIC ARCHIVE.)

It obviously proved easier to award prizes in the categories in which no distinction had to be made between what was mestizo and what was indigenous, as was the case with the prizes for the category "mixed groups: traditional ensemble and dance." In this category a special prize was awarded to a group from Tinta, two first prizes—one to a group from Quiquijana and another from San Pablo—and two second prizes—one for the group Mosoq Llaqta from the city of Cuzco and another for the group Paucarttica from the district of San Jerónimo. For those familiar with the geography of Cuzco it is obvious that the special prize and the two first-place prizes were given to groups that were more distant from the city. This made them seem more indigenous to the intellectuals and artists in Cuzco, as is confirmed by the comments made by the press.[40] Journalists perceived the Mosoq Llaqta and Paucarttica groups as more mestizo than the others because they were obviously connected with the city of Cuzco (the district of San Jerónimo is very close to the city, and Mosoq Llaqta was founded by people who lived in it). However, the music and dance genres performed by these two groups were not markedly different from those played by the groups that were considered more indigenous.[41]

The extolling of mestizo art and identity was even more propitious in the

1939 contest, as this was one of the central events in the celebrations held for the Fourth Centennial of the birth of the Inca Garcilaso de la Vega, the symbol of the cuzqueño and in general of the Andean mestizo identity. This was the contest in which Andrés Alencastre (Killco Huarak'a) proved to be an outstanding representative of the burgeoning costumbrista theater of a neo-Indianist type with his play *challakuy.* Consider, for instance, the following comment made in the press:

> The people from Canas then staged the drama—which is in every sense of the word—'challacuy,' an original piece by Kilko Waraka. This is no mere attempt, as the author modestly calls it; this is a play which is just as good as any play either in national or foreign theater. *In it the author expounds the thesis of neo-Indianism and the defense of the mestizo people through the speeches of his main characters and the denouement of the play, precisely in relation to the significance of the life and works of the Inca Garcilaso.* "Challacuy" is thus a work with which we can claim we have an *authentic neo-indigenous cuzqueño theater.* . . . [A]t the end [the public] forced the author to come out to the stage to give him a standing ovation, an homage that, as far as we can recall, had never been given to a playwright in Cuzco.[42]

Alencastre and his group participated with theater and music in the third contest, which was organized by the IAAC in 1940, and also won the applause of the cuzqueño public. The following year they did not participate, probably because the prestige Alencastre had achieved at the regional and the national levels did not allow him to.[43] The third and fourth contests had fewer participants, and only four and three qualifying rounds were required, respectively. These two contests were the last of this type (music, dance, and theater) that the IAAC would organize as an institution, but its members would continue promoting them as part of the celebrations held for Cuzco Day and Cuzco Week. Some of the contestants in previous contests would continue participating, and new ones appeared who had been encouraged by the competitions (see fig. 13).

One of the groups formed and later reorganized as a result of the contests sponsored by the Centro Qosqo and then by the IAAC, was one of the self-educated quena players that Ricardo Flórez reorganized in 1940 under the name Centro Artístico Ollanta (Ollanta Art Center). The passage cited at the beginning of this chapter shows that popular artists such as Flórez often

13. A folkloric group from Yanaoca, Canas, in the 1930s or 1940s. (PHOTO BY MARTÍN CHAMBI, MARTÍN CHAMBI PHOTOGRAPHIC ARCHIVE.)

resorted to the institutional support of the IAAC for funds, to use the premises, or simply to have their artistic endeavors recognized. We will see that such was the case with the Asociación Folklórica Kosko (Kosko Folklore Association), which was headed by self-educated musicians such as Manuel Pillco and Francisco Flórez, the brother of Ricardo.

It is true that one can find groups that were formed and headed by intellectuals and artists starting in the late 1920s, which may have seemed more authentic from the standpoint of some sectors in the cities of Cuzco and Lima (e.g., the Conjunto Acomayo, formed by Policarpo Caballero, or the K'ana-Layo, formed by Alencastre), but this was not the case with most of the groups that participated in the effervescent creative work studied here. The artistic creations of groups such as Paucarttica; ensembles from Tinta, Quiquijana, San Pablo, and Mosoq Llaqta; Manuel Pillco's group; and the Centro Artístico Ollanta, to name just a few, produced most of the artistic-folkloric output of the time.[44]

The Conjunto Obrero Huanacaure (Huanacaure Workers' Group), which participated in the four contests organized by the IAAC, is a final example of the various social sectors that participated in artistic-folkloric production during this period. This group was often praised by the press "because [it comprised] above all manual workers who cultivate the musical art with love (*cariño*) and devotion (*dedicación*)."[45] This group performed music, dance, and theater, and three of its members, including its director, Isidoro Leiva, attained their greatest success in the fourth contest, when they won three of the eight individual prizes awarded on that occasion.

An incident took place within the context of a competitive event—outside the by then traditional *santurantikuy*, which was organized every year by the IAAC—that allows us to see the kind of convergences and disagreements that took place throughout the decades when the cuzqueños tried to make their art, and their land in general, the focus of national and foreign attention. The major actor in this incident was a young but already renowned composer, violinist, and orchestral conductor, Armando Guevara Ochoa.

ELEVATING THE POPULAR SONG: THE NATIONALIST EFFORTS OF ARMANDO GUEVARA OCHOA

[Manuel Pillco] gave me the purest Andean folklore—how beautifully he played his harp, a harp virtuoso! Thus, we improvised on songs that had already been created, others that were mine, and others that were his, [and it was] a *fantastic counterpoint of love* (cariño) *and music*. . . . [He taught me] the indigenous stuff, the real huayno, the huayno that is the warmth of the soul.

My message is that we must not abandon what is ours; the huayno has to be in the soul of the individual. *We will never have a national identity as long as the huayno does not get in, as long as we are not vitalized by and rally behind the huayno* (nos animemos detrás del huayno)—the rest comes afterward. ARMANDO GUEVARA OCHOA[46]

A photograph of Armando Guevara Ochoa playing the violin as a child alongside Manuel Pillco (fig. 14) illustrates, in many ways, the fluid and productive interaction between musicians with a formal musical education (usually from wealthy families) and the self-educated ones of popular extraction, either rural or urban, which led to a prolific artistic-folkloric production in Cuzco between 1920 and 1950. As noted above, Guevara Ochoa, whom the specialists say is the Peruvian composer "who has most [successfully] disseminated his work around the world" and is the only symphonic composer of his time who remained faithful to the "popular thematic" or "folklore" (Pinilla 1985, 176) and learned "the purest Andean folklore" from the art of Manuel Pillco, "indigenous stuff, the real huayno." Although

14. Manuel Pillco on the harp and Armando Guevara Ochoa on the violin (Cuzco, 1930s). (PHOTO BY MARTÍN CHAMBI, MARTÍN CHAMBI PHOTOGRAPHIC ARCHIVE.)

Guevara Ochoa is in many ways unique at both the regional and the national levels, and his art cannot be considered typical of cuzqueño musical output, some aspects of his personal trajectory and his work let us see the complexities of, and the contradictions in, some of the spaces in which artistic-folkloric music developed in the period studied here.

Armando Guevara Ochoa was born in the city of Cuzco in 1926 to a wealthy family of good social standing. His father, Domingo Guevara Yañez, a physician, and his mother, Elvira Ochoa de Guevara, had "a property" (in Guevara Ochoa's words) in Corao, Pisac, which they visited particularly for popular festivals. This "was delightful" for Armando, as it allowed him to appreciate the music of the dances "with the syncope that characterizes them" and "the dissonance of the quenas," two musical characteristics that for him comprise the beauty of real Andean music.[47] But it was above all the early musical influences he received in his family's social circles in the city of Cuzco that enabled him to develop as a musician and composer while still very young. Guevara Ochoa told me that his house was a place where relatives, particularly those on his mother's side, and musician friends who participated in the city's artistic scene met to make music and share compositions.

It was in this milieu of parties and jams that Armando Guevara first interacted with Manuel Pillco, who would become his teacher, along with instructors his mother, a pianist, provided, many of whom were already renowned musicians in Cuzco: Roberto Ojeda, Baltazar Zegarra, and Juan de Dios Aguirre.[48] According to Guevara Ochoa, Manuel Pillco was not yet famous in the city, but his mother, as well as other musicians of the time, "loved Manuelito," which was why he frequented the house. Thanks to his mother Guevara Ochoa also listened to European classical music at a tender age, and it was from her that he received a mandate that touched him deeply and marked his musical career: "You will elevate popular songs like these great [musicians] do."[49]

Armando made his debut as a violinist in the Centro Qosqo when he was seven years old, and in Lima when he was nine, with his own compositions. His family nurtured his artistic talent, and, starting in his teenage years he moved between Cuzco and Lima, where he also received individual musical training from teachers such as Bronislaw Mitman, Pablo Chávez Aguilar, Rodolfo Holzman, and Virginio Lagui, among others (Pinilla 1988, 176; Escalante 1995, 361).

The early death of his mother when Armando was fifteen left a strong mark on him and led him to dedicate himself even more to composing musical works comparable to those of the European classical tradition but incorporating the Andean spirit. This kind of effort had been under way among cuzqueño musicians since the early twentieth century and had given rise to a nationalist music with strong highland roots. For Guevara Ochoa and other specialists, however, these musical works lacked the complexity required to attain recognition the world over. This conviction, which was the driving force in the work of Guevara Ochoa, led him into a series of confrontations, some of which were even with his cuzqueño teachers.

The contest organized by the IAAC in 1944 was one of the times Guevara Ochoa was forced to argue in public with his teachers Roberto Ojeda and Juan de Dios Aguirre. The contest was limited to three areas: music, literature, and painting. Perhaps it only focused on these three fields because that same year folkloric music and dance had already been represented in a regional contest organized in honor of Cuzco Day and Cuzco Week (see below). Under "music," the rules specified that only natives or residents of Cuzco could submit works "within any of the following genres: symphony, poem, valet [*sic*], suite, hymn, yaraví, dance, etc."[50] However, the works submitted by Guevara Ochoa could not be judged properly due to "the difficulties in their performance . . . particularly those written for an orchestra, because Cuzco does not have the required instruments and also due to the shortage of time."[51]

As a result of these and other "irregularities" regarding the decision taken in the music contest, in which the first prize went to Roberto Ojeda, his teacher, Armando Guevara sent letters of protest to the major newspapers of Cuzco.[52] These letters discussed the details of the contest, but what is worth stressing here is the call Guevara Ochoa made for Cuzco music to overcome the lack of musical technique and knowledge, which he believed were major limitations that prevented it from being appreciated throughout the world. One of the letters reads:

> I am not aware that the above cited doctors [Humberto Vidal, Rafael Yépez, Juan de Dios Aguirre, and Horacio Villanueva], friends I sincerely respect and appreciate, have followed any studies whatsoever in any musical academy, institute, or conservatory in order to become acquainted with all the rules that are required by the position of a musical composition examining jury. To judge a composition one must be deeply familiar with the rules of composing, which means having studied harmony, counterpoint, musical form (*forma musical*), instrumentation, etc., etc. . . .
>
> If we are to discard the technical part of our music, as Doctor Vidal says, how are we to enrich said music and do something to help it attain a privileged place?? What steps have we taken in so many years of labor with the same old monotony, a harmonic base so overused. With this alone we can do almost nothing. All peoples have their popular songs, but besides this they have a grand musical genre.[53]

Guevara Ochoa's desire to help cuzqueño music, and Andean music in general, develop until it reached the same standards as those of foreign works valued for their technical quality has been a constant issue throughout his life. But this composer is remarkable precisely because, despite the techniques he used, his work always remained close to the Andean traditions that inspired his love for this music at a very early age. Guevara Ochoa told me that when he was twelve or thirteen years old in Lima and his teachers imposed on him the use of "Western technique," he "rebelled" and, for instance, used in his compositions the syncope and dissonance he had perceived as essential in these traditions.[54] In his work, technique and the respect for Andean musical traditions have always gone hand in hand.

It was perhaps due to these confrontations, and/or to a growing desire to have Cuzco's musical production nourished or inspired by classical Western music, that the Asociación Orquestal Cuzco was formed in the city the year after the contest under the sponsorship of the IAAC and particularly of Humberto Vidal Unda. With his experience in obtaining subsidies for the IAAC, Vidal Unda, the first president of the Asociación Orquestal, used his influence among the cuzqueño political representatives in Lima to obtain a subsidy for this institution that lasted until 1959. The Asociación Orquestal Cuzco faded away when the subsidy was not renewed, but in its place there was the Escuela Regional de Música Leandro Alviña (Leandro Alviña Regional Music School), founded in 1951, which educated musicians in Western techniques in a far more formal way. The Orquestal intended to popularize the "musical riches" of Cuzco as well as the "creation of world[-renowned] artists" (Vidal de Milla 1982, 18). Armando Guevara Ochoa participated in the inaugural concert of this institution as a violinist and composer.

In the mid-1940s, Guevara Ochoa began to distance himself from his homeland, though not from its music, and he spent several years in Boston and then New York. In both places he earned part of his living by playing the violin and continued his studies, always with private teachers, among whom figured one of Russian nationality whose last name was Slaminski. According to Guevara Ochoa, this teacher persuaded him to focus on composing. The achievements of Guevara Ochoa include not just his five hundred compositions (which include dozens of symphonic pieces, chamber music pieces, folkloric pieces, and military marches, among others) but also having had them performed in London, Paris, Moscow, Beijing, Madrid, Mexico City, and Caracas, among other major cities. The performance of one of his works at Carnegie Hall in New York City when he was twenty-two was a particular highlight.

Throughout his life Guevara Ochoa periodically returned to Lima and Cuzco. He conducted the National Symphonic Orchestra in Lima and headed the Escuela Regional de Música in Cuzco.[55] In 1999, when he returned to Cuzco to settle down, the Instituto Nacional de Cultura, the highest governmental institution in cultural affairs, named him a "Living National Cultural Patrimony." Since then he has had a permanent position in this institution from which he promotes musical activities in Cuzco.

A formal musical education in the techniques and repertoires of so-called Western (mostly European and North American) music was still rare among cuzqueño musicians at the time when Armando Guevara Ochoa already shone as a composer and interpreter (this changed somewhat with the establishment of the Escuela Regional de Música in 1951). This was perhaps reflected in the first and only contest the IAAC ever organized (in 1947) exclusively for music. Only two compositions were submitted to this contest, which stipulated that the musical compositions must be "written and harmonized for the piano"[56] and submitted in three copies, one of which would be sent to the Conservatorio Nacional de Música.[57] One of the two pieces, a "suite" entitled "Corpus del Cuzco," composed by Baltazar Zegarra, received one of two second prizes, while the other was declared ineligible. A first prize was not awarded, "as the musical works presented are not of sufficient quality to make them worthy of such a distinction."[58]

This somewhat frustrated attempt to "elevate" cuzqueño musical compositions to the standards of erudite Western music, as well as the establishment of the Asociación Orquestal Cuzco, may be considered a partial response to the call Guevara Ochoa made because of the misunderstandings caused by the music contest the IAAC had organized in 1944. The type of musical production that Guevara Ochoa wanted, which is still being called for by cuzqueño musicians, has been minimal in comparison with the vast musical output—not so erudite and of a more self-educated type—that increased within the context of performances for tourists and as part of the regional folklore contests that became increasingly popular. Since 1944 the most propitious context for the organization of this type of contest has been the celebrations held for Cuzco Day and Cuzco Week.

CUZCO DAY AND CUZCO WEEK: THE FORMALIZATION OF SPACES FOR FOLKLORIC ART

It was in the midst of the promotional enthusiasm of the IAAC, and particularly thanks to the proposals made by the indefatigable activist of cuzqueñismo Humberto Vidal Unda, that Cuzco Day was established in 1944 and Cuzco Week the following year. To describe here all the elements that came together to establish these celebratory events, and the different types of impact the activities they comprised had on the consolidation of cuzqueñismo, would be very ambitious indeed. I have discussed several of these aspects elsewhere (Mendoza 2000, chap. 2; 2001, chap. 2), as have other scholars (Tamayo Herrera 1981, 172–75; Vidal de Milla 1982, 26–63; Aparicio 1994; De la Cadena 2000, 152–76). I will therefore concentrate on those that will help us see how these occasions from the beginning became—and still are—the major official spaces wherein folklore performances are held both on the stages and throughout the streets of Cuzco.

The establishment of these festivals can be understood as the culmination of a gradual process of crystallization of cuzqueñismo that had been taking place since the early twentieth century, with the key presence of artistic-folkloric production. A regional identity, as well as proposals for national and American identities, had been developing in Cuzco, with the participation of artists from its various rural and urban sectors and through theater (Incaic or costumbrista), music, and dance, that endeavored to place this region in the forefront of national and international attention. As noted, this feeling had been definitely encouraged for several decades by the idea that Cuzco should become a sort of Mecca of international tourism. Both processes—the prolific artistic-folkloric activities that promised a successful celebration at the level of public forms of expression and the great promise of tourism as a burgeoning activity in Cuzco—were among the most significant factors that came together at this time to encourage individuals such as Vidal Unda, as well as other contemporary artists and intellectuals, to organize these festivals.

Although at first the idea was just to establish a one-day celebration of Cuzco, in December 1944 it was decided, following a suggestion made by the president of the Republic himself, and with his official (legislative and financial) support, to establish Cuzco Week the following year, from June 24 to July 1.[59] The former date had been proposed and defended by Vidal Unda against others, such as the birth date of Garcilaso de la Vega and Túpac Amaru and the Spanish foundation of the city of Cuzco. The reasons he gave that won the day were as follows:

> First, because on that date the Incas celebrated the great festival of Inti Raimi as that day corresponds to the winter solstice, that is, an astronomical event celebrated all over the world.
>
> Second, because this is the day of a popular celebration [the feast of Saint John], and we are told that a resolution taken by an Indigenista Congress decreed that this no longer is the Day of the Indian, which has been set for April 12.

Third, because among the classical dates available, none is more suitable to attract tourism and hold festivities because on those days it does not rain and it is close to the Corpus Christi festival.[60]

These practical reasons for celebrating Cuzco Day on that date, as well as the more general reasons Vidal Unda gave to justify the need for establishing the festival, makes it evident that for him it was essential to choose a ritual that could be of interest and/or meaningful not just for the region but for all of Peru and the world. The most obvious and direct approach was therefore to evoke the glorious Inca past, which was something that could be clearly recognized at those levels. Vidal Unda wrote, "The Inti Raymi festival could easily become one of the major festivals in the world, like the Holy Week of Seville, [or] the Carnival of Venice. These feasts give life to those townspeople. . . . The government itself should provide us with facilities: landing runways, paved roads. . . . New industries derived from tourism could be born" (Vidal de Milla 1982, 33).

Although extolling the Inca past may seem to contradict the neo-Indianist ideology and practice advocated by Vidal Unda and other intellectuals and artists, it is not so if we bear in mind that Vidal Unda decided to promote this Inca representation for economic and practical reasons. The reasons he gave for the establishment of the festivals were first all of an "emotional" kind meant to "stimulate and strengthen the cuzqueñista feeling." They were also of a historical, political, and ideological nature so as to argue again that Cuzco should be considered the "fountainhead of Peruvianness." Finally came the economic and practical considerations, as the festivals would provide new opportunities for the development of industry, farming, livestock, and art and above all would make tourism "a main source of revenue in Cuzco."[61]

Vidal Unda obviously resorted to a ritual from the Inca past in order to draw national and international attention to Cuzco, but he did so as part of his efforts to make the cuzqueños value their contemporary society and culture—and see them valued by others, too—and attain an economic development not just through their traditional economic resources but also realizing their future economic potential, particularly through tourism. His economic, practical, political, historical, and emotional intentions came together in the following statement, presented in the first assembly held to organize Cuzco Day:

> It is not a question of just adding one more day to the civic calendar, to have it go by with popular indifference, reduced to just a few official events. We need to carry out a true spiritual revolution in the children of Cuzco in particular and of the country in general in regards to the meaning of our land. It is sad to have to admit—but it must be said—that a large group of young people have forgotten their land, and worse, many are even ashamed of being cuzqueños. . . . The foreigners who visit this land never forget it. But we, cuzqueños, Peruvians, are perhaps those who have most forgotten it. A day must therefore be devoted to the memory of our land, to extol its values and explain and learn its deep significance among us. . . . That day all cuzqueños must gather and cast aside their resentments, to prepare the general plan of its progress and establish its needs.[62]

With his many years of experience promoting cultural activities that would inspire cuzqueñismo, this intellectual and self-taught artist used the burgeoning folkloric art as an important way to enhance these festivals. As I have pointed out elsewhere (Mendoza 2000, 63; 2001, 102), Vidal Unda was the major promoter of having folkloric groups from outside the city of Cuzco participate in the contests and several other events that were held during the first and subsequent celebrations of Cuzco Day and Cuzco Week.[63] The participation of this type of group in the artistic circles of the city, and in general of artists of peasant and popular urban origin, was strongly encouraged by Vidal Unda when he organized *La Hora del Charango,* as well as in the contests organized by the IAAC. Although the participation of these folklore groups in the celebrations held for Cuzco Day played a major role from the beginning, their participation became even more important in the second year, when Cuzco Week was established (see figs. 12 and 13).

The staging of the Inti Raymi ritual was meant for the consumption of foreign and Peruvian tourists from the beginning, and its importance increased with time. This does not mean that this symbolic act was of no significance, nor that it had no impact on the people of Cuzco, for throughout time the ritual inspired many efforts and gave rise to debates regarding the elements it should contain to make it a more accurate depiction of the Inca past.[64] Nor does it mean that the ritual did not produce a hierarchical image, for it clearly evoked the submissiveness of all the inhabitants of the empire to the sun, the supreme god, and the Inca, the sun's representative on earth (Mendoza 2000, 64; 2001, 104).

I discovered the significance of these two aspects in 1990 when I was at a meeting held to make the depiction even more faithful to the historical past, as well as to increase its significance for the people of Cuzco. It was clear then that the progressive cuzqueño intellectuals and artists who wanted to have the Inti Raymi more attuned to the cuzqueños of all social classes, not just an idealized depiction of a despotic empire essentially meant for tourists, could see quite obvious contradictions (Mendoza 2000, 64; 2001, 104). The contradictions were perhaps similar to the ones faced by the neo-Indianists who established the ritual.[65] There is no denying that the symbolic power of the idealized Inca past that places Cuzco in the forefront of Peruvian and international attention still greatly influences how cuzqueños depict their society and culture. Even so, no analysis can be made of the meaning the Cuzco Day and the Cuzco Week celebrations have for the cuzqueños, and the role of folklore in them, based only on an incomplete assessment of the Inti Raymi or on the speeches delivered in official ceremonies.[66]

In December 1944, the performance of so-called "folkloric" or "traditional" (*típicos*) groups from Cuzco and the other provinces was scheduled for the twenty-second. That night, these same groups held what was called a Gran Función de Arte Peruano (Gala Performance of Peruvian Art) in the Teatro Municipal.[67] The following day they held a Gran Verbena Popular (Great Evening Festival) in the main square, which included plays, fireworks, and bonfires.[68] On the twenty-fourth, the central day of the celebrations, the groups had two major performances. One was a parade in front of the grandstand, "playing the best numbers of their repertoire" immediately after the Inti Raymi was over (a "performance of an evocative nature"), and the other was during the "popular feasts" (*diversiones populares*) in the place where a farming, livestock, and industrial exhibition was being held.[69] The next day, which was the last of the festival, the groups performed in another nocturnal, open-air celebration on the premises of the farming and livestock exhibition.

It was during the first Inti Raymi, while the folklore groups were performing, that tragedy struck Pancho Gómez Negrón. Thanks to his wide recognition, his performance in this first Inti Raymi was much anticipated by the cuzqueños (Valencia Espinoza 1994). Unfortunately it caused the accident that left him in poor health and eventually led to his demise.

Artistic-folkloric activities had an even more important place in the program of the second year. Artists from several parts of Cuzco and Puno performed on the twenty-fourth immediately after the Inti Raymi, and at night they also played in the *verbena* (evening festival) held in the main square. "Vernacular art concerts" were alternately held in the Cine Colón and the Teatro Municipal on the twenty-fifth and for eight more consecutive nights; these events culminated with a special ceremony in which prizes were presented to the winners of the contest organized by the committee.[70] The folklore groups participated in several other public events, such as a *verbena y baile popular* (evening festival and popular dance) at the Santa Clara Central Market, which was organized by the Market Workers' Union on July 30, and in another event held that same night in the main square of Cuzco, which was "attended by a large public."[71]

The vernacular art concerts were part of a contest held during Cuzco Week. It was at this contest that what is now known as the "second" anthem of Cuzco was first heard, that is, the huayno *Valicha* (Calvo 2002).[72] This huayno, composed by Miguel Ángel Hurtado, a native of Acopía (in Acomayo), recounts in Quechua the love of a country woman, Valicha, who goes to the city to work in the chicherías and becomes a mestiza. The song to Valicha thus epitomizes in many ways, as Calvo admits, the ideal of the cholo or chola and the mestizo or mestiza defended by the neo-Indianists (2002, 17). The "official" anthem of Cuzco had been inaugurated on the first Cuzco Day. The lyrics, written by the poet Luis Nieto Miranda, and the music, by Roberto Ojeda Campana, had won their respective contests sponsored by the Comité Pro-Celebración del Día del Cuzco (Committee for the Celebration of Cuzco Day).

After plans for the establishment of Cuzco Day were under way in the IAAC, the responsibility for its organization and financing was transferred to the committee, albeit with members of the IAAC still actively participating. Formed initially with forty-four members—"heads of cultural, sports, workers, and social institutions of Cuzco such as the archbishop, the mayor, the head of the Supreme Court, etc." (Vidal Unda 1945, 8), practical considerations reduced its leadership to a seven-man Executive Committee presided over by the prefect (governor) of the Department of Cuzco, with Humberto Vidal Unda as secretary.

Since the first celebration of Cuzco Day, which was attended by President Manuel Prado, who had been invited by the committee, this festival has become a time when a series of cultural, civic, and political events are held in addition to the artistic-folkloric ones. Special radio programs, gala performances, circus and cinema shows, military and school parades, sporting events, and inaugurations of important buildings (such as the opening of the tourist hotel El Cuadro in 1944) and public works, among other activities, have been held since the first years when Cuzco Day and Cuzco Week were celebrated.

A couple of months after the second Cuzco Day, an institution was officially established that gathered several self-taught artists from inside and outside Cuzco in an attempt to attain a prominent place within the city's burgeoning artistic-folkloric scene. This new institution took advantage of the support provided by the IAAC, as well as the gap left by the almost defunct Centro Qosqo. It included members from both institutions in key management positions, in part to validate its artistic activities in the eyes of cuzqueños, Peruvians, and tourists. This was the Asociación Folklórica Kosko (Kosko Folklore Association), which in 1951 officially inherited the name Centro Qosqo, which it would strengthen and eventually turn into the premier folklore institution of Cuzco.

THE ASOCIACIÓN FOLKLÓRICA KOSKO: AN EFFORT FROM BELOW

With no background decorations, with no curtains or stage for their performance, in this presentation the costumed dance groups (*comparsas*) and the song duets, as well as the collective dances, were expressed successfully, with good taste, love, [and] identification with the scenes and feelings that were being presented and stylized. . . . *The group has improved so much that it awakens in the spectator that indescribable emotion that stirs the heart and shakes the innermost corners of the soul.* EL SOL, EMPHASIS ADDED

In 1945 a group of self-taught musicians, dancers, and actors in the city of Cuzco, some more experienced than others, took advantage of the existing resources in the regional artistic-folkloric milieu and decided to "establish an institution of a cultural and artistic nature that would group all practitioners and followers of native music in order to improve and coordinate vernacular art in Cuzco," which they called the Asociación Folklórica Kosko (AFK).[73] Several sources recall that the Centro Qosqo was "completely dormant" at the time and in the city's art scene there was no institution with the scope and characteristics the Centro had possessed a few years before.[74] It was then that the efforts for, and the leadership in, staging and styling the artistic practices that could be considered folklore were undertaken by individuals who were not intellectually, socially, or artistically recognized in the urban milieu but felt called on to spearhead the development of this art.[75]

One of the artists who headed this group was the experienced Manuel Pillco, who had already gained recognition in the art circles of the city of Cuzco. He included in the institution his eldest son, Reynaldo Pillco Oquendo, age eleven, who was a violinist and would in time become one of the most important conductors of the Centro Qosqo's orchestra; years later he conducted the first album recordings of the Centro.[76] This kinship between members of the group was not uncommon in the Asociación Folklórica and other associations, and so we find that in its early years it included the brothers Simón and Evaristo Tupa, Ricardo and Francisco Flórez, and Florencio and Manuel Ichillumpa.

The Flórez brothers, both self-taught quena players (Francisco also had some acting experience), had been participating for more than a decade in the art circles of the city of Cuzco in several venues (contests, stage performances, radio programs, and family parties) (see fig. 10). Their artistic activities obviously did not provide them with significant financial support. Francisco was a "part-time worker" while Ricardo was a manual laborer at the University of Cuzco.[77] Being a worker or an artisan was not uncommon among the self-taught musicians of the time. For instance, the Ichillumpa brothers (both of whom were quena players) earned their living making hats in the neighboring district of San Sebastián.[78]

Neither was it uncommon for "popular" musicians in this period to be church musicians at one point or another in their careers (Pilco Paz 2005). Manuel Pillco began as a church musician and remained so until his death, in addition to his job as a pyrotechnician. His latter activity was recognized in the same year that the asociación was established, when he was given a diploma during the celebration of the first Cuzco Week.[79] Cosme Licuona, a respected chapel master and organist in the parish of San Sebastián, as well as a connoisseur of popular music (yaravíes, huaynos, marineras, etc.), was another founder of the AFK.[80] Like he did with Manuel Pillco, Licuona taught other popular musicians through church music. Such was the case of Fidel Zanabria (1911–2003), a native of Lucre (in the province of Quispicanchis) and another founding member of the AFK who worked for a time as the organist at the Jesuit church in the city of Cuzco but left this position due to financial problems and worked for several decades in a textile factory.[81] Another founding member of the AFK was Zenón Usca, the church organist in the neighboring district of San Jerónimo, who for several years had been participating in the artistic life of Cuzco city through the contests as a member of a theater, music, and dance group formed in that district.

Among the musicians who have contributed most to the development of both lay and religious music, special reference must be made to one of the most outstanding musicians, and one of the few still alive, master Ricardo Castro Pinto (b. 1906), a singer and organist and nowadays the chapel master of the Cuzco Cathedral. According to Pilco Paz (2005), Castro Pinto began his career in music through the church. He was in charge of maintaining order in the cathedral when he was ten as a verger and then joined its children's choir (188). While a teenager, Castro Pinto was in charge of ringing the church bells and became a tailor's apprentice (184). He gradually developed as an organist and eventually became one of the most important popular and church musicians in Cuzco. Castro Pinto was one of the founders and leaders of the AFK.

Not all of the artists who joined the AFK in its early years were musicians, dancers, or actors with experience in the artistic circles of the city. Such was the case of the quena player Evaristo Tupa (1928–2006) who in 1946—he was eighteen at the time—was invited by Manuel Pillco to join the association, which his brother Simón had already joined. Born and raised in the peasant community of Chocco, district of Santiago, Cuzco province, Señor Evaristo gave me the following account of his introduction into the musical circles of Cuzco city:

> I played on my own—I come from the countryside, [which] is not too far away. . . . I grazed my sheep, and I grabbed my small quena and played just like that—I liked to play like that. My brother played the *pampapiano* and he was already being hired to play at parties and festivals; he took me [with him], and I already knew how to play a little, so I just went with him, played with him [at] his engagements. And then it happened that Señor Manuel Pillco had his group. . . . I don't know where he saw me, he heard about me . . . [then he said] come with me to this and that engagement. . . . So I must have surely done something [right] there. . . . He took me to the Centro Qosqo [AFK] in 1946. Then I went . . . from that day to the present.[82]

Don Evaristo also said that he was unable to make a living playing music even though he played every now and then at social events, so he was forced to seek another occupation in the city of Cuzco and would "just have to learn another craft."[83] So he became interested in photography. On settling in Cuzco he lived for four years in the house of Manuel Pillco, and it was thanks to this friendship that he made the required contacts to become an assistant to a photographer. Señor Pillco was acquainted with several photographers in Cuzco, perhaps thanks to his friendship with Martín Chambi, and he placed Evaristo first the helper of a man called González and finally a helper in the Chambi studio (in 1957), where he worked until his death. Evaristo Tupa was a member of the Centro Qosqo's ensemble until the moment of his sudden death in 2006.

The case of Evaristo Tupa is not unique. There is, for instance, the case of Reynaldo Baca Cuba (1930), who also joined this group in 1946 without having had any real experience in the city's art circles. According to Señor Baca's account, it was almost by chance that he joined the AFK one day when he was sixteen. He had gone as usual to escort his elder sister Carmen (or Carmela), who participated in the activities of the association. She had been a member of the group from the beginning. The AFK did not have enough male members for the dances they were going to perform, and Baca Cuba was asked to join "at least as a filler" (Baca n.d., 1).[84] His onstage performance was perfect in every way, and so he was asked to join the group, which he did, and he stayed as a dancer until 1960. From that date on he has remained a member of the ensemble or music department of the Centro Qosqo as a guitar player and has even served as its conductor (1).

Like Carmela Baca, the women who joined the Asociación did so as dancers and singers. Although in the first half of the twentieth century some women from the well-to-do sectors of Cuzco did practice music, for instance, by playing the piano, as did the mother of Armando Guevara Ochoa, it was strange to see a woman acting in public as a musician or playing an instrument.[85] This had not changed dramatically by the late twentieth century or the early twenty-first. Even so, the participation of women in folklore groups was essential if this art was to develop properly from the moment when the Misión Peruana de Arte Incaico was first established, for songs and dances were and still are key elements in it. Along with Carmela Baca, Hilda and Fulvia Carbajal, Ubaldina Delgado, Lola and Luisa Tupayachi, Jesús

Gonzáles, and Graciela Alfaro joined the AFK in its early days and several more came as the group evolved.[86]

When the group of popular musicians decided to establish itself as an asociación folklórica, it sought the protection, support, and sponsorship of the Instituto Americano de Arte, on whose premises the Asociación was founded. At its first official meeting or assembly, which was presided over by Humberto Vidal Unda, the photographer Martín Chambi was named president while Vidal Unda himself, Dr. Domingo Velasco Astete, and the industrialist Carlos de Luchi Lomellini were named honorary presidents. The first three were members of the IAAC, while the latter obviously was a major figure in the social and economic world of Cuzco. This tactic of naming patrons or giving out honorary positions was also used by the members of the AFK in art, and from their very first year they invited Roberto Ojeda, Baltazar Zegarra, and Juan de Dios Aguirre, perhaps the three most renowned musicians in the Cuzco musical circles, to act as musical "consultants," while José Luis Ramírez, Manuel Pillco, and Ricardo Castro Pinto were appointed as directors. According to Reynaldo Pillco, this institution was established by several amateur musicians who then invited musicians such as Ojeda, Zegarra, and Aguirre "to honor the group."[87] The final tactic used was to request the participation of "protecting members" who were either intellectuals or individuals with social standing in the city of Cuzco, several of whom had already been members of the Centro Qosqo and/or members of the IAAC (e.g., Rafael Aguilar, Luis Felipe Paredes, José Ignacio Ferro, and Luis A. Pardo).

The drive and organization in these early years came, however, from the self-taught artists and others, most of whom had not yet received artistic or social recognition in the city, although they gradually would.[88] For instance, in these early years Julio Benavente Díaz joined the group, and his participation helped him to ultimately shine not just in the region, but also throughout the country. This musician, as well as several others in the AFK—many of whom were at that time the best-known artists in Cuzco (Manuel Pillco, Roberto Ojeda, Baltazar Zegarra, and Andrés Alencastre among them)—also joined another institution at one time or another (some for only brief periods), the Conjunto Folklórico de la Corporación Nacional de Turismo.

This "divisionism"—this is what they called it—notwithstanding, the AFK persisted, using the premises of the IAAC until 1949 and then moving to its own premises, which, though rented and modest, did give it greater institutional autonomy. That same year the AFK made a successful tour of Arequipa and began to stage regular performances for tourists, as well as in several major civic and religious events in the city of Cuzco.[89] Slowly, renowned artists with more formal training in their art and more affluent economic positions (e.g., Roberto Ojeda, Andrés Alencastre, and Antonio Alfaro), as well as up-and-coming ones who were self-taught and came from popular sectors (e.g., Evaristo Tupa, Fidel Zanabria, and Ricardo Castro Pinto), drew ever closer in the artistic activities of the city through the AFK.

The repertoire that this institution included in its various performances in Cuzco and Arequipa had a marked continuity with that which had coalesced in the Centro Qosqo around 1935. Although these artists were still creating new pieces that tried to partially reconstruct customs or festivals in places distant from the city of Cuzco, were modifying or elaborating popular choreographies or musical pieces from the department, or were simply composing new huaynos and yaravíes, the predominant characteristics in these performances may be placed in the three classifications I suggested in chapter 3 (Mendoza 1998; 2000, chap. 2; 2001, chap. 2) and were of course permeated by the sentimental themes of nostalgia and love for one's beloved or land or birthplace. The warlike and aggressive spirit of the past that still survives, particularly in some provinces distant from the city of Cuzco; the bucolic and lethargic yet at the same time industrious lives led by contemporary peasants and their Inca ancestors; and the festive and licentious spirit that bursts out during celebrations, particularly those of a carnivalesque kind—these were themes that abounded in the pieces performed by the AFK.

For instance, it was around this time that Ascensión de la Sota, a member of the AFK, choreographed *wayna chura* (a dance that exalts the bravery of the *Qorilazo*—see chapter 3) and, along with Lizardo Pérez, choreographed *Elmicha* and *phallchay* (both dances that depict courting among the young, particularly during Carnival). Finally, it was also during the early years of the AFK that Julio Benavente staged his "cuadro vivo costumbrista" (living costumbrista tableau)[90] called *las hilanderas* (spinning women), which had characteristics similar to Roberto Ojeda's *awajkuna.* All of these pieces were often included in the programs of the AFK, side by side with some that had become classic numbers since the time of the misión, for example, the *danza de la flecha* (*wachi'j tusuy*), *Kosko piris, los llameros, k'achampa,* and *awajkuna.*

After the devastating earthquake of 1950, when the Conjunto de la Corporación de Turismo ceased to exist, the members of the AFK decided to "write the birth certificate" of their institution, which amounted to giving it a legal existence (Castro Pinto 1999). It was in this context that someone came up with the idea of merging this rising institution with the dormant Centro Qosqo.[91] In a general assembly held on the premises of the AFK, its president officially asked the members of the Centro Qosqo to merge the institutions as the latter was "in an indefinite recess."[92] The document sealing the merger was read and approved at this meeting. It reads as follows.

> The following, former members of the Centro Ccoscco de Arte Nativo, hereby give our all-encompassing powers to the leaders of the Conjunto de Arte Folklórico Ccoscco [AFK], so that, given the total lack of activities of the former entity for several years, it [the latter] may take the name of the former and reorganize it according to its bylaws. Which is to say that with the Centro Ccoscco de Arte Nativo—an institution officially recognized by Ministerial Decree (Resolución Ministerial) No. 149 of 17 November 1933—dissolved, said name will be taken by the Conjunto Ccoscco [AFK] along with all of the prerogatives and rights provided by the official recognition.[93]

This assembly formed a reorganizing commission that included Andrés Alencastre, Andrés Zamora, Crizólogo Carazas, and Lizardo Pérez.[94] The new board of the reinvigorated institution took office in January of 1952, and in June it staged the drama *Ollantay* on the occasion of Cuzco Week. The Centro Qosqo began staging the Inti Raymi the following year and would do so on many occasions up to the present day.[95]

The Centro Qosqo was rejuvenated immediately after the earthquake, when Cuzco became even more clearly a center of tourism for foreigners. From this moment on, the institution made the shows staged for tourists one of its most important activities. The support given to the development of tourism, both by local sources and the state, evidently increased with the reconstruction of the city after the earthquake. As was noted in depth in chapter 3, not only was the promise of tourism present in the contemporary regionalist and nationalist projects, but institutional measures had also been taken—some of them by the state—to make Cuzco the most important Peruvian tourist center. This was shown by the establishment of the Corporación Nacional de Turismo and its departmental office in Cuzco in 1946, which then formed its own Conjunto Folklórico (Folklore Group).

THE CORPORATION'S ENSEMBLE: THE STATE, TOURISM, AND ARTISTIC-FOLKLORIC PRODUCTION

Although the creation of a folklore group in the newly established departmental office of the Corporación Nacional de Turismo was a local cuzqueño initiative, to a certain extent it can be claimed that this was the first instance of a folkloric group being organized and financed by a government entity. This support emerged because of Cuzco's promise as a major center of international tourism. Before the corporación was established, successive administrations had only shown a sporadic interest in tourism—for instance, when a Central Commission for Advertising and Tourism (Comisión Central de Propaganda y Turismo) was established for the Fourth Centennial in 1933 or when Giesecke was asked in 1936 to study the potential for international tourism in Peru—but this had not taken permanent shape at an institutional level. Until then, in international events where other nations discussed their touristic potential, the Peruvian government had relied on the Touring and Auto Club of Peru (Touring y Automóvil Club del Perú, Touring henceforth), an institution that was a branch of an international organization (the International Association of Recognized Auto Clubs). This institution represented Peru in the first South American Congress on tourism, which was held in 1928.[96]

My interest in briefly reviewing some aspects of the conjunto established by the Corporación Nacional de Turismo, Oficina de Cuzco (henceforth Corporación) is to illustrate how by the late 1940s tourism and folkloric-artistic activities were strongly connected in the city of Cuzco. This strong connection also marked the institutional life of the Centro Qosqo, the major organization of an artistic-folkloric nature, as well as other folklore institutions such as Danzas del Tawantinsuyo (Dances of Tahuantinsuyu), which was formed in the early 1960s due to a division within the Centro Qosqo. In the 1960s both institutions vied to catch the attention of the tourists and for recognition as the premier representative of Cuzco folkloric art. In the end (see the "Epilogue"), the Centro Qosqo remained the most respected folklore institution in the region.

Although a municipal office to help tourists visiting the region had been established in 1936 in response to many local requests, tourism as such required a more coordinated and regulated approach than this office could provide. We saw that the IAAC took over some of the tasks related to tourism, but this institution was in no way an entity devoted to its organization and promotion. So in Cuzco the Touring took over the administrative duties required by this activity, and in 1940 it established an office in Cuzco city under the direction of José Gabriel Cosio. A newspaper article published in Lima in which Cosio was interviewed noted that the flow of tourists to Cuzco was on the rise partly because at that tragic moment (during the Second World War) Europe was "closed to this type of activity."[97] In this interview Cosio pointed out that in 1940 about a thousand tourists (mostly from the United States and Argentina) had visited the archaeological sites in Cuzco.[98]

The Touring's delegation there, he claimed, had provided the tourists with "all [the] information and all the facilities" they needed, including "guides (*cicerones, guías*), carriers, and lodging."[99]

By 1946 there were many printed materials to guide the tourist on his or her visit to Cuzco. These materials, which were added to those developed in the 1920s (see chapter 3), included the "Guía del Cuzco para Turistas" (Tourists' Guide to Cuzco, 1941),[100] by Humberto Vidal Unda, and a detailed pamphlet prepared by the Touring (1946).[101] This guide emphasized the fact that, besides several hotels, Cuzco now had a tourist hotel that met international standards (the Hotel President Prado, inaugurated in 1944), with a capacity of 180 guests.[102] It was in this context, in which the provision of facilities for tourists visiting Cuzco was increasing, that the Peruvian government established the Corporación Nacional de Turismo in 1946.

In that year, the director of the newly established Corporación asked Albert Giesecke (who had in previous years helped the Touring in its task of promoting tourism in Peru) to act as its representative "in carrying out all the steps he deems useful and essential to the exchange of tourists between the United States and Peru."[103] In compliance with this task, Giesecke presented the following month a memorandum with his most pressing suggestions so that the Corporación could take advantage of the contacts he had established with the corresponding firms to stimulate the flow of tourists to Peru.[104] Shortly after presenting this document, the Corporación asked Giesecke to take an active role in the establishment of the tourist guide school in the city of Cuzco, as he was believed to be "in a position to make the correct assessment of the professional abilities of the representatives in that region" due to his close acquaintance with Cuzco.[105] Thus, right from the beginning Giesecke played a major role in the central organization of the Corporación in Lima, as well as in the departmental office in Cuzco.

One example of the important role Giesecke had in the Corporación is that he was named this institution's representative to the commission organizing the First National Congress on Tourism, an event that the Corporación itself was organizing.[106] The event was held in Lima in 1947, and in it a great variety of matters were discussed and decisions taken with regard not just to foreign but also to internal tourism. In the congress the Cuzco delegation included, among various petitions meant to improve the facilities for tourists in this region, that it be declared the "Capital Turística del Perú" (Tourist Capital of Peru).[107] The rise of Cuzco as a tourist center intensified with the approval of this request that same year, with the construction of the zigzag road that facilitated visiting Machu Picchu, and with the establishment of regular commercial flights to Cuzco (the last two events in 1948).

By early 1947—the year of the congress on tourism—the folklore section of the Corporación's Cuzco office had been established at the behest of Humberto Vidal Unda, with the activities of the Conjunto Folklórico in the forefront of its activities. This group, which paid those who participated in its artistic activities (this was new in Cuzco), attracted several members of the AFK at one time or another, particularly those who were already renowned in the artistic circles of Cuzco. The musicians and choreographers who joined this group at some point and had also been members of the AFK included Roberto Ojeda, Baltazar Zegarra, Julio Benavente, Manuel Pillco, Andrés Alencastre, Ricardo Castro Pinto, Lizardo Pérez, Ascensión de la Sota, and Antonio Alfaro.[108]

As head of the folklore section and the Corporación's Conjunto, Humberto Vidal Unda intended to turn both into formal centers for the collection of folklore materials throughout the region in order to disseminate these materials by staging them and thereby promoting tourism. The Corporación's folklore section was closely connected to the IAAC in various ways and continued the work carried out by the latter of collecting and recording on calendars and files information on festivals, music, and dances.[109] These materials, properly "refined" (*depurado*) and elaborated, would become the basis for the Conjunto's performances.[110]

A glance at the materials included in their programs and the *fichas coreo-*

gráficas (choreographic index cards) in the Conjunto's folklore archive shows that the parameters found in the design of the AFK's repertoire also structured the design of the Conjunto's performances. Many of the numbers performed by the former were also performed by the Corporación's Conjunto. For instance, we can see the recurring performance of classical numbers of the cuzqueño repertoire such as *awajkuna, k'achampa, danza de la flecha, pajonal chumvibilcano,* and *Inti Raymi.* The carnivalesque theme remained a key one; the *carnaval tinteño* was often performed by the Conjunto, as well as at carnivals from the neighboring department of Apurímac.[111]

New arrangements, or *captaciones* (in which local practices are imitated but re-created for the stage), show this continuity in numbers. Examples include the *chiaraje* or *c'iaraqhe* dance, a festive ritual activity enacted during Carnival that one of the folklore index cards collected by the Corporación's Conjunto described as "The battle between the various peoples of Canas, [in order] to prognosticate a good or bad year for their harvests, and it is at the same time a competition of physical strength."[112] This same card gives a detailed description of the attire the dancers had to wear, the choreography, and the main song that accompanied the dance.[113] The following is the description given of the choreography:

> *First Figure, First Movement.* The men come out of the back corners of the stage in a column, with an aggressive attitude. [They move at a] normal walking pace. Behind them the women enter the stage six a-side [six from each side], and finally the musicians appear playing the traditional pinkuyllu, and place themselves at the back of the stage.
>
> *Second Movement.* Two groups of men face one another and throw stones at each other with slingshots, to both the head and the feet. To avoid the stones they jump, moving their heads and bodies, while the women sing the following song. . . .
>
> *Second Figure, First Movement.* When the battle is over each side forms a circle, half of it formed by the women and the other one by the men, thus ending the dance and the tableaux.
>
> *Note.* One may fall during the combat and is immediately picked up and removed from the stage.[114]

The Conjunto had a short life span, just like the Corporación Nacional de Turismo itself, for both ceased operations after the 1950 earthquake. The

"Epilogue" shows that the task of reorganizing tourism in the region after the earthquake was taken over first by the Junta de Reconstrucción y Fomento (Reconstruction and Development Junta) and then by the Corporación de Reconstrucción y Fomento (Reconstruction and Development Corporation, CRYF). The Conjunto had performed not just for tourists and the local public in Cuzco but in Arequipa and Lima. Vidal Unda even wanted to give the Conjunto an international scope, alongside the development of tourism. In other words, the folkloric art of Cuzco would be *apreciado* (appreciated) above all as part of a package that promoted tourism in the region. Among other points, the "General Guidelines" of the Conjunto specified, "Since the objectives of the Corporación de Turismo include sending a theatrical company (*cuadro teatral*) to the main cities abroad in order to advertise tourism, the Conjunto Folklórico will primarily focus its efforts on ensuring [that] the group (*cuadro*) formed in Cuzco is chosen for this task due to its preparation and performance."[115]

In the late 1940s, the artistic-folkloric activities found a direct incentive in the growing interest in, and the presence of, foreign tourists in Cuzco. While the desire to consolidate the identity of Cuzco as Peru's tourist capital moved to the forefront, the efforts to make Peru and the rest of America find an inspiration for the consolidation of the national and continental identities in Cuzco's expressive culture took a backseat. The hope that Cuzco would have a prominent place on the national and international map rested increasingly on its future as a tourist center. This trend had existed in the region before the 1950 earthquake, but it was intensified by the tragedy. Although it cannot be conclusively stated that there is an intrinsic connection between producing art for tourism and the stagnation of creativeness and inspiration, it can be pointed out that the standards of the 1920s and mid-1940s seem to have become stagnant in the late 1940s with regard to the production of folklore in the institutions that promoted or presented it in the region.

This, of course, does not mean that artistic-folkloric production also stagnated outside this realm of representation. Quite the contrary—the definition of individual and group identities through dance, music, and drama was revitalized once the world of "folklore" had been validated as an artistic practice to be respected and admired rather than rejected or scorned. I hope to have shown here that the appraisal made of this space for folklore was a clear achievement of the creative effervescence that resulted from the fluid exchanges between artists and intellectuals from various social sectors of Cuzco. These cuzqueños generated—and joined in—common feelings and thoughts that coalesced in musical pieces, dances, and dramas they could clearly call their own: cuzqueño, Peruvian, and Hispanic American.

The parameters laid out in this period, which constantly surfaced in contests and staged performances, influenced the dominant ideas regarding what was to be considered indigenous or mestizo in Cuzco and what was traditionally (*típico*) cuzqueño. But the production that was already classified as folklore, and took place as part of religious or secular celebrations of various types held in Cuzco, always went beyond these parameters, giving rise to conflicts and making evident contradictions in the regional contests or festivities there. In these, it became possible, just as in 1927, for something new to be considered "traditional" or "genuinely" cuzqueño.

EPILOGUE *Who Will Represent What Is Our Own? Some Paradoxes of Andean Folklore Both Inside and Outside Peru*

> Faced with the outcry and unanimous protest of the people and representative institutions of Cuzco due to the *decision reached by the Casa de Cultura, to appoint a black group as the representative of Peruvian folklore in the world event in Mexico,* the decision is presumably going to be annulled and vernacular groups characteristic of our highlands will [instead] be appointed.
>
> This was stated by speakers for Corporación de Turismo del Peru (the Peru Tourism Corporation or COTURPERU) and the Casa de La Cultura, but the latter is still undecided.
>
> Several institutions in Lima that are devoted to genuine Peruvian folklore and vernacular art also joined in the protests that have broken out, not just in Cuzco but also in various parts of the country, since the Peruvian art groups were marginalized. . . .
>
> *If the mistake is rectified, then Cuzco will be [present] in the Mexican world event because if the participation of the black group is canceled, the only city with a priority would be the Archaeological Capital City of America.*
>
> "CUZCO DIRÍA PRESENTE EN MÉXICO," EMPHASIS ADDED

> The arrival of the Centro Qosqo to Lima was preceded by a huge display of publicity. . . . The prestige of the Santa Clara institution in its half century of existence, to which we must add its organization and performative quality, gave rise to this publicity. . . . *Tonight, our fellow countrymen* (paisanos) *will have the great responsibility of showing that Cuzco should have represented Peru in the Mexican Cultural Olympics.* EL COMERCIO, EMPHASIS ADDED

In the late 1960s, when the physical and cultural presence of Andean migrants in Lima had become undeniable (Matos Mar 1984; Cotler 1978), and when the music from highland provinces was increasingly inundating public spaces in Lima, as well as the recording industry and radio stations (Nuñez Rebaza and Lloréns 1981; Lloréns 1993; Romero 2002a), the cultural institutions and groups devoted to highland folkloric art were given a slap in the face. Their efforts to have the huayno and other Andean styles accepted as genuine representatives of the Peruvian majorities were once again cast aside in a most conclusive way when the Casa de la Cultura, the national institution in charge of cultural affairs at the time, decided to entrust a group called Teatro y Danzas Negros del Perú (Black Theatre and Dances from Peru) with the task of representing Peru.[1]

Despite protests against "Limeño centralism,"[2] this group, which was headed by Victoria Santa Cruz, who in time became a renowned practitioner of Afro-Peruvian art, went to Mexico as the Peruvian representative in the Cultural Olympics held at the same time as the Olympic Games in Mexico in 1968.[3] To the best of my knowledge, this Lima-based institution was the first the Peruvian government sent to an international event as a representative of the entire nation.[4] In 1923 the government had denied any kind of support to the Misión Peruana de Arte Incaico, and this effort had been undertaken thanks to the cooperation of the Argentinean Comisión Nacional de Bellas Artes and a group of Cuzco artists and intellectuals.

The proposals for a national identity that Cuzco artists and intellectuals had developed in their artistic-folkloric repertoire and performed with success in Lima and other departments, as well as abroad (in Argentina, Bolivia, Chile, and Uruguay), were not chosen as the ones that could best represent the entire nation. Although just a couple of months after the debate about who should represent Peru began a sudden change in the Peruvian government (with the military coup of General Juan Velasco Alvarado) and its cultural policies would endeavor to place the significance of Andean culture at the forefront of the public's attention, this did not change the fact that by this decade the criollo proposal for a national identity had been accepted by the most powerful social, political, and economic groups in Peru. In the 1950s these groups had chosen the coastal criollo tradition, and the Limeño one in particular—which idealized some aspects of the Afro-Peruvian population and incorporated some of its musical traditions—as most representative of the Peruvian people (Llorens 1983, 78–79). The government's promotion of "criollo [culture] as the popular-national [culture]" gradually increased, and during the Velasco regime criollo music was used in government publicity (80).[5]

A decade before the debates over the question of who would represent Peru in Mexico, the worldwide fame of a Peruvian singer who presented herself as an "Inca princess" without any governmental promotion had already raised another paradox for the cuzqueños regarding who had the right to represent the national and Andean traditions outside Peru. The art of this singer, who went under the name Ima Sumac—which was already quite esoteric and commercial in the 1950s—was acclaimed by the public in many different countries as representative of Andean traditions, the Inca in particular. Ima Sumac became a world famous exotic star by monopolizing the mystery and exoticism of the Inca past and the increasingly publicized archaeological site of Machu Picchu and by taking advantage, as noted by Limansky, of the fact that after the Second World War the North American and European public was in search of "distraction," "diversion," and "escapist entertainment" in general (2003, 3).

The accounts of the personal and artistic life of Zoila Augusta Emperatriz Chávarri del Castillo (Ima Sumac) are full of fantasies and sometimes contradictions.[6] Although it is known that she was born in Cajamarca and lived in Lima as a teenager, her exact place and date of birth (1924 or 1927) and the way in which her extraordinary talent was "discovered" are debatable. Strangely, besides the fact that both of us have the same first name, her life and mine crossed indirectly through my mother (whose first name is also Zoila and went by her maiden name of Beoutis), who was a schoolmate of this singer in Lima. I therefore have my own account of her "discovery" as a singer, which I heard for many years before I dreamed of writing this book.[7]

Even more important than this personal anecdote is to see how the artistic career of Ima Sumac intersected with those of the main characters in this book. In the 1940s, when her career was developing on Peruvian and Latin American stages and her repertoire was mostly formed by representative styles of Peru's Andean traditions, Ima Sumac and her manager and husband, Moisés Vivanco, became interested in three Cuzco artists who were prominent on the regional and national scene: Manuel Pillco (harpist), Augusto Navarro (who played the guitar and the harmonica at the same time), and Víctor Qawana (quena player). Ima Sumac and Vivanco asked these three artists first to go to Lima and then to accompany her on a tour of Mexico. This meeting, which, according to Reynaldo Pillco[8] took place in 1947, proved ill-fated because after playing together in Lima the quena player was run over by a car while Manuel Pillco was unable to travel because the

Mexican embassy denied a visa to his son Reynaldo, who was then a minor and had come with him to Lima. Manuel did not want to let his son return to Cuzco on his own and so decided not to go to Mexico.

Shortly after this, Vivanco and Ima Sumac, who were living in the United States, formed a permanent artistic troupe with which they traveled all over the world.[9] Her success had an ambiguous reception among Peru's Andean artists. Some were pleased that a Peruvian artist had attained such a high degree of recognition in the world, but others were dissatisfied with the type of art she was presenting and the image she sometimes projected of Peru's Andean people. In 1950 Ima Sumac left behind her previous image as an interpreter of Andean folklore and, dressed in "costly gowns and exotic Peruvian jewelry," she began to perform "quasi-operatic compositions of intricate vocal filigree often enhanced by bizarre impressions of nature" (Limansky 2003, 2–3).

When Ima Sumac and Vivanco (who were now U.S. citizens) and their artistic troupe returned to Peru for a tour in 1959, their visit was immersed in controversy. For some years José María Arguedas, a major government official in cultural affairs at the time, had harshly criticized the style and repertoire that Ima Sumac and Vivanco presented to the foreign public (Romero 2001, 98). When they visited Peru in 1959, it was probably in response to the critiques of Arguedas that Vivanco called him "plagiarist number one in Peru."[10] The artists also received a hostile reception by the Arequipa public. According to a Cuzco newspaper, on their arrival in Arequipa, "they whistled and hooted rejection because with her statements this renegade Peruvian [Ima Sumac] had often made her countrymen look savage and primitive; she may be admired for her art, but her unworthy attitude as a Peruvian can never be forgiven."[11]

Ima Sumac apparently did not have such a hostile reception in Cuzco, and the local press limited itself to reprinting articles or commenting on what had been written elsewhere. According to a statement made to the press, Ima Sumac's first visit to Cuzco with the "Vivanco Production Stars" (the name of the artistic troupe) was the result of her desire to "get acquainted with the historical Inca legacy of Cuzco expressed by its ruins as an homage to her former fatherland and as proof that, despite her new nationality, she is still a 'daughter of the sun' and of Inca ancestry."[12] After giving several performances in Cuzco, Ima Sumac left for Arequipa, where her experience was far from pleasant.

In the 1950s, while Ima Sumac was becoming famous throughout the world, the people of Cuzco were devoting themselves to the reconstruction of their capital city and to devising projects for the economic and social development not just of the city but of the whole region (Guillén 1982, 1). It was perhaps as a part of this reconstruction drive that the Centro Qosqo was rebuilt to become the most respected cultural institution promoting folklore to this day, even though in the 1960s it had been closely rivaled by the Danzas del Tawantinsuyo group, with which it competed neck to neck for the title of best representative of Cuzco folklore. The government scorned both of them, however, when the Peruvian delegation that was to be sent to Mexico was chosen in 1968.

Although Cuzco groups continued touring Peru and South America, and still received the attention and recognition of the public, the hope that Cuzco and/or highland art would be recognized as the national art slowly faded away due to events like the one recounted at the beginning of this epilogue. But at a regional level the stimulus provided by the growth of tourism and the state, particularly during the Velasco administration, consolidated and stimulated the practice of this activity at an institutional level—both private and governmental—and in the festive practices of all cuzqueños.

CHANGES AND CONTINUITIES: THE PLACE OF FOLKLORE IN CUZCO SINCE 1950

I have explained elsewhere (Mendoza 2000, 65–69; 2001, 104–11) that the earthquake of May 21, 1950, which destroyed or damaged most of the buildings in the city of Cuzco, accelerated several changes that were already taking place in the region and also added new dimensions to the perspectives developed by Cuzco intellectuals and artists regarding their proposals for a regional and national identity. While the state and international organizations took over the reconstruction and promotion of the region, migration from the countryside to the major cities and new areas of colonization in the lowlands, the pressure the peasantry exerted on the lands of the haciendas, the pauperization of rural areas, and the peasant unionist movements took on new force.

The United Nations and technicians from the United States actively participated, along with agencies created by the Peruvian government, in the reconstruction of Cuzco. In 1952 the Junta de Reconstrucción y Fomento (Reconstruction and Development Junta) was established, and in 1956 it became the Corporación de Reconstrucción y Fomento (Reconstruction and Development Corporation or CRYF). This institution attracted several intellectuals and artists from the city of Cuzco who were members of the Centro Qosqo and the IAAC, and its activities in the economic, cultural, and political life of the region continued up to 1972. The new nature of the city as a tourist and urban center surrounded by shantytowns took shape throughout the reconstruction. A major element of the new promotion of tourism was the renewed impulse given to artistic-folkloric activities.

At the same time that the increase in the number of foreign and Peruvian tourists flowing to Cuzco stabilized,[13] the Centro Qosqo, thanks to the efforts of the Asociación Folklórica Kosko, emerged as the major institution in the city that promoted folkloric art. Reorganized and revitalized, the Centro toured the southern Peruvian highlands in 1953 (see fig. 15) and in 1956, after many administrative proceedings undertaken by its members, the municipality of Cuzco granted it a plot of land on which to build its own premises. Although the building was not completed until 1973 due to the lack of resources and financial support, for the members of the Centro Qosqo this grant amounted to a major show of recognition. Desirous of being once more prominent and recognized in Peru and abroad, the performing troupe of Centro Qosqo toured Lima in 1958 and Chile in 1959.[14] Both tours were highly successful, but it is the latter that many of the old members of the Centro Qosqo fondly recall as they were considered cultural ambassadors of Peru and were allowed to visit the *Huáscar,* a Peruvian warship that was seized during the War of the Pacific (1879–83).[15]

As part of its renewed activities, in 1957 the Centro Qosqo revived a failed attempt the IAAC had made to sponsor a beauty and traditional dress contest and proposed it as part of the celebrations held in Cuzco Week.[16] The main inspiration came from the artist and choreographer Juan Bravo, who formed the Danzas del Tawantinsuyo group in 1961 along with other artists from the Centro Qosqo. The establishment of this group by members of the Centro Qosqo began a process that continued its development throughout the following decades. In this process, some members of the Centro Qosqo dropped out as active members in order to form other folklore institutions based in the city of Cuzco and their own folklore groups, which would compete for the attention of the local public and tourists in the region. Such was the case of the renowned folklore institutions of Cuzco called *Ricchariy*

15. Centro Qosqo before an artistic tour (Cuzco, 1950s). (PHOTO BY EVARISTO TUPA, EVARISTO TUPA PRIVATE ARCHIVE.)

Wayna (Wake Up Young Man) in 1972 and *Filigranas Peruanas* (Peruvian Filigree) in 1981. Some members joined these other groups only for a time and then returned to the Centro Qosqo.[17]

In 1961, after several misunderstandings and clashes over a tour of Mexico the Centro Qosqo had tried to arrange, some of its members established the Danzas del Tawantinsuyo. This group was successful in Peru and South America probably thanks to Raúl Montesinos, its main impresario; its choreographer, Juan Bravo; and its musical director, Ricardo Castro Pinto. It soon rivaled the Centro Qosqo for the position of best representative of cuzqueño and Peruvian art. For instance, thanks to its own efforts, in 1962 the Centro Qosqo took part in the first international folklore dance festival held in Santiago del Estero, Argentina, and the following year Danzas del Tawantinsuyo participated in the first Latin American folklore festival held in Manizales, Colombia, where it won first place. Danzas del Tawantinsuyo, which, according to many of the artists it included at the time, had begun a new style trend in Cuzco folklore in order to attract the attention of tourists and other publics, was particularly successful in the 1960s, but its regional and national significance declined in the following decade.[18] By then the practice and teaching of folklore had gained a new impulse under the sponsorship of the government of General Juan Velasco Alvarado, which began with a coup d'état in October 1968.

Although the "military revolution" of Velasco must be understood within the context of a long-term struggle to reform the Peruvian political system and transform the structures of dominant power, and even though its revolutionary effort "from the top down" failed in many respects (Rénique 1988, 212–307), it still represented a milestone in the presence of the highlands and Andean culture on the national scene (Turino 1991; Mendoza 2000, 68–72; Mendoza 2001, 109–15). The Velasco regime not only officially brought to an end the hacienda system in the countryside and promoted regional autonomy, at least theoretically, it also fostered its own program for the incorporation of folkloric music and dances in "a truly national integrated culture that fully assumes our multicultural reality" (Instituto Nacional de Cultura 1977, 7; 2001, 109–15). In his desire to establish "permanent channels of cultural interrelation" (Instituto Nacional de Cultura 1977, 3), Velasco used the educational system and the two most important institutions he created, the Sistema Nacional de Apoyo a la Movilización Social (National System of Support for Social Mobilization, or SINAMOS) and the Instituto Nacional de Cultura (National Institute of Culture), as replacements for the old Casa de la Cultura.[19]

On the other hand, once a series of regulations had been promulgated governing telecommunications, folkloric music, the Quechua language, and Andean music in particular began appearing on radio and TV programs from which they had previously been excluded. These regulations, Lloréns points out, "were no longer used" after the shift to the more conservative administration under General Morales Bermúdez (1975–80), and so Andean music lost ground in the "stations hostile to national music" (1983, 128). Even so, says Lloréns, "the [number of] radio programs for highland people from the provinces who were living in Lima continued growing throughout these years" (128) and the Andean presence expanded.

As noted elsewhere (Mendoza 2000, 71–72; 2001, 113–14), in Cuzco the major entities promoting folklore prior to the Velasco regime were private ones (with occasional and indirect government support), but the state began to have a more direct role during the military regime. Although the trend that led to the proliferation of folklore contests and performances in Cuzco had begun some decades earlier, and despite the fact that the municipality of Cuzco had established the Comisión Municipal de la Semana del Cuzco (as a replacement for the Comisión Organizadora de los Festejos del Cuzco) in 1967, just before the advent of the Velasco regime, thus giving a new impulse

16. The Centro Qosqo ensemble in 1971. (PRIVATE ARCHIVE OF THE PILLCO FAMILY.)

to the contests held on the occasion of the Inti Raymi, it is clear that the support the state gave to folklore had a major impact on the region and throughout Peru.[20] The support given by the government stimulated the establishment of new groups and folklore institutions, as well as of contests and performances in this genre that all kinds of Cuzco institutions (schools, ministries, unions, sports leagues, clubs, parishes, and so on) carried out.

The Velasco administration and the subsequent Morales Bermúdez regime also contributed to the development of Cuzco as a tourist and folklore center throughout the 1970s through international agreements favoring touristic infrastructure (the most significant of which was an agreement reached with UNESCO) and through creating favorable conditions for the investment of capital by the old cuzqueño landowners and others from Lima and abroad (see fig. 16). Although Cuzco was already being transformed into a tourist paradise in the 1960s, it was only in the following decade that tourism began to have a significant economic impact on the region and the capital city became a cosmopolitan center full of hotels and souvenir shops. Although the economic impact of this activity has never been easy to measure—according to some local scholars it has never reached its potential (Aguilar, Hinojosa, and Milla 1992; Guillén 1982; Lovón 1982)—the effect its development has had on the creation of a cuzqueño identity, as well as on the production and re-creation of ethnic and racial categories through artistic-folkloric production, does seem more straightforward.

In the early 1990s one could see in Cuzco that if the growth of tourism in the region and the government's promotion in the 1970s had had a significant effect on the consolidation of the feeling of pride cuzqueños had for their folklore and in the expansion of the spaces where it is practiced, what had crystallized in the late 1940s as the parameters with which to judge what was considered "traditionally" cuzqueño, be it "mestizo" or "indigenous," were still highly prominent. This does not mean that creativity had stagnated at the level of festive practices, that the repertoire had stopped expanding, or that the parameters had not been constantly questioned in various situations. But the criteria and repertoire the artists and intellectuals had developed in order to define what the cuzqueños, Peruvians, or perhaps other Americans could consider "their own" in the late 1940s were still being reinforced in contexts wherein certain specialists were called on to judge cuzqueño traditions.

OUR FOLKLORE IS WORTHY OF PRIDE AND ADMIRATION

This book had its inception in the late 1980s and early 1990s when I learned about the pride that Cuzco musicians and dancers took in their art, which they deemed folklore, be it in local festivities or on the stage. I likewise could not avoid noting that this field, which involves everyone from peasants in distant provinces to the city's major cultural institutions, was always a contentious and privileged space where cuzqueños defined social and ethnic/racial identities. I discovered, for instance, that the most popular dances among those that were believed to be traditional in Cuzco had in fact begun to appear as such in the 1970s after being questioned and provoking disputes in the regional contests organized on the occasion of Cuzco Week (Mendoza 2000, 77; 2000, 120–23). The so-called Paucartambo dances, which are considered to be "mestizo dances" throughout the region, were performed both by members of small, mostly Quechua-speaking peasant communities in their local festivals and in the regional pilgrimage to the shrine of the Lord of Qoyllurit'i, as well as daily by the Centro Qosqo in its shows for tourists.[21]

Another instance that showed how struggles for the creation and redefinition of identities in Cuzco are a constant within folklore, and which I met with when I was beginning my studies in the region, is the strong presence of music and dances from the Altiplano (the highland plateau shared by Bolivia and the Puno department) in Cuzco in the late 1980s, which I have studied in previous works (Mendoza 2000, chap. 6; 2001, chap. 6). The cuzqueños of younger generations identify themselves with these styles, and, although they do not deny the existence of "traditional" Cuzco dances, they find that these traditions have serious limitations. They identify instead with an Andean tradition they consider to be more "modern," urban, and cosmopolitan, one they have made their own.

The fact that so-called Altiplano music and dances were viewed this way by the young had a lot to do with the international prestige that a generic "Andean" style had already acquired. This style was born in the Bolivian tradition of urban folkloric music in the 1960s and 1970s and was first spread throughout Europe by Bolivian and Chilean musicians (Wara Céspedes 1984; Leitchman 1989). The latter had performed in Bolivian folklore *peñas* (nightclubs) on their way into exile (Wara Céspedes 1984, 228). This is why the style that was popularized in North American and European circles as "Andean" has a clear Bolivian imprint. Although the charango was accepted within the Cuzco urban tradition—*La Hora del Charango* had much to do with this—the fact that this instrument figures prominently in the Bolivian tradition reinforced the interest in it by younger generations of Cuzco musicians.

Faced with the popularity of Altiplano music and dances among the young and the fact that Peruvian and foreign tourists expect to hear the "Andean" music style in Cuzco—at least since the 1980s—cuzqueño artists have confronted a new set of contradictions and paradoxes, which deserve a detailed study. For me, one of the most interesting aspects of the debate regarding the so-called invasion of Altiplano music styles in Cuzco was the finding that the young dancers and musicians who were repressed in the name of the "cuzqueño tradition" defended their right to carry out their practices by defining them as folklore. In doing so they endowed these practices with a validity that is hard to deny even though this folklore is not cuzqueño alone but is shared with other Andean countries.

Although the field of folklore will remain contentious as long as it is being vitally re-created and renovated by the cuzqueños, it cannot be denied that this field acquired an unquestionable validity in the late 1950s thanks to the complex processes partially illustrated in this book. What I have also tried to show is that, unlike what other perspectives claim—including some of my own in the past—this field developed and became consolidated thanks to a complex and fluid interaction between artists and intellectuals from various urban and rural social sectors of Cuzco throughout the first half of the twentieth century. A repertoire and series of parameters that were meant to guide what was deemed representative of the cuzqueño—or Peruvian—identity, within both a mestizo and an indigenous tradition, also crystallized in this period. Although the categories *mestizo* and *indigenous,* as this book shows, are somewhat simple and problematic when one tries to place many cuzqueño artistic practices in convenient categories, they are still used in the region in various contexts, particularly in contests and staged performances. In my opinion, in the late 1950s the cuzqueños would widely accept a repertoire as their own or "traditional" (*típico*) not because it was the result of manipulation or was imposed by the indigenista or neo-Indianist intellectual and artistic elites but because it emerged from a complex process of exchange in the spaces discussed in this book.

After the 1950s, artistic-folkloric production, which had been closely connected in the city of Cuzco with the political proposals of a regional and national identity throughout the first half of the twentieth century, found itself increasingly removed from these projects and perhaps more dependent on the goal of having Cuzco firmly established as a tourist center. The desire to represent Peru endured in the artistic-folkloric activities of Cuzco in subsequent decades, as is shown by the offense taken by Cuzco artists when they were not chosen to represent Peru in Mexico in 1968. But perhaps the desire to present a tradition to a public composed of tourists consistently and schematically, along with the feeling that an opportunity had been lost vis-à-vis a state that did not recognize them as the fountainhead of national art, came together in the 1960s and caused the Cuzco intellectuals and artists to become concerned with reinforcing and somehow freezing the repertoire and parameters that had crystallized by then rather than allowing them to evolve. So it was that these parameters and the repertoire became canons that had to be reinforced by the cultural institutions in the city.

For me there are at least three major, interrelated reasons to revisit and try to understand the complexity of the process of intellectual, sentimental, and artistic creation that unfolded in Cuzco in the first half of the twentieth century, particularly in 1920–50. First, in this way we can learn a major lesson regarding the potential that Peru may still hold for the creation and promotion of spaces that enable a fluid exchange among artists, intellectuals, and politicians belonging to different social sectors in Peruvian society. This could prove useful for the development of political and social ideological proposals that include the voice or the feelings of more social sectors than those that are usually included in these proposals.

Second, examining the efforts by Cuzco's artists and intellectuals to place at the center of the nation the feelings and desires of the highland majorities —which had long been marginalized or silenced through various mechanisms—demonstrates their regional and national significance and at the same time defends them from the harsh and one-sided criticism they receive. Despite all the contradictions and paradoxes in the discourse and actions of the proposals of mestizaje made by some of the neo-Indianists mentioned in this book, we must not forget that these intellectuals and artists tried to place the indigenous culture at the center of an "Andean state" and so turn it into public culture at the historical moment when the "criollo state" did not include Andean culture in that space (Klarén 2001, 217). Among the positive results attained by the efforts of the neo-Indianists we have the validation and invigoration of a fruitful field of creative action that would be classified as "folklore." The neo-Indianists took this field as a source of inspiration for their social and political proposals at the national level at a time when these "folkloric" practices were marginalized and disdained by the socially and politically dominant groups in the region and the country.

Third, and perhaps as a more general and theoretical point, I would note that in understanding the complexity of the interaction between the cuzqueño artists and intellectuals, which gave rise to what we have come to know as indigenismo and neo-Indianism, we also realize that, as Williams suggested, the qualitative changes that took place from the 1920s to the 1950s cannot be considered the "epiphenomena" of institutional changes or "secondary evidence" of the changes that took place in the social and economic relations between or within classes (1977, 131). In order to understand the complexity of what was taking place in Cuzco society at the level of the proposals for a regional, national, and American identity, we need to get inside the social experience of the actors, to understand what they thought and how they felt when they were united in the common purpose of "creating our own."

...... *Notes*

INTRODUCTION: REVISITING INDIGENISMO

1. In the following text, the reader will notice that Cuzco is spelled in different ways. This is due to a great extent to the fact that the name was originally Quechua and there was no written language there prior to the Spanish colonization of Peru. In Quechua, the name has a guttural sound that is represented (depending on which system is adopted) with either a *q* or a double *c*, that is, *Qosqo* or *Ccoscco*. The Spaniards decided to use the name *Cuzco*, which is how it appears in the dictionaries of the Real Academia de la Lengua Española. Many of the contemporary inhabitants of Cuzco spell the name with an *s*, as *Cusco*, and I used this spelling in previous publications in English. The name also appears spelled with a *k* in some of the documents and texts I cite, so the reader will likewise find the form *Kosko*.
2. The volume edited by Gisela Cánepa Koch (2001) is a major effort in the reassessment currently under way within Peru's social sciences of the field commonly known as *folclor* or "traditional culture." In the introduction, Cánepa Koch provides a theoretical elaboration of the significance of the "performative approach."
3. For instance, Michael Herzfeld (1986) clearly illustrates how the work done by folklorists in the case of Greece proved crucial to the development of a Greek national identity, as it established the necessary connections between an idealized past and what began to be considered the continuity of this cultural heritage among members of the present-day peasant majority. As we shall see, although this type of effort is similar to those undertaken in the early twentieth century by some of Cuzco's indigenista intellectuals, this attitude cannot be extended to all who promoted folkloric practices.
4. I admit that I, too, made this mistaken assessment in previous studies (Mendoza 1998, 2000, 2001) and did not fully appreciate the complex nature of this phenomenon.
5. The term *captación* refers to a particular piece of music or dance choreography, a combination of dance choreography and music, or a combination of dance

choreography, music, and theatrical representation that is the result of an observation purportedly made by the author or authors, who in turn modify or stylize those forms in order to present them to a different audience. During the period I am discussing here, most often the observations were purportedly made in rural contexts in Cuzco and the *captaciones* were presented at events in Cuzco city and eventually in Lima and other countries. From the perspective of those who created captaciones, the observed forms had no known authors or were the product of communal ancestral practices. Therefore, they were just called folklore.

6. As in previous studies, I use the definition of *class* presented by Bourdieu (1987), who claims that classes are correlative and shaped by various kinds of power relations. Social classes are historically defined not only by their members' possession of similar economic capital but also similar cultural (or "informational") capital, social capital ("which consists of resources based on connections and group membership"), and symbolic capital ("which is the form the different types of capital take once they are perceived and recognized as legitimate") (4).
7. De la Cadena's study tries to approach the world of artistic-folkloric production from this perspective, considering it to be a result of manipulation and stylization carried out by artistic and intellectual elites. This study also makes the mistake of viewing these artistic activities as mere reflections of the political, economic, or social aspects of the time that ensnared the indigenista and the neo-Indianists in social and racial hierarchies. This causes the author, whose work is so insightful in other respects, to lose sight of the significance of artistic-folkloric practice in shaping and creating the indigenista and neo-Indianist proposals and ultimately in transforming the cuzqueño society of their time. Although I do not deny that rigid social hierarchies and racism were a part of the everyday experience of many cuzqueños, I concur with those scholars who believe that the greatest limitation of this study is that it overemphasizes the extent to which both cuzqueño society and the indigenista or neo-Indianist efforts of the early twentieth century were dominated by those elements and racism in particular. De la Cadena thus loses sight of the achievements of these movements as well as the complexity of the dilemmas their representatives had to face (Krüggeler 1999; Klaren 2001).

   A new and innovative study was published as the Spanish edition of this book went to press, which analyzes different local and foreign discourses on Cuzco between 1900 and 1935 (López Lenci 2004). López Lenci's book pays more attention to the cuzqueño artistic-folkloric field from the perspective of discourse analysis than do previous studies of indigenismo and neo-Indianism.
8. As noted elsewhere (Mendoza 2000, 2001), the glorified memory of the Incas had already been used in Peruvian history with different goals in mind, including an attempt by landed elites in the seventeenth and eighteenth centuries to establish their legitimacy through the visual arts (Mannheim 1991, 73).

9. The text is quoted in Aparicio 1994, 134–35.
10. The term *criollo* was originally used in the Latin American colonial period to name the people of Spanish descent born in the colonies. This term has, since approximately the end of the nineteenth century, applied to a repertoire of popular music and dance genres identified with coastal culture that later became nationally popular.

1. THE MISIÓN PERUANA DE ARTE INCAICO

1. It is worth recalling that in Cuzco Quechua drama was highly developed, particularly in the colonial period, and it is possible that it has endured since that time (Itier 1995, 16).
2. Of Itier's (2000) four stages in the history of Incaic theater, "The first extends from a waiting period in the 1870s to the creation of the first modern dramas in the 1890s and 1900s; the second comprises the period 1913–16, when we find a strong increase in the number of theatrical performances in the city of Cuzco; during the third period, from 1917 to 1921, many cuzqueño theatrical companies toured outside the region, in Puno and Bolivia, as well as Arequipa, Lima, and other cities in Peru, northern Chile, and Ecuador, thus turning Incaic drama into a national and even pan-Andean phenomenon; [finally,] from 1922 on, the Incaic theater retreated to the Cuzco region and was no longer perceived as avant-garde drama. It was then abandoned by the local and national intellectual elites and became a part of popular culture, enduring in the provinces of the department of Cuzco until about 1960" (10–11).
3. Itier (2000) points out that "a large popular public, probably mostly monolingual, attended the performances. Quechua dramatic performances were probably the only space in Cuzco at the time where people from different social strata could share the same cultural and intellectual experience, and they therefore represented one of the few venues in which the presence of a national community, over and above the ethnic and cultural differences separating the different groups in everyday life, was evident" (37).
4. I would like to thank César Itier for the information he provided in June 2005 regarding this and other points in connection with the drama *Ollantay*, about which he expects to write soon.
5. An interesting debate took place in the Cuzco newspaper *El Comercio* in 1939–41. See, for example, "*Ollantay* en Buenos Aires," *El Comercio* (Cuzco), October 31, 1939, 1; "*Ollantay* en Buenos Aires: Al Señor Pancho Fierro, Atentamente," *El Comercio* (Cuzco), November 24, 1939, 2; "Notas Sobre el '*Ollantay*' de Ricardo Rojas," *El Comercio* (Cuzco), January 1, 1940, 1; "Los Dramas Quechuas el *Ollantay*," *El Comercio* (Cuzco), July 28, 1940, sec. 2, 1; and a series of articles by José Gabriel Cossío entitled "Otra vez el Drama '*Ollantay*' en el tapete de la discusión," *El Comercio* (Cuzco), November 26, 1941, 1; November 28, 1941, 1; December 2, 1941, 1; December 4, 1941, 1; December 5, 1941, 1.

6. A recording of this theme is included on the Pillco family's compact disc (CD) *Violins from the Andes*, as well as in the *Música del Qosqo* cassette collection (see the discography in this volume).
7. For instance, Pío W. Olivera, Calixto Pacheco, and others remained anonymous (Ojeda 1987, 11).
8. Harawi was one of the most widespread genres in the pre-Columbian Andean world and still survives in some rural areas of Peru (See chap. 2) where performances retain a close connection to specific vital contexts (Romero 1988: 243).
9. As Romero explains, when Andean music began to be studied in the early twentieth century it was common for "contemporary Andean culture to be considered a direct extension of Inca culture, devoid of any changes or transformations, as well as for Andean music to be deemed a homogeneous entity, with no local or regional variations" (1988, 223).
10. Ojeda (1987) notes that in 1959, following an initiative of the newspaper *El Sol*, "and with the support of representative institutions, it was agreed to name Francisco Gonzáles Gamarra, Juan de Dios Aguirre, Baltazar Zegarra, and Roberto Ojeda the Big Four of Cuzco Music (Los Cuatro Grandes de la Música Cuzqueña)" (53).
11. This hymn is one of the key musical themes in the Inti Raymi, the most important present-day cuzqueñista ritual, which is discussed in chapter 5. A recording of this theme is included on Centro Qosqo's album *Qosqo Llaqta*, as well as in the *Música del Qosqo* cassette collection (see the discography).
12. For a detailed discussion of the characteristics of traditional Andean music, see Romero 1988, 223–55.
13. For a discussion of this subject, see Ojeda 1987, 49, 59.
14. Itier (2000, 75) also points this out. His fourth stage would have begun in 1922 and extended to about 1960, by which time it existed only in the provinces of the department of Cuzco (2000, 11). By 1930 or 1940, the so-called *comedia costumbrista*, which denounced *gamonalismo*, had to a great extent displaced the Incaic theater (27).
15. See "El Teatro Incaico," *El Comercio* (Lima), reproduced in *El Comercio* (Cuzco) September 5, 1924, 2.
16. See, for instance, the use of these terms in articles in the Buenos Aires press reproduced in "La Compañía Incaica en Buenos Aires: Debutó con Éxito," *El Comercio* (Cuzco), November 24, 1923, 5; and "La Compañía Incaica en Buenos Aires," December 5, 1923, 2.
17. "El Teatro Incaico," *El Comercio* (Cuzco), September 5, 1923, 2, reproduced from *El Comercio* (Lima).
18. "El Teatro Incaico," *El Comercio* (Cuzco), September 5, 1923, 2.
19. Although in the early twentieth century in Argentina there were some defenders of the indigenista conception of nationhood, as well as a large peasant popula-

tion representative of an indigenous tradition, most of the intellectuals who supported the Argentinean state's nation-building project supported the idea that the country was fully white (Chamosa 2004).

20. "La Compañía Incaica en Buenos Aires: Debutó con Éxito," *El Comercio* (Cuzco), November 24, 1923, 5.
21. Ibid.
22. Although the misión did not go to Chile, its performance in Buenos Aires was discussed in a Chilean magazine.
23. "La Compañía Incaica en Buenos Aires: Debutó con Éxito," *El Comercio* (Cuzco), November 24, 5.
24. A recording of this composition is included on Centro Qosqo's album *Qosqo Llaqta*, as well as in the cassette collection *Música del Qosqo* (see the discography).
25. "La Misión Peruana de Arte Incaico Juzgada por Chile," an excerpt from the magazine *Zig Zag* (Santiago de Chile) reproduced in *El Comercio* (Cuzco), April 5, 1924, 4.
26. A recording of this piece is included in the cassette collection *Música del Qosqo* (see the discography).
27. Pablo, his son, notes that his favorite instrument was the violin (Ojeda 1987, 68).
28. As I have explained elsewhere (Mendoza 2000, 150; 2001, 226), the huayno (also spelled *wayño, wayñu,* or *wayno*) is one of the most important song and dance genres in Peru (particularly in the highlands) and other Andean countries. The styles vary, but the huayno usually ranges between a binary and a tertiary rhythm with a 2/4 or 4/4 time. A classic study of the Cuzco huayno is Roel Pineda 1956. Recorded examples appear in all of the sources included in the discography.
29. *Urpi*, or "dove," is the most common metaphor a man uses in the Quechua language to describe the woman he loves.
30. See the complete lyrics from which these stanzas were taken in Oróz 1999, 13; Elizabeth Mamani Kjuro translated them from Quechua to Spanish.
31. Itier 2000, 75, citing the memoirs of Luis Valcárcel.
32. "La Compañía Incaica en Buenos Aires" (*El Comercio* [Cuzco], November 15, 1923, 3) reproduces a note published in *El Diario* (Buenos Aires) on October 27. "Compañía Peruana de Arte Incaico" (*El Comercio* [Cuzco], October 2, 1923, 2) reproduces an article published in *El Tiempo* (Lima).
33. "La Compañía Incaica en Buenos Aires" (*El Comercio* [Cuzco], November 15, 1923, 3), reproduced from *El Diario* (Buenos Aires).
34. "La Compañía Incaica en Buenos Aires: Debutó con Éxito," *El Comercio* (Cuzco), November 15, 1923, 3.
35. Pillco, who is briefly mentioned below, is extensively discussed in chapter 2.
36. "La Compañía Incaica en Buenos Aires: Debutó con Éxito" (*El Comercio* [Cuzco], November 24, 1923, 5) reproduces an article originally published in *La Nación*

(Buenos Aires). It is also possible that there were piano performances, either solo or accompanied by the choir.

37. See the various examples of this style in the recordings of the Centro Qosqo listed in the discography.
38. "La Compañía Incaica en Buenos Aires," *El Comercio* (Cuzco), December 5, 1923, 2, reproducing an article from *La Nación* (Buenos Aires).
39. For the complete lyrics and a translation into Spanish, see Montoya, Montoya, and Montoya 1987, 332–33.
40. The music of this dance, as performed by a typical orchestra of the Centro Qosqo, is included on the CD *Qosqo Takiyninchis* (see discography).
41. See "Compañía Peruana de Arte Incaico," *El Comercio* (Cuzco), October 2, 1923, 2, which reproduces an article published in *El Tiempo* (Lima). See also "La Compañía Incaica en Buenos Aires," *El Comercio* (Cuzco), November 15, 1923, 3.
42. "La Compañía Incaica en Buenos Aires" (*El Comercio* [Cuzco], December 5, 1923, 2) reproducing an article published in *La Nación* (Buenos Aires).
43. *El Comercio* (Cuzco), November 24, 1924, 5, reprinted from *La Nación* (Buenos Aires).

2. CULTURAL INSTITUTIONS AND CONTESTS

1. See Mendoza 2000, chap. 2; 2001, chap. 2.
2. As was explained in the previous chapter, most of these individuals belonged to the middle and upper classes of the city of Cuzco (in some cases they had not been born in the department), had secondary or university educations, had formal musical or artistic training, and were under a cosmopolitan influence (which means they were acquainted with the classical and contemporary repertoires that had spread from Europe and the United States and probably knew how to read and write music).
3. Pillco Familia n.d., 1. This text was prepared by the family for its use in the liner notes of the CD *Familia Pillco: Violins from the Andes,* TUMI United Kingdom, 2001.
4. Although I was not personally acquainted with Manuel Pillco, the recording his grandson and another cuzqueño musician—Darwin Del Carpio—made in 1990 in Spanish clearly shows that Quechua's phonetics and grammatical structure pervaded his use of Spanish, which was often combined with Quechua words.
5. Zoila Mendoza, interview with Reynaldo Pillco, Cuzco, July 1996.
6. Pillco Familia n.d., 1.
7. In order to appreciate Pillco's special style one should listen to the two harp solos he played on two of the recordings listed in the discography. These pieces are "En mi pobreza" (composed by Pillco himself) on the album *Sacsayhuaman* and "Melodías en Arpa" on the album *Danzas del Tawantinsuyo.*
8. On the yaraví in Peru, see Romero 1988, 245–46; Estenssoro 1989, 30–37; Raygada 1936; Pagaza Galdo 1961; and Pilco Paz 2000, 2002.

9. Nowadays the harawi can be described, as Romero (2002b) does, as "a genre of monophonic singing that consists of a musical phrase repeated several times with melismatic passages and long *glissandos*" (39), and the yaraví as "a soft lyrical genre of mestizo song with a ternary rhythm and a binary form" (43). Examples of yaravíes are included in most of the recordings listed in the discography, but I recommend listening to those performed by the Pillco family.
10. See Pilco Paz 2000, 2002.
11. Manuel Pillco, interview with Enrique Pilco and Darwin del Carpio, 1990.
12. In the 1990 interview with Enrique Pilco and Darwin del Carpio, Manuel Pillco pointed out that he established an organization to play for the Señor de los Temblores on Easter Monday, for Saint Matthew and the Virgin of Bethlehem. He presumably established the first of these institutions in 1938–40.
13. See Pilco Paz 2000, 2002; Olsen 1986–87; and Romero 1998.
14. See Pilco Paz 2002. It is possible that for the performance of his church music Manuel Pillco, like other musicians, also used a modified harp with a longer and triangular body (see figs. 1 and 14). However, his grandson Enrique pointed out to me that perhaps the domingacha was the one his grandfather used most because it is the smallest and easiest to carry (Zoila Mendoza, interview with Enrique Pilco Paz, Seville, March 2002).
15. Zoila Mendoza, interview with Reynaldo Pillco, 2001.
16. Zoila Mendoza, interview with Reynaldo Pillco, Cuzco, July 1996.
17. Ibid.
18. Enrique spells his name with just one *l*, as Pilco. He is currently engaged in doctoral studies in France, where he is studying anthropology and the Andean tradition of church music.
19. Zoila Mendoza, interview with Enrique Pilco Paz, Seville, March 2002. After reading an earlier draft of this chapter, Enrique specified that he had not meant to say that no other harpist would ever attain a mastery equal to or greater than that of his grandfather. What he wanted to emphasize in the interview was the mastery of his grandfather. In the same interview he explained that what specifically caught his attention was the ability his grandfather had to make the left hand work independent of the right, thus complementing the work of the latter but without being subordinate to it. This, he noted, is something rarely found nowadays.
20. This piece, performed by Manuel Pillco himself, is included on the Centro Qosqo album *Saqsayhuamán*. A new version appears on the CD *Familia Pillco: Violins from the Andes*. Both are listed in the discography.
21. The Pillco family describes his participation in the liner notes to *Familia Pillco: Violins from the Andes;* and Pillco Familia n.d.
22. See "Compañía Peruana de Arte Incaico," *El Comercio* (Cuzco), October 2, 1923; and "La Compañía Incaica en Buenos Aires," *El Comercio* (Cuzco), November 15, 1923, 3.

23. "La Compañía Incaica en Buenos Aires: Debutó con Éxito," *El Comercio* (Cuzco), November 24, 1923, 5, reproduced from *La Nación* (Buenos Aires).
24. The biography of Humberto Vidal Unda, prepared by his sister Delia, also lists Max Galdo and Domingo Rado as two of the participants who met in the tearoom in order to establish the institution (Vidal de Milla 1982, 15).
25. Zoila Mendoza, interview with Reynaldo Pillco, Cuzco, July 2001.
26. See the reference to this title (*nombramiento*) in chapter 2.
27. "Formemos un Centro Musical," *El Comercio* (Cuzco), March 26, 1927, 2.
28. Ibid.

29. Vivanco (1973) points out the great support that the colony from Ancash in Lima gave to their department's delegation. The colony issued a flyer instructing its members to cheer the seventy-strong Ancash delegation, and the support given was apparently massive (36). Furthermore, Hector Beoutis says that his father, Alejandro Beoutis (a deceased great-uncle of mine), who hailed from the department of Junin and resided in Lima, was a major sponsor of the artistic delegations from the department that participated in the Amancaes festival, providing them with room and board while they stayed in Lima (Zoila Mendoza, interview with Héctor Beoutis, Lima, December 2002).
30. "La Fiesta de San Sebastián y Este Cronista," *El Comercio* (Cuzco), January 19, 1927, 2.
31. Ibid.
32. "Post-Scriptum Acerca de un Concurso de Música Nacional," *El Comercio* (Cuzco), July 13, 1927, 3. The five well-known Russian "authors" are the composers Balakirev, Rimsky-Korsakov, Cui, Mussorgsky, and Borodin.
33. One comment published in *La Nación* of Buenos Aires regarding the performance of the Misión Peruana commended "the work of art, of the Russians, for instance" and declared that it was now "the turn of musicians, painters, poets to do [the same]. Then the art of these nations will be a faithful expression of the American spirit" ("La Compañía Incaica en Buenos Aires: Como Fue la Función de Despedida," *El Comercio* [Cuzco], December 11, 1924, 2).
34. "A Favor de la Música Aborigen: Una Iniciativa Interesante Encaminada a Propiciar para Octubre Próximo un Certámen en el Que Intervengan todos los Músicos del Departamento, de Manera Especial, los Indígenas," *El Comercio* (Cuzco), September 16, 1927, 2.
35. The individuals who signed this call were Alejandro del Carpio, Roberto Ojeda, Antonio Alfaro, Julio Rouvirós, and Alberto Negrón.
36. "A favor de la Música Aborigen: Una Iniciativa Interesante Encaminada a Propiciar para Octubre Próximo un Certámen en el Que Intervengan todos los Músicos del Departamento, de Manera Especial, los Indígenas," *El Comercio* (Cuzco), September 16, 1927, 2.
37. "Comentarios de la Redacción: Certámen de Musica Incaica," *El Comercio* (Cuzco), September 17, 1927, 4.

38. "A Favor de la Música Aborigen: Una Iniciativa Interesante Encaminada a Propiciar para Octubre Próximo un Certámen en el Que Intervengan todos los Músicos del Departamento, de Manera Especial, los Indígenas," *El Comercio* (Cuzco), September 16, 1927, 2.
39. See Mendoza 1998; 2000, chap. 2; 2001, chap 2.
40. The genre known as marinera originated on the coast and already had this name in the late nineteenth century (Romero 1988). This music and dance tradition was becoming popular in the Andes by the early twentieth century. The marinera and the huayno gradually came together in the Andes in various combinations, of which the best known today is the marinera with a huayno fugue.
41. "Un Concurso de Música Autóctona: Bases Suscritas por el 'Centro Musical Cusco,'" *El Comercio* (Cuzco), September 23, 1927, 3.
42. See Lloréns 1983 on the spread of foreign genres in this period through new media such as the phonograph. See also the comment by Antonio Garland in "Post-scriptum Acerca de un Concurso de Música Tradicional," *El Comercio* (Cuzco), July 13, 1927, 3, regarding the perceived threat posed by the tango's popularity in Peru.
43. "A Favor de la Música Aborigen: Una Iniciativa Interesante Encaminada a Propiciar para Octubre Próximo un Certámen en el que Intervengan todos los Músicos del Departamento, De Manera Especial, Los Indígenas," *El Comercio* (Cuzco), September 16, 1927, 2.
44. "Un Concurso De Música Autóctona: Bases Suscritas por el 'Centro Musical Cusco,'" *El Comercio* (Cuzco), September 23, 1927, 3.
45. Ibid.
46. "La Audición de esta Noche: Interesante Concurso de Música Aborigen en Homenaje a la Fiesta de la Raza, Gran Éxito de la Bella Iniciativa del Centro Musical Cusco," *El Comercio* (Cuzco), October 14, 1927, 2.
47. The program described *ccori ñusta* as a "mestizo dance" (ibid.). Velasco Astete died in 1925.
48. The other members were Ricardo Flórez, J. Gamarra, O Saavedra, and E. Tapia (ibid.).
49. Ibid.
50. Ibid.
51. Ibid.
52. Ibid.
53. Ibid. Kashua is the same as qaswa.
54. Ibid.
55. "Arte Nativo: La Fiesta De Anoche En El Excelcior Música, Canto Y Danza Las más Dilectas Manifestaciones De La Sensibilidad Terrígena, Reseña Del Certámen y Comentarios," *El Comercio* (Cuzco), October 21, 1927, 5.
56. Ibid.
57. Ibid.

58. Guevara Ochoa is discussed in chapter 5.
59. Zoila Mendoza, interview with Armando Guevara Ochoa, Cuzco, December 2002.
60. "Arte Nativo: La Fiesta De Anoche En El Excelcior Música, Canto Y Danza Las más Dilectas Manifestaciones De La Sensibilidad Terrígena, Reseña Del Certámen y Comentarios," *El Comercio* (Cuzco), October 21, 1927, 5. The article points out that half of the proceeds from the show were to be used to build a maternity ward in the central hospital.
61. At this point Ricardo Flórez was not yet a famed musician, but the following year he was asked to go with the members of the Centro Musical to the contest at Amancaes.

62. "Arte Nativo: La Fiesta De Anoche En El Excelcior Música, Canto Y Danza Las más Dilectas Manifestaciones De La Sensibilidad Terrígena, Reseña Del Certámen y Comentarios," *El Comercio* (Cuzco), October 21, 1927, 5.
63. Ibid.
64. Ibid.
65. Ibid.
66. Versions of this composition are available on the CD *Qosqo Takiyninchis* and in the cassette collection *Música del Qosqo*, both of which are listed in the discography.
67. "Arte Nativo: La Fiesta De Anoche En El Excelcior Música, Canto Y Danza Las más Dilectas Manifestaciones De La Sensibilidad Terrígena, Reseña Del Certámen y Comentarios," *El Comercio* (Cuzco), October 21, 1927, 5.
68. Romero (2001) points out that until around 1940 the Andean musicians in Lima who played at Amancaes and in other places dressed themselves in the cuzqueño regional style that was considered Inca (95–96). Núñez and Lloréns (1981, 55), as well as Romero (2001, 93), note that Arguedas also wrote at the time that Andean music was called Inca music.
69. For instance, an editorial in *El Comercio* (Cuzco) pointed out that "among others we have the art mission headed by the musician Señor Ojeda and the stage director and choreography expert Señor Rouvirós, the same [group] that had achieved brilliant triumphs five years before in Buenos Aires and Montevideo" ("El Concurso de Baile i Música Nacional de Amancaes," *El Comercio* [Cuzco], June 20, 1928, 2).
70. One comment reads, "[The] far bigger cuzqueño [group] would have been unable to participate in the contest had there been specific and conclusive rules. Because its members, who have worked and rehearsed since 1923, the year they went to Buenos Aires, Montevideo, and La Paz, cannot pretend to be on par with the rest" (reproduced from an unidentified Lima newspaper in "Notas de Arte," *El Comercio* [Cuzco], August 11, 1928, 5).
71. The following individuals participated in both missions: Julio Rouvirós, Roberto Ojeda, Alejandro del Carpio, Guillermo Gallegos, Eduardo Polo, Pedro Campero, Luzmila Luna, Benigno Ttito, and Angélica Álvarez ("Misión Cuzqueña de Arte Incaico," *El Comercio* [Cuzco], August 25, 1928, 4).

72. The other participants who had not been members of the La Misión Peruana were Aída Medrano de Castillo, Francisco Luglio, Aniceto Villafuerte, Visitación Luna, Angélica León, Max Letona, J. F. Castillo, the boy Eleodoro Alfaro, and Andrés Izquierdo (ibid.).
73. A version of *pajonal chumbivilcano* is included in the cassette collection *Música del Qosqo*, which is listed in the discography.
74. The authorship of *Suray Surita* and *pariwana* is likewise disputed. See Ojeda 1987: 56. However, Roberto Ojeda called *pajonal chumbivilcano* one of "my compositions" in an interview given before the misión left for Lima to participate in the contest ("Artistas Cuzqueños en Lima," *El Comercio* [Cuzco], June 16, 1928, 4).
75. Rozas (1991) says of *pajonal* that "Alberto Negrón Romero (1989) is the one who created this wayno, which has spread throughout all of the southern Peruvian Andes. There are thus many instrumental and choral versions of it, and it is even considered 'folkloric' " (27).
76. "Alrededor del Certámen Artístico de Amancaes," *El Comercio* (Cuzco), July 11, 1928, 1.
77. Ibid.
78. In his biography of Policarpo Caballero, Esteban Ttupa (1988) cites an article from *La Crónica* (Lima) in which the terms *authentic gentlemen* and *authentic Indians* are used (20); this same article was reprinted in "Notas de Arte," *El Comercio* (Cuzco), August 11, 1928, 1.
79. Article published in *La Prensa* (Lima), reprinted in "Notas de Arte," *El Comercio* (Cuzco), August 11, 1928, 1. Rado can be seen in figure 9, where he is second from the left in the second row standing.
80. Recordings of this composition are included on *Violins from the Andes* and *Música del Qosqo*, both of which are listed in the discography.
81. "Alrededor del Certamen Artístico de Amancaes," *El Comercio* (Cuzco), July 11, 1928, 1.
82. This piece is included on *Violins from the Andes,* which is listed in the discography.
83. Zoila Mendoza, interview with Diómedes Oróz, Cuzco, July 1994.
84. Both events are discussed in chapter 3.
85. See Romero 2001, chap. 4. See my discussion of coliseos in chapter 3.

3. TOURISTIC CUZCO

The first epigraph to this chapter is from "Neoindianismo," *El Sol* (Cuzco), July 28, 1928, 3. The second epigraph is from "Cuzco La venerable," *El Comercio* (Cuzco), November 9, 1933, 4.

1. Valcárcel himself said he and García were great friends and collaborated in many projects but "fell [somewhat] apart" in the mid-1920s: "Around 1925 we regrettably fell apart. Uriel wanted to be the president of the university without having the support of most of the professors, including myself. In 1927 I published

Tempestad en los Andes [Storm in the Andes], and his book, *El Nuevo Indio* [The New Indian] came out afterward. Whereas I contended that there was only one Indian from antiquity to the present day, he spoke of the coming of a new Indian. Therefore, we found ourselves on opposite sides with respect to the way we conceived the Indian. In Cuzco they presented us, me as someone who preserved the ancient [and was] unable to see the new elements the Indian had appropriated as his own and Uriel Garcia as the promoter of the modern Indian" (1981, 210).

2. See the discussion of these issues in the introduction to this volume.

3. See Tamayo Herrera 1981, 112–13, for references to knowledge of the site prior to the "discovery."
4. The Archivo Albert Giesecke (Albert Giesecke Archive, AAG) holds several letters exchanged between Giesecke and Bingham regarding the archaeological explorations of the latter. When I consulted this archive it was in the safekeeping of the Centro de Estudios Rurales Andinos "Bartolomé de las Casas" in Cuzco, but it is now once again under the care of the Giesecke family in Lima. Some of the documents in this archive are numbered, but others are not, so I only give the document number in the former case.
5. The abundant and rich materials in the AAG should be a major source for many studies regarding the important connections Giesecke established between Cuzco and Lima, Cuzco and other countries, and Lima and other countries.
6. For more details on the manipulation of the information, see Mould de Pease 2000, 137–38; and Tamayo Herrera 1981, 112–15.
7. See Albert Giesecke, "Breves Apuntes de la Vida y Obra de Hiram Bingham," April 12, 1961, document in the AAG.
8. José Gabriel Cosio, "Una excursión a Machupiccho, ciudad antigua," *Revista Universitaria* 2 (September 1912): 2–22, quoted in Tamayo Herrera 1981, 114.
9. See Albert Giesecke, "Hiram Bingham y el hotel Machu Picchu," October 10, 1960, 2, document in the AAG.
10. Albert Giesecke, Letter to the "Señor Prefecto del Departamento del Cuzco y Presidente de la Comisión Oficial Especial para celebrar el cincuentenario del descubrimiento de Machu Picchu por Hiram Bingham," July 23, 1961, AAG.51.648, p. 3.
11. Ibid.
12. By then Giesecke had already held a position at Cornell University for two years (*Revista Universitaria* 1960, 24).
13. Thanks to a proposal made by cuzqueño intellectuals and politicians, Albert Giesecke was invested with honors by Congress in Lima, on December 18, 1951, for the many significant contributions he had made to Cuzco and Peru. A document entitled "Sesión Efectuada el 18 de diciembre de 1951: Condecoración del Doctor Alberto A. Giesecke," held in the AAG, is a transcription of the

speeches read at the ceremony. Quoted in the text is a speech delivered by the cuzqueño representative, Garrido Mendívil (p. 2).

14. Ibid., 3.
15. This plebiscite was to decide the geopolitical future of the Peruvian departments of Tacna and Arica which had been fought over during the recent war between Peru and Chile. Subsequently Tacna remained part of Peru and Arica became part of Chile.
16. This would be an interesting subject for an in-depth study, which the abundant documentation held by the AAG would allow.
17. Letter to the "Sr. Ministro de Relaciones Exteriores, Dr. don Alberto Ulloa Sotomayor," Miraflores, July 24, 1936, p. 1, enclosed with the report that Giesecke presented to the Minister of Foreign Affairs, AAG.
18. "Informe dirigido al Sr. Ministro de Relaciones Exteriores, Dr. don Alberto Ulloa Sotomayor," Lima, July 24, 1936, 30, AAG.
19. See law no. 7688, in Municipalidad del Cuzco 1990, 355; and "ley para la Celebración del Cuatricentenario del Cuzco," *El Comercio* (Cuzco), September 26, 1933, 2.
20. See "Una oficina de Turismo en el Municipio," *El Comercio* (Cuzco), January 28, 1935, 2, in which the establishment of this office is demanded; and "El Turismo en el Cuzco," *El Comercio* (Cuzco), April 4, 1936, which was written after the office was established.
21. Dirección General de Hacienda, signed Eleodoro Freyre, letter to "Señor Doctor Alberto A. Giesecke," March 6, 1934, AAG 47.596.
22. See ibid.; and "La Ley Para La Celebración del Cuatricentenario del Cuzco," *El Comercio* (Cuzco), September 26, 1933, 2.
23. Quoted in *El Comercio* (Cuzco), March 8, 1937, 2.
24. "La necesidad de Reglamentar el Turismo," *El Comercio* (Cuzco), February 18, 1937, 2.
25. See Corporación de Turismo del Perú, signed Benjamín Roca Muelle, president, letter to "Señor Doctor Alberto A, Giesecke," Lima, June 9, 1965, AAG.
26. See Centro Qosqo de Arte Nativo 1988, 1; and Oróz 1989, 1. The decree is dated November 7, 1933.
27. "Bases Para un Concurso Musical: Brillante Iniciativa del Centro Ccoscco," *El Comercio* (Cuzco), June 16, 1933, 1, 4.
28. Ibid.
29. Ibid.
30. "Un Concurso de Música Autóctona: Bases Suscritas por el 'Centro Musical Cusco,'" *El Comercio* (Cuzco), September 23, 1927, 3.
31. "Bases para un Concurso Musical: Brillante Iniciativa del Centro Ccoscco," *El Comercio* (Cuzco), June 16, 1933, 1, 4.
32. Ibid.

33. "Gran Concurso Musical," *El Sol* (Cuzco), January 28, 1931, 4.
34. "Un Concurso de Música Autóctona: Bases Suscritas Por El 'Centro Musical Cusco,'" *El Comercio* (Cuzco), September 23, 1927, 3.
35. "Bases Para Un Concurso Musical: Brillante Iniciativa del Centro Ccoscco," *El Comercio* (Cuzco), June 16, 1933, 1, 4.
36. See Mendoza 2000, chap. 4; and 2001, chap. 4, where I show through the study of the dance called *los majeños* in 1940 that the landowners were already interested in participating in *comparsas* (dance groups) during religious festivals.
37. "Bases Para Un Concurso Musical: Brillante Iniciativa del Centro Ccoscco," *El Comercio* (Cuzco), June 16, 1933, 1, 4.

38. See a passage cited by Itier (2000, 63) that criticizes a popular representation of the immolation of Cahuide in the fortress of Sacsayhuamán in 1924.
39. Itier gives the example of Zenón Usca, a church singer and humble resident of the district of San Jerónimo who wrote and staged plays with Inca themes, and the company and drama group (*compañía y un conjunto dramático*) formed by Ascensión Gallegos, which presumably reached Lima (1995, 40).
40. On the political processes that took place in the southern highlands in the twentieth century, see Rénique 1991.
41. *El Sol* (Cuzco), July 21, 1934, quoted in Itier 2000, 84. Itier does not give the title of the article or the page numbers.
42. *El Sol* (Cuzco), July 28, 1934, 1, quoted in De la Cadena 2000, 134. De la Cadena does not give the title of the article or the page numbers.
43. "La Ley Para La Celebración del Cuatricentenario del Cuzco," *El Comercio* (Cuzco), September 26, 1933, 2.
44. *El Sol* (Cuzco), June 10, 1934, quoted in Itier 2000, 84. Itier does not give the title of the article or the page numbers.
45. See "Orden de los premios del Certamen Nacional," *El Sol* (Cuzco), February 21, 1935, 3. According to this article, the Conjunto Acomayo ended up in fifth place in the category "Inca music" and was awarded for this a gold medal, a diploma, and one hundred dollars. Esteban Ttupa (1988, 20) also recorded these prizes. The article points out that the Centro Qosqo—no position is given—along with eight other groups from various parts of Peru, received a diploma, a gold medal, and fifty dollars. Just as in the Amancaes contests, this one included the category "criollo music."
46. Reproduced in "Actuación Artística," *El Sol* (Cuzco), February 20, 1935, 2. The document does not identify the minister by name.
47. Ibid.
48. Program, "Presentación del conjunto 'Centro Ccoscco de Arte Nativo,'" February 5, 1935. Document in the private archive of the Pillco family.
49. See the list of the members of the delegation in "Una Carta del Centro Ccoscco," *El Sol* (Cuzco), February 21, 1935, 3. The list only mentions nineteen individuals and does not include Manuel Pillco. Humberto Vidal Unda, the Centro's secre-

tary, notes in another article, however, that the delegation had twenty-four members. Bearing in mind a previous pattern, it is likely that the list published in the press does not include the members of the traditional ensemble that we know accompanied the group. Manuel Pillco was a member of the Centro Qosqo's traditional ensemble. The fact that Pillco kept the program of this performance in Lima in his personal archive is one more reason to believe that he went on the journey.

50. "Actuación Artística," *El Sol* (Cuzco), February 20, 1934, 2.
51. See the article on this performance in *El Sol* (Cuzco), July 21, 1934, quoted in Itier 2000, 84. Itier does not give the title of the article or the page numbers.
52. "Una Carta del Centro Qosqo," *El Sol* (Cuzco), February 21, 1935, 3.
53. "Una Carta del Centro Qosqo" (ibid.) mentions, for instance, the exclusion of Roberto Días Robles, "the famed cello player whom critics say is one of the best players of this instrument in Peru . . . ; Augusto Navarro, *rondinista* (a person who plays the harmonica), the only one who has managed to enter the Casino of Viña del Mar in Chile and has attained achievements that honor Cuzco; Domingo Rado, a renowned composer; Eduardo Zavaleta, a violinist with a good record in Amancaes itself in the capital city; Francisco Gómez Negrón; and others [who] have been replaced with young men who, although they have good intentions, are just being initiated into art in one sense or another."
54. Ibid.
55. Ibid.
56. Ibid.
57. Program, "Presentación del conjunto 'Centro Ccoscco de Arte Nativo,' " February 5, 1935. Document in the private archive of the Pillco family.
58. Ibid.
59. A recording of *wifala* is included in the *Música del Qosqo* collection, which is listed in the discography.
60. Recordings of this piece are included in *Violins from the Andes* and *Música del Qosqo*, which are listed in the discography.
61. This section in the yaraví follows one that reads, "The birds when they sing love warbles, how sad it is to wake up when one knows [he has awoken] to suffer. My lover you were yesterday, [and] now you've left me, knowing that for you I sacrificed my mother's love. Her heart I tore apart, evil woman how badly you've repaid me" (Oróz 1999, 45).
62. As Paúkar (1947) describes the *pariwana*, "The heron or marabou from my country is the *pariwana*, a beautiful bird that is a symbol of Peru [and] is snow white on the back and the wings and is of a red-blood [color] below these, as well as on the chest. It became an Indian totem in primitive times [and] a messenger of love. Beautiful Indian ladies confessed their sentimental problems to it, their joys and innermost sorrows. '*Pariwana*' is a plaintive and nostalgic song solo" (26).

63. Program, “Presentación del conjunto ‘Centro Ccoscco de Arte Nativo,’ ” February 5, 1935. Document in the private archive of the Pillco family.
64. Ibid.
65. Here are two stanzas from each of these popular huaynos. For the complete lyrics, see the text these passages were taken from, cited below.

Ingrata	Ingrate
Ingrata como pretendes abandonarme	Ungrateful [woman], how can you think of leaving me
Quieres quitarme la única flor de mi esperanza	You want to take away from me the only flower of my hope
Borraste con tu infamia mi fiel cariño	With your infamy you erased my faithful love
Cómo pretendes recuperar lo que has perdido . . .	How can you think of recovering what you have lost . . .
(Oróz 1999, 17)	
Picaflor	Hummingbird
Quisiera ser picaflor,	I would like to be a hummingbird
Y que tu fueras clavel;	And you a carnation
Para chuparte la miel,	To suck your honey
Del capullo de tu boca	From the bud of your mouth
Me miras, te ríes,	You look at me, you laugh
Pero no sabes ingrata,	But you don’t know, you ungrateful one
Que tengo otra mejor que tú . . .	I’ve got someone better than you
(Escobar and Escobar 1981, 487)	

In Quechua poetic language, the man is a hummingbird that approaches a woman to woo her.

66. Program, “Presentación del conjunto ‘Centro Ccoscco de Arte Nativo,’ ” February 5, 1935. Document in the private archive of the Pillco family.
67. A version of this theme is included on the compact disc *Qosqo Takiyninchis*, which is listed in the discography.
68. *Charki* or *ch’arki* is salted and dried meat (hence the English word *jerky*), and *chuño* is dried potato. Besides being widely eaten by the Andean people in general, both items are considered the typical fare of the traveling *llameros.*
69. Program, “Presentación del conjunto ‘Centro Ccoscco de Arte Nativo,’ ” February 5, 1935. Document in the private archive of the Pillco family.
70. The lyrics are quoted from Centro Qosqo de Arte Nativo 1960, 6, and were translated into Spanish by Elizabeth Mamani Kjuro. Another version of this huayno was collected and translated by Gabriel and Gloria Escobar (1981, 295).

4. *LA HORA DEL CHARANGO*

1. This passage is quoted from a personal document provided by Delia Vidal De Milla in which she recalls in a paraphrased way the words of Vidal Unda in the epigraph above. She prepared this document following a request made by Julio Benavente Díaz, who wanted information on *La Hora del Charango*. The document was signed by her on May 13, 1977, and is a part of the Archivo Privado Humberto Vidal Unda (APHVU).
2. See, for instance, the accounts of its significance in Aparicio 1994, 136–38; and Vidal de Milla 1982, 113.
3. A *chicheria*, to which Don Julio referred in the epigraph, is a kind of pub where Andean people drink the traditional fermented beverage called *chicha* (corn beer). Such places are mostly associated with the lower classes.
4. The montera, a flat hat that some peasants in Cuzco wear, connotes an Indian identity. It used to be worn by both men and women, but it nowadays is characteristic mostly of women.
5. *Maqt'a* is a Quechua term that literally means "young man." In the Cuzco context the term is often used as a synonym for *cholo* either in a demeaning way or simply to indicate an association with the Andean indigenous element.
6. The meaning of the mermaid figure in charango music is explained later.
7. I transcribed the lyrics from Julio Benavente Díaz's compact disc *Charango and Songs from Cuzco,* which is listed in the discography. Calvo (1999, 122) also transcribed this huayno with some variations. A recording of the piece is included on the CD.
8. For instance, the charango has a prominent place in the music of renowned groups such as Inti Illimani, which has appeared in Chile but primarily popularized Andean music in Europe. I will return to this kind of "Andean music" in the epilogue.
9. Testimony of Don Julio Benavente, taken from Calvo 1999, 117. Turino (1984) likewise believes that the first two of these reasons may have contributed to the preference shown for the small size of this instrument (255). As for the third reason given by Don Julio, during the last fifteen years, as I have explored the musical circles of Cuzco, I have heard similar comments made by charango players who claim that the size of the instrument had its origin in the ease with which it could be hidden from the Spaniards.
10. See Parejo 1988, 9; and Calvo 1999, 117, where Don Julio himself says the vihuela is the predecessor of the charango.
11. Alberto Yábar Palacio, "De Nuestro Ambiente: *La Hora del Charango*," *El Sol* (Cuzco), June 5, 1937. The photocopy of this article in the APHVU has no page numbers.
12. Edmundo Delgado Vivanco, December 29, 1936, manuscript composition in honor of the charango, document in the APHVU.

13. His full name was Pedro Francisco Gómez Negrón. His parents were Eleuterio Gómez Pimentel and Donata Negrón.
14. The information regarding his journeys to the last two countries is contradictory. On the one hand, Valencia Espinoza claims, using information provided by Gómez's daughter, that he had to turn down the invitations from Chile and Argentina because he was unable to travel (1994, 155). On the other hand, De la Cadena claims that he traveled all over South America and implies that he went to Chile—where he was presumably endorsed by the famed Chilean poet Gabriela Mistral—and Argentina, where the people "shed nostalgic tears when they remembered their gauchos, whom Francisco Gómez Negrón resembled" (2000, 148).
15. Valencia Espinoza points out that Gómez Negrón had to turn down an invitation to visit Mexico and tour the United States because he did not receive the financial support of any institution (1994, 155). Valencia Espinoza likewise claims that after the death of Gómez Negrón the Centro Qosqo organized a collection to help his widow, though the funds raised never reached her (160). Finally, De la Cadena cites a 1948 newspaper article that mentions a collection made by the people of Colquemarca—where Gómez Negrón was born—in order to help pay for his medicines (2000, 148).
16. On the "conquest of the dial" by Andean music throughout Peru, and in general for a study of the development of Andean and criollo music in Lima with regard to the mass media, see Lloréns 1983. For the golden age of Andean music recordings, with an emphasis on huanca music, see Romero 2001, 113–21; 2002.
17. Cuzco Day and the Cuzco Week were established in 1944 (see chapter 5).
18. See "De Arte: Recital de Música Neo-Indiana en el Municipal," *El Sol* (Cuzco), March 6, 1942, 4; "De Arte: Gómez Negrón Alcanzó Éxito en su Presentación en el Municipal," *El Sol* (Cuzco), March 9, 1942, 4; and "De Arte: Segundo Recital de Música Neo-Indiana," *El Sol* (Cuzco), March 26, 1942, 4.
19. "De Arte: Gómez Negrón Alcanzó Éxito en su Presentación en el Municipal," *El Sol* (Cuzco), March 9, 1942, 4, emphasis added.
20. *Mejoral* is the name of a common analgesic in Peru. Gómez Negrón is playing with this meaning and the verb *mejorar,* "to feel better."
21. Valencia Espinoza (1994, 158–59) transcribes and translates this huayno.
22. I first heard an account of this story from Manuel Pillco in the 1990 interview recorded by his grandson and the musician Darwin del Carpio. Pillco spent a long time recounting it.
23. For different accounts of this tradition and a preliminary analysis of them, see Roca Wallparimachi 1999, 62–67.
24. Undated document in the APHVU entitled "Radioescuchas." The contents suggest that it belongs to one of the first programs staged in 1937.
25. Amaru, who is cited in the second epigraph, was the pseudonym of David Chaparro, a cuzqueño lawyer who was city mayor in 1911–12 and 1938–42. Cha-

parro is quoted from Amaru, "A Propósito: '*La Hora del Charango*,'" *El Sol* (Cuzco), June 8, 1937.

26. Recordings of pieces classified as Inca fox are included in the Centro Qosqo's cassette and compact disc listed in the discography. See also the list of pieces included in the program of June 28 and published in an article called "Radio Local," *El Comercio* (Cuzco), June 26, 1937. They include a piece called *munay soncco,* composed by Julio Cornejo and performed by the "Centro Musical Leandro Alviña," which was classified as Incaic jazz, and another number by the same composer called *al silencio de la noche,* which was classified as an Incaic fox.
27. See, for instance, Felipe Pinglo's concern regarding criollo music in Lloréns 1983, 51–52.
28. "Un Grupo de Artistas Han Establecido el 'Día del Charango,'" *El Sol* (Cuzco), December 23, 1936, emphasis added.
29. Julio C. Gutiérrez, "En la '*Hora del Charango*' de Anteanoche," speech delivered on April 26, 1937, and published in *El Sol* (Cuzco), April 28, 1937, emphasis added.
30. The epigraph above is drawn from Humberto Vidal Unda, "Amables Oyentes," an editorial comment delivered on *La Hora del Charango* in 1937, document in the APHVU.
31. The Yábar Palacio are well known in the region as a landowning family with large haciendas in the province of Paucartambo.
32. Alberto Yábar Palacio, "De Nuestro Ambiente: *La Hora del Charango*," *El Sol* (Cuzco), June 5, 1937. The photocopy of this article in the APHVU has no page numbers.
33. Ibid.
34. Ibid.
35. The idea that cuzqueños from various social classes could commingle thanks to the "solace" provided by the emotive power of the music broadcast during *La Hora del Charango* was present in several newspaper comments and the speeches made during the first months of the program. See, for instance, Amaru, "*La Hora del Charango*," *El Sol* (Cuzco), June 8, 1937; or "Radio Local," *El Comercio* (Cuzco), April 22, 1937. Photocopies of both articles in the APHVU do not include page numbers. See also a speech delivered by the intellectual Francisco Ponce de León, which was broadcast on April 12, 1937, in "Algunas ideas Sobre Música Peruana para la '*Hora del Charango*' del Lunes Doce de Abril de 1937," document in the APHVU.
36. Humberto Vidal Unda, "*La Hora del Charango*," *El Comercio* (Cuzco), June 12, 1937, 1.
37. Delia Vidal De Milla, interview with the author, 1996.
38. Humberto Vidal Unda, "*La Hora del Charango*," *El Comercio* (Cuzco), June 12, 1937, 1.
39. Alberto Yábar Palacio, "De Nuestro Ambiente," *El Sol* (Cuzco), June 16, 1937. The photocopy of this article in the APHVU has no page numbers.

40. Ibid.

41. See, for instance, a speech read by the intellectual Luis Felipe Paredes on *La Hora del Charango*, which was published in "Palabras del Doctor Luis Felipe Paredes Dichas desde la O.A.X.7 A," *El Tiempo* (Cuzco), April 21, 1937. The photocopy of this article in the APHVU has no page numbers. See also the speech delivered by the intellectual Francisco Ponce de León and broadcast on April 12, 1937, in "Algunas ideas sobre Música Peruana, para la '*Hora del Charango*' del Lunes Doce de Abril de 1937," document in the APHVU.

42. Huayno composed by the musician/singer Jorge Toribio Cárdenas Andrade, Cuzco, November 1938; the words in capital letters were emphasized by the composer. The text of the huayno is copied verbatim from a document in the APHVU. Its heading reads, "To the dynamic driving force of the 'HORA DEL CHARANGO,' Señor Humberto Vidal, sincerely and admiringly," and is signed "J. Toribio Cárdenas Andrade, Ciudad Milenaria, Noviembre 1938." The title of the huayno is "CHARANGUITO." According to a document appended to this composition that belongs to the APHVU, Cárdenas Andrade was just a fan of Vidal Unda who had never met him in person, at least not until he sent this second composition honoring the efforts of Vidal Unda in *La Hora del Charango* ("Carta al Señor Humberto Vidal, enviada por J. Toribio Cárdenas Andrade," Cuzco, November 24, 1938, APHVU). The first of these compositions is cited below. It is said that this admirer of Vidal's was a musician and singer (Zoila Mendoza, interview with Manuel Jesús Aparicio, Cuzco, August 2003) whose children, one of whom was also called Toribio and the other Teófilo, were also singers and formed the "Cuarteto Cuzco" around 1953–54 (Zoila Mendoza, telephone interview with Reynaldo Pillco, Davis, June 2004). Andrade Cárdenas was an artisan and merchant who had a small jewelry shop in the city of Cuzco (Zoila Mendoza, telephone interview with Reynaldo Pillco. Davis, June 2004).

43. "Palabras de José Uriel García dichas por intermedio de la O.A.X.7 A Con motivo del la Hora del Charango radiada anoche," *El Tiempo* [Cuzco], April 1, 1937; the photocopy of this article in the APHVU has no page numbers.

44. "El Día del Charango Será Semanal en Adelante, Los lunes, O.A.X.7 A Transmitirá Programas Folklóricos, " *El Comercio* (Cuzco), March 24, 1937, 2. *Melopoeia* is defined as a "rhythmic intonation (*entonación*) in which something in verse or prose can be recited" (Real Academia Española 2001, 1483).

45. The content of the first program was published in two local newspapers a few days after the event, probably in late March 1937. These documents are housed in the APHVU, though they do not include the dates or names of the newspapers.

46. This was found in the articles mentioned in the previous note, and only the last names of two of these artists are given: Cárdenas and Marroquín.

47. This information was found in the two articles cited in note 43, which published the repertoire of the first program.

48. "Sonado éxito alcanzó la audición de la Hora del Charango," *El Sol* (Cuzco), April 1, 1937. The photocopy of this article in the APHVU has no page numbers.
49. Ibid.
50. "Dos Excelentes Audiciones Irradió Anoche La O.A.X.7 A," *El Tiempo* (Cuzco), February 4, 1938, discusses an episode of *La Hora del Charango* and lists the following members of the Conjunto Leandro Alviña: José Castillo, Max Julio Galdo, Fortunato Ugarte, and Manuel Torres.
51. He graduated from the Colegio Nacional de Ciencias in 1929 (González 1999, 11–12).
52. Itier (2000, 84) cites an article in *El Sol* ([Cuzco], July 21, 1934) that mentions these performances, which were held in the Teatro Italia in the city of Cuzco. Itier does not give the title of the article or its page number.
53. See González 1999 for a study of the literary output and professional career of Alencastre. For instance, the author lists the invitations Alencastre received to meetings on "ethnic literatures" in Chile, Bolivia, Argentina, and Mexico and "his participation as speaker in the International Congress of Linguistics held in Bucharest, in Quebec on the subject of 'idiomatic Quechua-Spanish interaction,' and his much-talked about conference on Quechua on the radio and TV of Moscow in 1968" (15). Avendaño (1995) likewise points out that Alencastre traveled across America and Europe "giving recitals of his poetic output in Quechua" (468). De la Cadena (2000) cites Itier (1995) as saying that Alencastre was a great champion of the so-called mestizo Quechua and fostered the use of the people's colloquial language in the plays he staged; this was in marked contrast to the efforts of indigenistas in previous decades, who encouraged the use of Capac Simi (a more erudite Quechua, which was supposedly used by the Inca) in the plays (149). Gonzáles points out that Alencastre died in much the same way as his father, murdered by peasants who were struggling against the usurpation of their lands. This happened in 1984 in Pomabamba, where Alencastre had settled after his retirement from teaching (1999, 16).
54. "Fue singularmente interesante la octava '*Hora del Charango*' que irradió anoche la O.A.X.7 A," *El Tiempo* (Cuzco), May 18, 1937. The photocopy of this article in the APHVU has no page numbers.
55. "Se rindió cálido homenaje al maestro cuzqueño Baltazar Zegarra," *El Comercio* (Cuzco), May 3, 1938; "Se rindió anoche un emocionado y digno homenaje al maestro compositor Baltazar Zegarra," *El Sol* (Cuzco), May 3, 1938. Photocopies of both articles in the APHVU have no page numbers. Other groups based in Cuzco city that appeared on the program during its first two years were Huayna Cuzco, headed by Víctor Irarrázabal; Los Últimos; and El Trío Vicuña.
56. "Actuaron Anoche los conjuntos típicos de Acomayo, Quiquijana y Tinta," *El Comercio* (Cuzco), August 3, 1937, 5.
57. Ibid.

58. In the poem, the word *nervio* plays on both the idea of strength and power and its little-known meaning "strings" (e.g., for a charango).

59. A copy of this composition is in the APHVU, simply titled "Charango" (the words in capital letters were emphasized by the composer). In an accompanying document, Cárdenas Andrade asks Vidal Unda to "accept this insignificant and humble inspiration from your unknown friend. . . . I found it fitting to dedicate this work to you as proof of a sincere friendship and for the greatest event recorded in musical history, that is, national folklore, whose precursor you are at present" ("Carta al Señor Humberto Vidal, firmada por Jorge Toribio Cárdenas Andrade," Cuzco, July 1937, APHVU). In the letter that goes with the previously cited second composition of Cárdenas Andrade, the composer explains to Vidal Unda that it is a huayno accompanied by a charango. He suggests that "if it is not inconvenient I would be honored to play and sing [it], along with some friends, in the place you indicate" ("Carta al Señor Humberto Vidal enviada por J. Toribio Cárdenas Andrade," Cuzco, November 24, 1938, APHVU).

60. "Se Constituyó un Comité Organizador de la '*Hora del Charango*,'" *El Sol* (Cuzco), April 1938. The photocopy of this article in the APHVU has no page numbers.

61. The homage took place on May 2, 1938.

62. Julio Benavente Díaz, quoted in El Chuccchito 1999, 78. The italicized words are those emphasized by El Chucchito and those in capital letters are my emphasis.

63. According to El Chucchito (ibid.), Benavente Díaz was given the name "The Charango God" by a Lima magazine the day after he played a solo in Lima during a performance given by the Centro Qosqo, for he "caught the attention of the artistic circles of the capital city and of the public in general" (78).

64. Adelma Benavente, one of the daughters of Don Julio, says her father had a half brother called Juan de Dios, who was a teacher in Paruro, and Don Julio lived with him while he was in primary school. This half brother was also an amateur musician who played the guitar and sang. I am grateful to Adelma Benavente for having shared with me the information about her father presented in this chapter. My correspondence with her took place in March and July 2004.

65. The Centro Qosqo has only awarded the special status of "socios natos" to eleven individuals. According to their rules, this category includes those who "(1) were part of the Asociación Folklórica Kosko before it joined the CQAN; (2) helped the institution obtain its own building; (3) and have been active members for over fifteen (for women) or eighteen (for men) years." (Centro Qosqo de Arte Nativo 1988, 2–3). It is likely that Don Julio met all three conditions. The significance of the Asociación Folklórica Kosko in the reestablishment of the Centro Qosqo is discussed in the following chapter.

66. Both Calvo (1999) and El Chucchito (1999) state that this event in Lima was organized by the Corporación Nacional de Turismo, an institution that is discussed in the following chapter. Benavente was a member of the Conjunto Folklórico of this

corporation when it traveled to Lima that year. At that time he was also a member of the Asociación Folklórica Kosko, which is discussed in the next chapter.

67. Adelma Benavente says that Don Julio taught in Paruro, Anta, Huarocondo, Oropesa, Zurite, Lucre, and the city of Cuzco. (Zoila Mendoza, e-mail interview with Adelma Benavente, June 3, 2004).
68. According to his daughter Adelma, Don Julio was awarded a doctorate in audio-visual education (ibid.). The remaining information was taken from El Chucchito 1999, 77.
69. The Quechua lyrics of this song and their translation into Spanish by José María Arguedas are included in El Chucchito 1999, 78. A recording of these pieces is on the compact disc by Julio Benavente listed in the discography.

70. Although the exact date when this program was created is not recorded, it was still being broadcast in 1977. The document Delia Vidal De Milla prepared for Julio Benavente regarding the origins of *La Hora del Charango* (see note 2) says of the new program, "The work being carried out by Benavente and a group of practitioners of our art is worthy of support; let us hope that, as happened over forty years ago, all the best of our young people, in terms of Peruvian culture, appear on this program" (Delia Vidal De Milla, Cuzco, May 13, 1977, APHVU).
71. "La Hora Folklórica Peruana," *El Sol* (Cuzco), May 13, 1942, 2; "Segunda Hora Folklórica del Instituto Americano de Arte," *El Sol* (Cuzco), May 26, 1942, 4.

5. CREATIVE EFFERVESCENCE

The first epigraph to this chapter is from Alberto Delgado, "Nuestro Arte Nativo es la expresión original en que se trasunta la visión de América vista por los ojos americanos," *El Comercio* (Cuzco), October 31, 1941, 1, 6. Delgado was a poet and president of the Instituto Americano de Arte, Cuzco, in 1941. The second epigraph is from a letter to the "Señor Presidente del 'Instituto Americano de Arte,'" October 7, 1940, signed by Ricardo Flórez T[upayachi], president of the Centro Artístico 'Ollanta,' Archivo Institucional del Instituto Americano de Arte, Cuzco (AIIAAC). Among his other accomplishments, Flórez was a self-educated quena player.

1. Alberto Delgado, "Nuestro Arte Nativo es la expresión original en que se trasunta la visión de América vista por los ojos americanos," *El Comercio* (Cuzco), October 31, 1941, 1, 6.
2. Ibid.
3. "Estatutos del Instituto Americano de Arte del Cuzco, Finalidades," n.d., AIIAAC. This is probably one of the earliest documents and can be dated between 1937 and 1950.
4. Ibid.
5. "Acta de la Sesión Inaugural del Instituto Americano de Arte, Sección Peruana, Comité del Cuzco," Tuesday, October 5, 1937. Cuaderno de Actas No 1, Instituto Americano de Arte, Cuzco, 1937–38, AIIAAC.
6. For example, when distinguishing between peasant art in the provinces outside

Cuzco and that of the city dwellers, which was more stylized, Julio Gutiérrez, who went under the nom de plume of Pancho Fierro, mentioned the "cholos," as opposed to the "mestizos," when discussing the first contest of music and dance organized by the IAAC ("Se Impone el Arte Indígena," *El Comercio* [Cuzco], March 4, 1938, 1). Roberto Latorre also mentioned Santiago Rojas, an artisan from the province of Paucartambo who would become famous throughout the region after participating in the "Santurantikuy" contest (see below), as "a cholo who makes nice plaster figurines, a set of which managed to enter into a ministerial office (*repartición ministerial*) of the United States of North America" (Roberto Latorre, President of the IAAC, "Carta al Señor Álvaro Bedregal," October 13, 1947, 1, AIIAAC).

7. The epigraph is a quotation from José Uriel García Ochoa, "Llamamiento publicado en el diario El Comercio del Cuzco en setiembre de 1937," *Revista del Instituto Americano de Arte del Cuzco* 10 (1961): 263–65. This journal does not have a more precise date of publication.
8. Ibid.
9. "Acta de la Sesión Inaugural del Instituto Americano de Arte, Sección Peruana Comité del Cuzco, Cuaderno de Actas No. 1 del Instituto Americano de Arte, Cuzco, 1937–38," AIIAAC. The following persons were present at the opening session of the IAAC on October 5 and are included in the record: J. Uriel García (first president), José Gabriel Cosio, Víctor Guillén, Domingo Velasco Astete, Carlos Lira, Oscar Saldívar, Alfredo Yépez Miranda, Humberto Vidal, Víctor Navarro del Águila, Julio Rouvirós, Francisco Olazo, Julio G. Gutiérrez, and Roberto Latorre.
10. Ibid.
11. "Estatuto y Reglamento, Instituto Americano de Arte, Cuzco, 1961," 3, AIIAAC.
12. This appears in the "Estatutos del Instituto Americano de Arte del Cuzco, Finalidades," an undated document in the AIIAAC. It is not included in the bylaws of the institution printed in 1961.
13. Roberto Latorre, President of the IAAC, "Carta al Señor Álvaro Bedregal," October 13, 1947, AIIAAC.
14. "La 'Quincena de Arte Popular' organizará el Instituto Americano de Arte," *El Comercio* (Cuzco), November 4, 1935, 2.
15. Pancho Fierro [Julio Gutiérrez], "Santuranticuy ayer y hoy," *El Comercio* (Cuzco), December 23, 1937, 2.
16. "El Concurso que ha Provocado El Instituto Americano de Arte," *El Comercio* (Cuzco), December 15, 1937, 2.
17. Pancho Fierro [Julio Gutiérrez], "En Torno Al Concurso de Artes Plásticas Populares," *El Comercio* (Cuzco), January 8, 1937, 1.
18. Roberto Latorre, President of the IAAC, "Carta al Señor Álvaro Bedregal," October 13, 1947, AIIAAC.

19. Ibid.

20. "Concurso de Música y Danzas Populares Para Carnaval," *El Comercio* (Cuzco), February 7, 1938, 1.

21. José Uriel García was elected senator twice, in 1939 and 1950.

22. "Presupuesto del Instituto Americano de Arte Para el Año de 1943," January 1943, 1–4, document in the AIIAAC.

23. Roberto Latorre, President of the IAAC, "Carta al Señor Álvaro Bedregal," October 13, 1947, AIIAAC.

24. "El Instituto Americano de Arte y la Cátedra de Literatura Peruana," *El Comercio* (Cuzco), April 30, 1938, 2. This initiative was headed by Alfredo Yépez Miranda, the former chair of Peruvian literature, and by José Gabriel Cosío, the incumbent one, both of whom were members of the IAAC.

25. Roberto Ojeda, "Carta al Presidente del Instituto de Arte Americano," Cuzco, September 22, 1941, AIIAAC.

26. Víctor Guillén, President of the IAAC, "Carta a los Señores Roberto Ojeda y Juan de Dios Aguirre," April 11, 1942, AIIAAC.

27. "Presupuesto del Instituto Americano de Arte Para el Año de 1943," January 1943, 4, AIIAAC.

28. Víctor Navarro del Águila was born in Ayacucho but was one of the most active individuals in the cultural and academic life of Cuzco in the period studied here.

29. The epigraph is from "Cuarta Fecha Eliminatoria del Concurso de Música y Danzas Populares," *El Comercio* (Cuzco), February 22, 1938.

30. "Concurso de Música y Danzas Populares," *El Comercio* (Cuzco), February 7, 1938, 1.

31. "Para la Celebración del Centenario," *El Comercio* (Cuzco), February 28, 1939, 1.

32. "Concurso de Música y Danzas Populares," *El Comercio* (Cuzco), February 7, 1938, 1.

33. Ibid.

34. Prizes were awarded in the 1938 contest to four kinds of groups: (a) "mixed groups, traditional ensemble and dance"; (b) "estudiantina"; (c) "traditional Indian ensembles"; and (d) "harmonicas." In addition, there were ten individual prizes. "Finalizó Con Resonante Éxito Artístico El Concurso de Música y Danzas Populares," *El Comercio* (Cuzco), March 3, 1938, 6.

35. The rules for the second contest included under music were: (1) traditional ensembles; (2) estudiantinas and bands of strolling musicians (*rondallas*); (3) Indian bands; and (4) singing, popular songs, choirs, and solos. The rules for dance included: (1) Indian dances from popular folklore in groups; and (2) stylized dances, individual or in couples. The rules for theater were: (1) popular puppet theater; (2) unpublished comedies; and (3) parodies and dances of a pantomimic nature ("I. A. de A. Segundo Concurso de artes populares para el 12 de abril próximo, con motivo del Cuarto Centenario del nacimiento de Garcilaso de la Vega," *El Comercio* [Cuzco], March 2, 1939, 1).

36. "La Tercera fecha del Concurso de Música y Danzas Populares," *El Comercio* (Cuzco), February 18, 1938, 4.
37. "Finalizó con Resonante Éxito Artístico el Concurso de Música y Danzas Populares," *El Comercio* (Cuzco), March 3, 1938, 6.
38. I will return to this quena player in the epilogue.
39. "Finalizó con Resonante Éxito Artístico el Concurso de Música y Danzas Populares," *El Comercio* (Cuzco), March 3, 1938, 6.
40. See, for instance, newspaper stories that describe the Tinta and Quiquijana groups as "purely Indian," including "Conjuntos Indígenas Ocupan los Primeros Puestos en el Concurso de Música y Danzas Populares," *El Comercio* (Cuzco), February 26, 1938, 3.

41. See, for instance, the following newspaper comments on the Conjunto Paucarttica: "The 'Paucarttica' group from San Jerónimo. This group formed by Indians and mestizos played four numbers of carnivalesque music and dances in costumes that won the applause of the public; what particularly caught the [audience's] attention was a marinera with an original air, and the dances were also performed with much skill" ("Cuarta fecha Eliminatoria del Concurso de Música y Danzas Populares," *El Comercio* [Cuzco], February 22, 1938, 2).
42. "El Concurso regional de Música, Danzas, y Teatro Populares," *El Comercio* (Cuzco), April 27, 1939, 6.
43. See, for instance, the comments in "Posibilidades de Teatro Nativo en Killko Waraka," *El Comercio* (Cuzco), January 14, 1941, 1.
44. The work of these groups cannot be understood within the framework posited by De la Cadena (2000, chap. 3; 2001). Contrary to her claims, and even after acknowledging that the organization of spaces such as the IAAC contests was undertaken by artists and intellectuals from the city of Cuzco, the burgeoning artistic-folkloric production of the 1930s and 1940s cannot be understood primarily as a result of the efforts made by neo-Indianist artists and intellectuals to present a "festive Indian" or "mold Indian musical skills and form artists among the Indian pupils" (2001, 183–84). We find a far more complex picture than that which De la Cadena presents if we take a close look and study in depth the number and variety of artists, as well as the artistic output that was part of the contemporary creative process, who were trying to create a cuzqueño and Peruvian identity through folklore. Even considering the groups formed by Caballero and Alencastre, it would be all too easy to envision the work carried out by these groups as a result of the manipulation and depuration posited by De la Cadena (2000, chap. 3; 2001).
45. "Última Función Eliminatoria del Tercer Concurso Coreográfico-Dramático-Musical," *El Comercio* (Cuzco), December 28, 1940.
46. Zoila Mendoza, interview with Armando Guevara Ochoa, Cuzco, December 2002.

47. Ibid.

48. Ibid. In this interview Guevara Ochoa insisted that he owed these four musicians the early musical training that would mark his entire career. He claimed to have learned Indian music from Pillco, mestizo music from Ojeda and Zegarra, and ceremonial church music from Juan de Dios de Aguirre.

49. Ibid.

50. "El I. A. de A.-Cuzco, Concurso de Literatura, Pintura y Música 'María R. Vda. De la Torre," *El Comercio* (Cuzco), July 28, 1944, 3.

51. "Concurso Musical 'María R. Vda. De la Torre,' " in Cuaderno de Concursos, IAAC, July 24, 1944, AIIAAC.

52. See "Sobre el Concurso de Música Convocado por el I. A. de Arte," *El Comercio* (Cuzco), September 28, 1944, 5; and "Sobre el Concurso de Música convocado por el Instituto Americano de Arte," *El Sol* (Cuzco), October 5, 1944, 1.

53. "Sobre el Concurso de Música convocado por el Instituto Americano de Arte," *El Sol* (Cuzco), October 5, 1944, 1.

54. Zoila Mendoza, interview with Armando Guevara Ochoa, Cuzco, December 2002.

55. Guevara Ochoa directed the Escuela Regional de Música of Cuzco in 1981.

56. "Instituto Americano de Arte, Concurso de Música 1947," call for compositions, September 15, 1947(?), AIIAAC.

57. "Concurso de Música 1947, Acta de apertura," in Cuaderno de Actas de Concursos del IAAC, December 10, 1947, AIIAAC.

58. "Acta del 30 de diciembre de 1947," in Cuaderno de Actas de Concursos del IAAC, AIIAAC.

59. Law no. 10196, which was signed by President Manuel Prado on December 30, 1944, reads, "Art. 1. The days running from and including June 24 to the succeeding 1 July are declared 'Cuzco Week,' as from 1945 and in succeeding years, in order to organize evocative (*evocativas*) festivals."

60. Vidal Unda, 1945, 7. The article was originally published in *El Comercio* (Cuzco), March 14, 1944, under the title "El 24 de Junio" (Vidal Unda did not record the page number).

61. Vidal Unda in a 1944 radio program, quoted by his sister, Delia Vidal de Milla (1982, 31–33).

62. Vidal Unda, 1945, 7–8. This speech was delivered on March 2. 1944. In it, Vidal Unda drew on an article that was originally published in *La Crónica* (Lima), June 24, 1944. He did not record the title of the original article, nor did he record the page number of the newspaper.

63. These groups were not "forced" to participate, nor were they relegated to a marginal or subordinate role as suggested by Marisol De la Cadena (2000, 154–62). I do not agree with her suggestion that Vidal Unda and the artists and intellectuals who organized and carried out the Inti Raymi and other celebratory

events held around these dates were convinced that "the Indians were inferior and did not belong to the city but to the mountainous countryside" (162). Nor is it true that "indigenous dancers who danced in the periphery, represent[ed] the folkloric present for the consumption of tourists" (158).

64. The script that is still used for the staging was prepared in 1994. This work relied above all on two of the seven previous scripts. The first was the script supervised by José María Arguedas in 1952, when he was in the Ministry of Education. The second was produced by a forum established by the municipality in 1981, which presented its final draft in 1984 (Rozas 1994).

65. I concur with Klaren (2001, 217) that the Inti Raymi institution must not be analyzed using the model of "invented traditions" developed by Hobsbawm (1983), as it is documented that this ceremony has historical roots.

66. It is wrong to base, as De la Cadena does, the marginal role of folkloric groups in the Cuzco Day celebrations, as well as the belief the neo-Indianists had regarding the inferiority of the Indians and the idea that their proper place was not in the city but in the countryside, on just two aspects of the performance of the first Inti Raymi. The first point is that when the Inca enters the stage his subjects come down from the mountains dressed in different ways while others wave their arrows, indicating that they came from various parts of the empire. The second point is that groups of musicians and dancers from various places parade once the ritual is over, symbolizing the participation of the entire empire (De la Cadena 2000, 162). It must be pointed out with regard to the first point that these "Indians" were members of the group of actors that took part in the theatrical performance, not artistic groups arrived from outside Cuzco. There are two points that must be made also as far as the second aspect goes. First, the groups and individual artists that appeared once the ritual was over were much anticipated by the cuzqueños (and not just a spectacle for tourists), so that instead of seeing them as marginal they are rather like a climax. Second, these groups and artists staged several other performances throughout the festival, which gave them more relevance and significance than the theatrical staging of the Inti Raymi, which lasted less than two hours on the main day the first year it was staged (see Vidal de Milla 1982, 40).

67. "Día del Cusco: Programa general de festejos para el día del Cusco," *El Sol* (Cuzco), June 14, 1944, 3.

68. Ibid.

69. Ibid.

70. The awards ceremony apparently did not take place on July 1 as planned, for the results of the contest were announced on July 6. It was decided to award the first prize to the Conjunto Acomayo, the second to the Conjunto Folklórico Pucyura, and the third to the Conjunto Folklórico Ccanchis. Diplomas were awarded to the Conjunto Puno, the Conjunto Dramático Sihuarkkente, the Conjunto Folk-

lórico Salcca, the Conjunto Folklórico Pampeño Anta, the Asociación de Artistas Aficionados del Cuzco, the Asociación Folklórica Cuzco, the Conjunto Folklórico Hermanos Gonzáles-Artola, the Conjunto Cusipata, the Conjunto Pitumarca, and the Conjunto Teatro Popular de Títeres ("Resultado del Concurso de arte folklórico realizado en la Semana del Cuzco," *El Sol* [Cuzco], July 11, 1945, 2).

71. "Culminó exitosamente la celebración de la Semana del Cuzco," *El Sol* (Cuzco), June 2, 1945, 1.

72. Recordings of this piece are included on the Centro Qosqo's compact disc and cassette, as well as in the *Música del Qosqo* collection, all of which are cited in the discography.

73. "Acta de Constitución de la 'Asociación Folklórica Cuzco,' realizada el Domingo 22 de abril de 1945," AIIAAC. The name of this institution varies in the press and institutional documentation. It appears as: Asociación Folklórica Kosko, Conjunto de Arte Folklórico Kosko (in documents from this institution), the Conjunto Folklórico Kosko, or the Conjunto Folklórico Ccoscco. I have chosen to use Asociación Folklórica Kosko in this text as I heard it referred to that way most often.

74. The document that gave the Asociación Folklórica Cuzco permission to legally take over the name of the Centro Qosqo noted the "condition of total inactivity of the former entity [the Centro Qosqo] for several years" (Document on stamped paper, no. 7751515, September 15, 1951, Archivo Privado Familia Pillco, APFP). Ricardo Castro Pinto notes in a historical account of the Centro Qosqo that Rafael Yépez La Rosa left the presidency of the Centro "due to the lack of collaboration among the members" (1999, 10).

75. By 1945 an Asociación de Artistas Aficionados del Cuzco (Association of Cuzco Amateur Artists) had been established. The origins and impact of this institution merit more study, but it seems that it was a guild type of association, not one with aims similar to those proposed by the Centro Qosqo, which were now being proposed anew by the members of the Asociación Folklórica Kosko.

76. The first album recorded by the Centro was *Qosqo Takiyninchis* in 1964 (see the discography).

77. Zoila Mendoza, telephone interview with Reynaldo Pillco, Davis, June 2004. The part-time worker category usually is comprised of people who work with their hands or do not possess any specialized training.

78. Zoila Mendoza, e-mail interview with Enrique Pilco Paz, Davis, January 25, 2005.

79. "Resultado del Concurso de arte folkórico realizado en la Semana del Cuzco," *El Sol* (Cuzco), July 11, 1945, 2.

80. Mendoza, Zoila. E-mail interview with Enrique Pilco, Davis, January 25, 2005.

81. Pilco Paz (2005) gives an account of how Fidel Zanabria became an active unionist and in 1963 was jailed for several months.

82. Zoila Mendoza, interview with Evaristo Tupa, Cuzco, July 2003.

83. Ibid.

84. I was also told this anecdote in an interview I conducted with him in 1996 (Zoila Mendoza, interview with Reynaldo Baca Cuba, Cuzco, July 1996).

85. We have, for instance, the case of the daughters of Zenón Usca—a strange case, for they are organists and one of them is a popular musician who leads a musical group that plays at the popular festivals in the region.

86. No available list includes the names of all the women and men who were members of the AFK; these names were taken from printed programs of performances given by the association found in the APFP.

87. Zoila Mendoza, interview with Reynaldo Pillco, Cuzco, July 1996.

88. The following are some of the artists in this association who have not yet been mentioned: Abel Pinelo, Celio Condori, Florentino Aiquipa, Roberto Amao, Óscar Ochoa, Mariano Zárate, Manuel Juárez, Justo Guillén, Julio Miranda, Manuel Vergara, Braulio Mejía, Víctor Irrazábal, Juan Esqueiros, Manuel Zaavedra, Venturino Castillo, Gerardo Mendoza, Encarnación Cruz, Pedro Quispe, Daniel Castilla, Toribio Gamarra, Julio Villalobos, Simón Tello, and Juan Chara. The names were taken from the following documents: "Acta de Constitución de la 'Asociación Folklórica Cuzco,' Realizada el Domingo 22 de Abril de 1945" (AIIAAC); "Asociación Folklórica Cuzco, Junta Directiva Para el Año 1945" (AIIAAC); and "Asociación Folklórica Cuzco, Cuadro de Honor" (AIIAAC). After these two years more members joined, including Lizardo Pérez, who became a major dancer and choreographer first of the AFK and then of the Centro Qosqo.

89. The most important performances they gave in the region and throughout Peru included their participation in the artistic events that accompanied the Fourth National Eucharistic Congress, held in Cuzco in May 1949.

90. So it is described in the manuscript by Baca (1994).

91. According to Castro Pinto (1999), the idea first came to Alfredo Yépez la Rosa, one of the last presidents of the dormant institution (12). This information does not appear in any document. What does appear in the documentation cited below, as well as in interviews with other members of the CQAN and the AFK, suggests that it was an idea that originated with members of the AFK.

92. Cuaderno de Actas del Centro Qosqo de Arte Nativo, October 31, 1951.

93. Document on stamped paper, no. 7751515, September 15, 1951, APFP.

94. Cuaderno de Actas del Centro Qosqo de Arte Nativo, October 31, 1951.

95. In previous studies (Mendoza 2000, 2001) I claimed, based on one document (Oróz 1989) and before conducting an in-depth study of the institutional life of the Centro Qosqo and in general of all the cultural institutions in Cuzco, that the Centro Qosqo had been in charge of staging the Inti Raymi from 1944 to the late 1950s. Examination of the new documentation discussed in this chapter makes it clear that this was impossible, as the Centro Qosqo was dormant during those years.

96. "El próximo congreso suramericano de turismo y el Cusco," *El Comercio* (Cuzco),

March 15, 1928, 2. Aguilar, Hinojosa, and Milla (1992) indicate that matters related to tourism were handled by the Ministerio de Fomento y Obras Públicas (Ministry of Development and Public Works) up to 1932, but from that year until 1946 they were in the hands of the Touring (33).

97. *La Prensa* (Lima), January 17, 1941, reproduced in "Alrededor de mil Turistas visitaron las ruinas del Cuzco en el año 1940," *El Comercio* (Cuzco), January 25, 1941, 2.
98. According to the census conducted that year, the population of the city of Cuzco was 40,657.
99. *La Prensa* (Lima), January 17, 1941, reproduced in "Alrededor de mil Turistas visitaron las ruinas del Cuzco en el año 1940," *El Comercio* (Cuzco), January 25, 1941, 2.
100. This guide was the basis of a much more elaborate and detailed text published by Vidal Unda a few years later (1958) and is considered one of the most outstanding intellectual works on Cuzco, in fact better than any tourist guide prepared before or since (Flores Nájar 1994, 214).
101. See this pamphlet reproduced in "Estampa del Cuzco Imperial," *El Comercio* (Cuzco), March 9, 1946, 3.
102. Ibid.
103. "Carta de Benjamín Roca Muelle, Director-Gerente de la Corporación Nacional de Turismo al Señor Doctor Alberto A. Giesecke, Lima, 6 de Junio de 1946," AAG 57.1028.
104. "Memorandum para el Sr. Benjamín Roca Muelle con relación a datos de valor turístico para visitas de los EE.UU. de A, al Perú—Julio 1946," AAG. 57.1030.
105. "Carta de Benjamín Roca Muelle, Director-Gerente de la Corporación Nacional de Turismo al Señor Doctor Alberto Giesecke, 15 de Noviembre de 1946," AAG. 57.1031.
106. "Carta de Benjamín Roca Muelle, Director de la Corporación Nacional de Turismo al Sr. Doctor Alberto Giesecke, Lima 13 de Enero de 1947," AAG. 57.1033.
107. For a detailed list of all the requests made by the cuzqueño delegation, see "Primer Congreso Nacional de Turismo," *El Comercio* (Cuzco), June 2, 1947, 2.
108. This information was taken from programs of performances staged by the Conjunto de la Corporación found in the APFP.
109. For example, the Conjunto performed and rehearsed on the premises of the IAAC. On the other hand, several members of the IAAC, starting with Humberto Vidal Unda, performed with the Conjunto, including Roberto Ojeda, Andrés Alencastre, and Antonio Alfaro.
110. The first article in the "Reglamento Interno del Conjunto Folklórico" (p. 1), states that the "Conjunto Folklórico seeks to cultivate and purify Peruvian art in its theatrical manifestations, particularly in choreography, music, and drama" (document held in the APHVU).
111. It does not seem likely that this was the only noncuzqueño dance in the Con-

junto's repertoire because its archives include a detailed description of a dance from Ayacucho folklore called *arascasca,* as well as a description of how many members should participate and what they should wear (document in the APHVU). In the programs of the Conjunto we also find another dance from Ayacucho called *tojro k'asa* ("Distribución del Programa No. 3," APHVU).

112. "Ficha Coreográfica, Archivo de Folklore de la Corporación Nacional de Turismo-Oficina Departamental del Cuzco," "C'ia Raqhe," Date: 19–11–49, Informant: Dr. Andrés Alencastre (APHVU). See Remy 1991 for a critical picture of the way this ritual activity has been interpreted in discourses on violence in the Andes.

113. The description reads, "*Dress and Ornaments.-The men wear: c'llu* [or *chullo*] of Canas style, a montera in the Canas style with the '*walqana*' [a strap to hold the montera on the head] fixed at the chin, a *chamarra* [vest], trousers[,] *chumpi* [a woven belt], poncho tied at the waist, '*warak'a*' [handmade woolen slings] as combat weapons. *The Women.*-Montera '*lliqlla*' [a shawl worn over the back] from Castile, a petticoat adorned with an embroidered ribbon, '*q'epina*' [a shawl used to carry things on the back] crossed over the shoulder to the opposite side, a *chamarra* [sheepskin vest] adorned with frets and buttons" ("Ficha Coreográfica, Archivo de Folklore de la Corporación Nacional de Turismo-Oficina Departamental del Cuzco," "C'ia Raqhe," Date: 19–11–49, Informant: Dr. Andrés Alencastre [APHVU]).

114. Ibid.

115. "Reglamento Interno del Conjunto Folklórico," p. 1 (APHVU).

EPILOGUE: PARADOXES OF ANDEAN FOLKLORE

The first epigraph to this chapter is from "Cuzco diria presente en Mexico," *El Comercio* (Cuzco), September 26, 1968, 1. The second epigraph is from "Hoy es el día; Centro Qosqo en el municipal," *El Comercio* (Cuzco), September 21, 1968, 1.

1. The ethnomusicologist Heidi Feldman gave me the exact name of this entity in February 2005. Feldman is finishing a book on the Afro-Peruvian musical tradition.
2. For instance, a headline in *El Comercio* ([Cuzco], September 5, 1968, 1) read, "Cuzco Debía Protestar Por Centralismo en Folklore Nativo" (Cuzco Should Protest over Centralism in Native Folklore).
3. "400 millones de personas verán el folklore peruano" (*El Comercio* [Cuzco], August 24, 1968, 1) stated that thanks to satellite TV four hundred million people would watch this cultural event and hence the performance of the Peruvian delegation. It was also noted that sixty countries from five continents would participate in the sporting and cultural events.
4. A more detailed study of this first Peruvian delegation has yet to be conducted. Some newspaper items suggest that the delegation headed by Victoria Santa Cruz took with it the typical attire of several parts of Peru, including Cuzco, and that

dances from various parts of Peru would be performed, though by dancers from Lima (see ibid.).

5. In 1969, some members of the Teatro y Danzas Negros del Perú formed the group Perú Negro, and, although it was originally created to work in a tourist restaurant called El Chalán, it soon became popular and established a close relationship with the government of Juan Velasco and with the Instituto Nacional de Cultura, the institution that replaced the Casa de la Cultura in its cultural role. The information here presented was provided by Heidi Feldman and Javier León, the latter a student of criollo music in Peru, who, like Feldman, is completing a book on this subject.
6. The most recent and complete study that tries to apprehend the different personal, artistic, and specifically musical sides of Ima Sumac was written by Nicholas E. Limansky (2003). Limansky's planned biography of Sumac has not yet been published. I therefore give the page numbers of the printed document taken from the Web page.
7. My mother, Zoila Beoutis Joffré, is a native of the Andean region of the Mantaro Valley. In the late 1930s and early 1940s she was in high school in Lima and living in the house of her uncle, Alejandro Beoutis. who lived in this city. At the time she was friends with Zoila Augusta, who was studying at the same school. One day, when Zoila Augusta visited my mother at her uncle's house, Hélida Beoutis, my mother's cousin, was rehearsing music with Moisés Vivanco for a scheduled performance. It was then, on hearing the music, that Zoila Augusta (Ima Sumac) began to hum the song Vivanco and my Aunt Hélida were rehearsing. Vivanco heard her and called her over to hear her sing. It was then, according to the account of my mother, that Ima Sumac met and was discovered by Moisés Vivanco, who began to promote her as a singer.
8. Zola Mendoza, interview with Reynaldo Pillco, Cuzco, July 1996.
9. An article published in *El Comercio* ([Cuzco], July 21, 1957, 5) proudly ran the headline "Arpista Cusqueño de Orquesta Vivanco Triunfa en Jira de Ima Sumac por Grecia" (Cuzco Harpist of the Vivanco Orchestra Triumphs in Ima Sumac's Greece Tour). According to this piece, the harpist José Farfán Aldea, a native of the province of Paruro, had met Vivanco when he was playing in the coliseos in Lima (see chapter 3).
10. See "Voz de Ima Sumaj," *El Comercio* (Cuzco), December 7, 1959, 2. There Vivanco writes, "One of the individuals who most criticizes me is José María Arguedas, who, based on I do not know what merits, managed to become the director of culture in Peru. When we were students at San Marcos school, he plagiarized several folkloric compositions, taking them from a book written by myself and Gómez Negrón entitled *canto quechua*. Arguedas is considered to be the Number One plagiarist. And this is precisely one of the men who tries to connect my work with foreign music (*música ajena*)."

11. "Hostil Recibimiento Tributaron a Ima Sumac," *El Comercio* (Cuzco), August 18, 1959, 3. This article also points out that Mrs. Chávarri knew full well how to "exploit the pseudonym of Ima Sumac," that she "uses the prestige of Peru as an advertisement for her success," and that "she has not hesitated in concocting the crudest lies regarding the deification thousands and thousands of savage Indians in the Peruvian highlands have subjected her to" (3).
12. "Ima Sumac en el Ollanta," *El Comercio* (Cuzco), August 10, 1959, 1.
13. According to an article in *El Comercio*, the movement of tourists was as follows in those years: "In 1953 [the number of tourists] came to 5, 814, in 1954 to 6,903, in 1955 to 8,176, in 1956 to 5,163, and in 1958 to 17,486" ("El Turismo puede Batir Record en 1959," El Comercio [Cuzco], August 21, 1959, 1). Another article in this same newspaper, "23 mil turistas nacionales en 1960" (*El Comercio* [Cuzco], January 1, 1961, 2), reports that 23,642 tourists visited Cuzco in 1960 and less than half of these (10,249) were foreigners. A subsequent article corrected this number and claimed that 16,091 Peruvian tourists and 10,349 foreign ones arrived in Cuzco in 1960, while a total of 28,814 arrived in 1961 ("Turismo batió record en 1961," *El Comercio* [Cuzco], January 1, 1962, 1). According to this last article, then, the number of tourists in 1960 amounted to about 19 percent of the total population in the city.
14. According to Castro Pinto's account (1993, 13), in that year the Centro Qosqo had been asked to stage the Inti Raymi on the Pampa de Amancaes by the mayor of the Lima district of El Rímac but had refused to do so. The mayor apparently persisted through other means, but according to Castro Pinto it was a "fiasco." The Centro Qosqo therefore traveled as soon as possible to Lima with "an authentic delegation (*embajada*) of Cuzco art" (13).
15. In the interview given by Manuel Pillco that was recorded by his grandson and Darwin del Carpio, he proudly recalled this visit and how he was recognized as a great harpist in Chile. Castro Pinto (1999, 15) also emphasizes the significance this journey had for the cuzqueño artists who formed the Centro Qosqo.
16. In 1943 and 1944 the Instituto Americano de Arte tried to organize the Primer Concurso Departamental de Belleza y Trajes Indígenas y Mestizos (First Departmental Beauty Contest and Contest of Indigenous and Mestizo Dress) and even published the rules (see "Instituto Americano de Arte, Primer Concurso Departamental de Belleza y Trajes Indígenas y Mestizos, Bases," November 15, 1943, document in the AIAAC). According to the president of the IAAC, these contests did not take place due to the lack of "the required cooperation of the municipality" (Paredes 1945, 89). Both this aborted attempt and the contest organized by the Centro Qosqo in 1957 sought to showcase the physical beauty of the contestants and the variety of cuzqueño traditional costumes, but the name of the 1957 contest did not point this out explicitly. The Indigenous Beauty Contest (this did not include the mestizo category, as did the contest the IAAC tried to organize)

sponsored by the Centro Qosqo gradually became a part of Cuzco Week and was held up to the 1960s, but it lost relevance at the regional level after a few years after having been canceled on some occasions. For additional data on this contest, see De la Cadena 2000, 177–82, where the contest is interpreted in a perspective and an overall framework with which I differ.

17. For instance, it is known that Manuel and Reynaldo Pillco, Baltazar Zegarra, and Diómedes Oróz joined the Danzas del Tawantinsuyo and then returned to the Centro Qosqo.

18. For example, *El Comercio* made the following comment regarding a performance by Danzas del Tawantinsuyo: "It was likewise noted that the movements in some dances such as Q'anchi have been expanded, thus making the development of these vernacular dances more colorful" ("Ante Nutrida concurrencia Actuaron Danzas Españolas y Tawantinsuyo," *El Comercio* [Cuzco], April 10, 1962, 1). Contemporary artists also credit Danzas del Tawantinsuyo with being the group in which the female dancers first wore short skirts, thus making them look like the performers in a kind of "Andean can-can." I first heard this expression, which I find most appropriate for describing some of the pieces the Centro Qosqo still performs, being used by my friend, the cuzqueño intellectual and artist Carlos Gutiérrez.

19. The major national corporate organization for the development of the military's policies at the regional level was SINAMOS, whose goal it was to promote regional autonomy through the promotion of regional and local institutions and policies (see Rénique 1988, 215).

20. For instance, the Velasco regime established the Encuentros Inkarrí (Inkarrí Encounters). Inkarrí is a mythological figure in Andean oral tradition. Although it only lasted for a few years, it tried to persuade peasant communities to perform their own dances without resorting to intermediaries and sponsored competitions in districts, provinces, and departments, with the finals held in Lima. The important Festival Carnavalesco de Coya (Carnivalesque Festival of Coya) was created during the Morales Bermúdez administration and is still held today.

21. This is the most important pilgrimage in Cuzco and one of the biggest in all of the Andes (see Sallnow 1987; and Poole 1988).

Discography

This limited discography only includes a minimum number of available recordings of some of the musical pieces explicitly mentioned in the text. It in no way intends to cover the vast range of recordings of Cuzco music available for the period studied.

Benavente Díaz, Julio

Charango et chants du Cuzco/Charango and Songs from Cuzco. CD. OCORA, Radio France (CD C 559037), 1988.

Centro Qosqo de Arte Nativo

Saqsayhuamán, LP. IEMPSA (LD 1763), n.d.

Centro Qosqo de Arte Nativo. Cassette. Centro Qosqo de Arte Nativo, n.d.

Qosqo Llaqta, LP. IEMPSA (ELD–02–01.11), 1984.

Qosqo Takiyninchis. CD. IEMPSA (CD 91150069), n.d. Original LP, 1964 (LD 1446).

Danzas del Tawantinsuyo

Danzas del Tawantinsuyo, LP. IEMPSA (LD 1304), n.d.

Municipalidad del Cuzco

Música del Qosqo. Four cassettes and booklet. Municipalidad del Qosqo, 1991.

Pillco Family

Familia Pillco, *Violins from the Andes.* CD. TUMI Music (LC 3885), 2001.

...... *Bibliography*

ARCHIVES

Archivo Albert Giesecke (Albert Giesecke Archive, AAG), Centro Bartolomé de las Casas, Cuzco city, currently in the possession of the Giesecke family, Lima.

Archivo de Folklore de la Corporación Nacional de Turismo (Folklore Archive of the National Tourism Corporation, AFCNT), Cuzco city.

Archivo Institucional del Centro Qosqo de Arte Nativo (Institutional Archive of the Centro Qosqo de Arte Nativo, AICQAN), Cuzco city.

Archivo Institucional del Instituto Americano de Arte de Cuzco (Institutional Archive of the Instituto Americano de Arte de Cuzco, AIIAAC), Cuzco city.

Archivo Privado Familia Pillco (Private Archive of the Pillco Family, APFP), Cuzco city.

Archivo Privado Humberto Vidal Unda (Humberto Vidal Unda Private Archive, APHVU), Cuzco city.

Cuzco Municipal Library Archive, *El Comercio* of Cuzco Collection, Cuzco city.

El Sol Newspaper Archive, Cuzco city.

Fototeca Andina Photographic Archive, Centro Bartolomé de las Casas, Cuzco city.

Martín Chambi Photographic Archive, Cuzco city.

Aguilar, Victor, Leonith Hinojosa, and Carlos Milla. 1992. *Turismo y Desarrollo: Posibilidades en la Región Inka.* Cuzco: Centro de Estudios Regionales Andinos Bartolomé de las Casas.

Aparicio, Manuel. 1994. "Humberto Vidal Unda: Siete décadas de usqueñismo." In *Cincuenta Años de Inti Raimi,* ed. Carlos Milla, E. Miranda, and E. Velarde Pérez, 125–64. Cuzco: Empresa Municpal de Festejos del Cuzco and Municipalidad del Qosqo.

——. 2000. "Cuscología y sus Orígenes." In *Desde Afuera y Desde Adentro: Ensayos de Etnografía e historia del Cuzco y Apurímac,* ed. Luis Millones, Hiroyasu Tomoeda, and Tatsuhiko Fujii, 95–122. Osaka: National Museum of Ethnology.

Ares Queija, Berta. 1984. "Las Danzas de los Indios: Un camino para la evangelización del virreynato del Perú." *Revista de Indias* 44, no. 174: 445–63.

Avendaño, Ángel. 1999. *Diccionario Enciclopédico del Qosqo.* Cuzco: Municipalidad del Qosqo.

Baca, Reynaldo. N.d. "Breve Biografía de Reynaldo Baca Cuba." Cuzco, manuscript.

——. 1994. "Repertorio de Danzas de Los Programas." Cuzco, manuscript.

Béhague, Gerard. 1996. "Latin American Music, c. 1929–c.1980." In *The Cambridge History of Latin America.* Vol. 10: *Latin America since the 1930s: Ideas, Culture, and Society,* ed. Leslie Bethel, 307–63. Cambridge: Cambridge University Press.

Bourdieu, Pierre. 1987. "What Makes a Social Class? On the Theoretical and Practical Existence of Groups." *Berkeley Journal of Sociology* 32:1–17.

Calvo Pérez, Julio. 1998. *Ollantay: Edición Crítica de la Obra Anónima Quechua.* Cuzco: Centro Bartolomé de las Casas.

Calvo, Rossano. 1999. *La Tradición: Representación de la Urbe Andina Cusqueña en el Siglo XX.* Cuzco: Municipalidad de Santiago.

——. 2002. "Valicha Canción e Identidad." *Tampu Revista de Cultura Andina* 2, no. 4: 15–17.

Cánepa Koch, Gisela. 2001. "Introducción: Formas de cultura expresiva y la etnografía de 'lo local.'" In *Identidades Representadas, Performance, Experiencia, y Memoria en los Andes,* ed. Gisela Cánepa Koch, 179–212. Lima: Fondo Editorial de la Pontificia Universidad Católica.

Cantwell, Robert. 1992. "Feasts of Unnaming: Folk Festivals and the Representation of Folklife." In *Public Folklore,* ed. Robert Baron and Nicholas Spitzer, 263–305. Washington, D. C.: Smithsonian Institution Press.

Castro Pinto, Ricardo. 1999. "Breve Reseña Histórica del Centro Qosqo de Arte Nativo." In *Centro Qosqo de Arte Nativo Bodas de Diamante, 1924–1999,* ed. Centro Qosqo de Arte Nativo, 10–15. Cuzco: Navarrete.

Centro Qosqo de Arte Nativo. 1960. "Coros y Danzas Folklóricas." Cuzco, manuscript.

——. 1988. *Estatuto del Centro Qosqo de Arte Nativo.* Cuzco: Centro Qosqo.

Chamosa, Oscar. 2004. "Indigenous or Criollos: Defining Race and Ethnicity in Argentina's Calchaqui Valley, 1890–1930." Paper presented at the panel "Comparing Indigenismo," Twenty-fifth Latin American Studies Association Congress, October 7–9, Las Vegas.

Cotler, Julio. 1978. *Clases, Estado, y Nación en el Perú.* Peru Problema, no. 17. Lima: Instituto de Estudios Peruanos.

Daniel Ivonne. 1995. *Rumba: Dance and Social Change in Contemporary Cuba.* Bloomington: Indiana University Press.

De la Cadena, Marisol. 2000. *Indigenous Mestizos: The Politics of Race and Culture in Cuzco, Peru, 1919–1991.* Durham: Duke University Press.

——. 2001. "Mestizos-indígenas, Imágenes de autenticidad, y des-indianización en la ciudad del Cuzco." In *Identidades Representadas: Performance, Experiencia, y Memoria en los Andes,* 179–212. Lima: Fondo Editorial de la Pontificia Universidad Católica.

Deustua, José, and José Luis Rénique. 1984. *Intelectuales, indigenismo, y descentra-*

lismo en el Perú, 1897–1931. Cuzco: Centro de Estudios Regionales Andinos Bartolomé de las Casas.

Eco Musical. 1943. *In Memoriam Daniel Alomía Robles* Año II, No. 10, Julio. Lima y Buenos Aires: Talleres Gráficos "Optimus."

El Chucchito. 1999. "Julio César Benavente Díaz y Su Charango," In *Centro Qosqo de Arte Nativo Bodas de Diamante, 1924–1999,* ed. Centro Qosqo de Arte Nativo, 76–80. Cuzco: Navarrete.

Erlmann, Veit. 1992. " 'The Past Is Far and the Future Is Far': Power and Performance among Zulu Migrant Workers." *American Ethnologist* 19, no. 4: 688–709.

——. 1996. *Nightsong: Performance, Power, and Practice in South Africa.* Chicago: University of Chicago Press.

Escobar, Gloria, and Gabriel Escobar. 1981. *Huaynos del Cusco.* Cuzco: Editorial Garcilazo.

Estenssoro, Juan Carlos. 1989. *Música y Sociedad Coloniales: Lima, 1680–1830.* Lima: Editorial Colmillo Blanco.

——. 1990. "Música, discurso, y poder en el régimen colonial." Master's thesis, History Department, Pontificia Universidad Católica del Perú.

——. 1992. "Los bailes de los indios y el proyecto colonial." *Revista Andina,* 10, no. 2: 353–89.

——. 2003. *Del Paganismo a la Santidad.* Lima: IFEA (Instituto Francés de Estudios Andinos) e Instituto Riva Agüero.

Fabian, Johannes. 1990. *Power and Performance: Ethnographic Exploration through Proverbial Wisdom and Theater in Shaba, Zaire.* Madison: University of Wisconsin Press.

Flores, Nájar. 1994. "Notas para la historia del turismo en el Cusco." *Revista del Instituto Americano de Arte de Cusco,* no. 14: 209–14.

García, José Uriel. 1930. *El Nuevo Indio.* Cuzco: Editorial Rozas.

——. 1949. *Pueblos y Paisajes Sud Peruanos.* Lima: Editorial Cultura Antártida.

Gonzales Jiménez, Odi. 1999. *Taki Parwa/22 Poemas Kilku Warak'a.* Cuzco: Biblioteca Municipal del Cusco.

Guillen, Jesús. 1982. *El Desarrollo del Cusco: Balance de unas Ilusiones, 1959–1982.* Cuadernos para el debate regional, no. 7. Cuzco: Centro de Estudios Rurales Bartolomé de las Casas.

Guss, David. 2000. *The Festive State: Race, Ethnicity, and Nationalism as Cultural Performance.* Berkeley: University of California Press.

Herzfeld, Michael. 1986. *Ours Once More: Folklore, Ideology, and the Making of Modern Greece.* New York: Pella.

Hobsbawm, Eric. 1983. "Introduction: Inventing Traditions." In *The Invention of Tradition,* ed. Eric Hobsbawm and Terence Ranger, 1–14. Cambridge: Cambridge University Press.

INC Perú (Instituto Nacional de Cultura, Perú). 1977. "Bases Para la Política Cultural de la Revolución Peruana." *Runa* 16:3–7.

Itier, César. 1995. *El teatro quechua en el Cuzco.* Vol. 1: *Dramas y comedias de nemesio Zúñiga Cazorla.* Lima: Instituto Francés de Estudios Andinos, Centro Bartolomé de las Casas.

——. 2000. *El Teatro Quechua en el Cuzco.* Vol. 2: *Indigenismo, Lengua, y Literatura en el Perú Moderno.* Lima: Instituto Francés de Estudios Andinos, Centro Bartolomé de las Casas.

Kirshenblatt-Gimblett, Barbara. 1998. *Destination Culture, Tourism, Museums, and Heritage.* Berkeley: University of California Press.

Klarén, Peter. 2001. Review of *Marisol de la Cadena, Indigenous Mestizos. Dispositio/n* 24, no. 51: 213–20.

Kristal, Efraín. 1987. *The Andes Viewed from the City: Literary and Political Discourse on the Indian in Peru, 1848–1930.* New York: Peter Lang.

Krüggeler, Thomas. 1999. "Indians, Workers, and the Arrival of Modernity: Cuzco, Peru, 1895–1924." *The Americas* 56, no. 2: 160–88.

Lauer, Mirko. 1997. *Andes Imaginarios: Discursos del Indigenismo 2.* Lima: Casa de Estudios del Socialismo, Centro Bartolomé de las Casas.

Leitchman, Ellen. 1989. "Musical Interaction: A Bolivian Mestizo Perspective." *Latin American Music Review* 10, no. 1: 29–52.

Limansky, Nicholas E. 2003. "Yma Sumac." *The Legacy of the Diva* [online]. http://www.divalegacy.com (accessed July 1, 2007).

Lloréns, José Antonio. 1983. *Música Popular en Lima: Criollos y Andinos.* Lima: Instituto de Estudios Peruanos.

López, Rick. 2004. "Intellectuals, the Popular Classes, and the State: Integrating the Mexican Cultural Nation, 1916–1940." Paper presented in the panel "Comparing Indigenismo," Twenty-fifth Latin American Studies Association Congress, October 7–9, Las Vegas.

——. 2006. "Two Ways of Exalting Indianness," In *The Eagle and the Virgin: Nation and Cultural Revolution in Mexico, 1920–1940,* ed. Mary Kay Vaughan and Stephen Lewis, 23–42. Durham: Duke University Press.

López Lenci, Yazmín. 2004. *El Cucco, paqarina moderna: Cartografía de una modernidad e identidades en los Andes peruanos (1900–1935).* Lima: Concytec y Fondo Editorial, Universidad Nacional Mayor de San Marcos.

Lovón, Gerardo. 1982. *Mito y Realidad del Turismo en el Cusco.* Cuzco: Centro de Estudios Rurales Andinos, Centro Bartolomé de las Casas.

Mannheim, Bruce. 1991. *The Language of the Inka since the European Invasion.* Austin: University of Texas Press.

Matos Mar, José. 1984. *El Desborde Popular y Crisis del Estado: El Nuevo Rostro del Perú.* Lima: Instituto de Estudios Peruano, Centro Bartolomé de las Casas.

Mendoza, Zoila. 1998. "Defining Folklore: Mestizo and Indigenous Identities on the Move." *Bulletin of Latin American Research* 17, no. 2: 165–83.

——. 1999. "Genuine but Marginal: Exploring and Reworking Social Contradictions through Ritual Dance Performance." *Journal of Latin American Anthropology* 3, no. 2: 86–117.

——. 2000. *Shaping Society through Dance: Mestizo Ritual Performance in the Peruvian Andes.* Chicago: University of Chicago Press.

——. 2001. *Al Son de la Danza: Identidad y Comparsas en el Cuzco.* Lima: Fondo Editorial de la Pontificia Universidad Católica.

Montoya, Rodrigo, Edwin Montoya, and Luis Montoya. 1987. *La Sangre de los Cerros: Urqukunapa Yawarnin.* Lima: Centro de Estudios Peruanos Sociales, Azul and Universidad Naccional Mayor de San Marcos.

Mould de Pease. 2000. "Apuntes interculturales para la historia inmediata de Machu Picchu: Las funciones de Hiram Bingham y Albert Giesecke," *Revista del Archivo Regional del Cusco* 15 (June): 133–47.

Municipalidad del Cusco. 1990. *Cusco . . . Testimonios.* Cuzco: Municipalidad del Cusco.

Navarro del Águila, Victor. 1944. "Calendario de Fiestas Populares del Cuzco." *Revista del Instituto Americano de Arte de Cuzfco* 3, no. 3 (January–June): 37–80.

Nettl, Bruno. 1997. "Native American Music." In *Excursions in World Music,* ed. Nettl, Bruno, Charles Capwell, Isabel Wong, and Thomas Turino, 251–68. 2nd ed. Upper Saddle River, N.J.: Prentice Hall.

Nuñez Rebaza, Lucy, and Jose Lloréns. 1981. "La Música Tradicional Andina en Lima Metropolitana." *América Indígena* 41, no. 1: 53–74.

Ojeda, Pablo. 1987. "Importancia de la Música Cusqueña en el Desarrollo de la Música Peruana." Cuzco, manuscript.

Olsen, Dale. 1986. "The Peruvian Folk Harp Tradition: Determinants of Style." *Folk Harp Journal* 53:48–54; 54:41–48; 55:55–59; 56:57–60.

Oróz Villena, Diómedes. 1989. "Breve reseña histórica del 'Centro Qosqo de Arte Nativo,' " Cuzco, manuscript.

——. 1999. *Cancionero de Aniversario, Centro Qosqo de Arte Nativo.* Cuzco: Instituto Nacional de Cultura.

Pagaza Galdo, Consuelo. 1963. "El Yaraví." *Revista del Instituto Americano de Arte de Cuzco,* no 11.

Paredes, Luis Felipe. 1945. "Memoria leída por el Dr. Luis Felipe Paredes, presidente cesante del instituto, correspondiente al año de 1944." *Revista del Instituto Americano de Arte de Cuzco* 4:88–92.

Parejo, Rafael. 1988. "Julio Benavente Díaz: Charango and Songs from Cuzco." Text for the compact disc of the same name, 9–12. Ocora: Radio France.

Paúkar, Martín. 1947. "Música, danzas y cantos del Cuzco." *Revista de Intituto Americano de Arte de Cuzco* 5 (November): 25–30.

Pilco Paz, Enrique. 2000. "Velada de Lunes Santo En la Catedral del Cusco, Simbolismo y Ritual." Thesis, Anthropology Licenciatura, Universidad Nacional San Antonio Abad del Cuzco, Cuzco.

———. 2001. "Cantos Liturgicos Quechua." Discographic Project, United Nations Educational, Scientific and Cultural Organization. Manuscript.

———. 2005. "Maestros de capilla, mestizaje musical, y catolicismo en los andes del sur." *Revista Andina* 40:179–208.

Pillco, Familia. N.d. "La Música del Cusco a Través de Tres Generaciones." Cuzco, manuscript.

Pinilla, Enrique. 1988. "La Música en el Siglo XX." In *La Música en el Perú*, 125–213. Lima: Patronato Popular y Porvenir Pro Música Clásica.

Poole, Deborah. 1988. "Landscapes of Power in a Cattle-Rustling Culture of Southern Andean Peru." *Dialectical Anthropology* 12:367–98.

———. 1990. "Accomodation and Resistance in Andean Ritual Dance." *Drama Review* 34, no. 2: 98–126.

———. 1997. *Vision, Race, and Modernity: A Visual Economy of the Andean Image World.* Princeton: Princeton University Press.

Portocarrero, Gonzalo, and Patricia Oliart. 1989. *El Perú Desde la Escuela.* Lima: Instituto de Apoyo Agrario.

Raygada, Carlos. 1936. "Panorama Musical del Perú." *Boletín Latinoamericano de Música* 11 (April): 169–213.

Real Academia Española. 2001. *Diccionario de la Lengua Española.* 22nd ed., 2 vols. Madrid: Real Academia Española.

Remy, Maria Isabel. 1991. "Los discursos sobre la violencia en los Andes: Algunas reflexiones a propósito del Chiaraje." In *Poder y Violencia en Los Andes*, compiled by Henrique Urbano, 261–97. Cuzco: Centro de Estudios Regionales Andinos, Centro Bartolomé de las Casas.

Rénique, José Luis. 1988. "State and Regional Movements in the Peruvian Highlands: The Case of Cusco, 1895–1985." Ph.D. diss., History Department, Columbia University.

———. 1991. *Los Sueños de la Sierra: Cusco en el Siglo XX.* Lima: Centro de Estudios Peruanos Sociales.

Revista Universitaria. 1960. "Homenaje al Dr. Alberto A. Giesecke." *Revista Universitaria* 49, no. 2: 9–28.

Roca Wallparimachi, Demetrio. 1999. "El Tema de Juan El Bandolero." In *Centro Qosqo de Arte Nativo Bodas de Diamante, 1924–1999*, ed. Centro Qosqo de Arte Nativo, 62–67. Cuzco: Navarrete.

Roel Pineda, Josafat. 1959. "El Wayno del Cuzco." *Folklore Americano* 6–7: 129–246.

Romero, Raúl. 1988. "La Música Tradicional y Popular." In *La Música en el Perú*, 216–83. Lima: Patronato Popular y Porvenir Pro Música Clásica.

———. 1998. "Perú." In *Garland Encyclopedia of World Music: South America, Mexico, Central America and the Caribbean.* New York: Garland.

———. 2001. *Debating the Past: Music, Memory, and Identity in the Andes.* Oxford: Oxford University Press.

——. 2002a. "Popular Music and the Global City: Huayno, Chicha, and Tecno-Cumbia in Lima." In *From Tejano to Tango: Latin American Popular Music,* ed. Walter Aaron Clark, 217–39. New York: Routledge.

——, ed. 2002b. *Sonidos Andinos: Una Antología de la Música Campesina del Perú.* Lima: Pontificia Unversidad católica del Perú, Instituto Riva Aguero y Centro de Etnomusicología Andina.

Rowe, William, and Vivian Schelling. 1991. *Memory and Modernity: Popular Culture in Latin America.* New York: Verso.

Rozas Aragón, Abel. 1991. "Música del Qosqo," Companion pamphlet to the music anthology. Cuzco: Municipalidad del Qosqo.

——. 1994. "El Guión del (Inti Raymi), Introducción." In *Cincuenta Años de Inti Raimi.* ed. Carlos Milla, E. Miranda, and E.Velarde Pérez, 91–95. Cuzco: Empresa Municpal de Festejos del Cuzco and Municipalidad del Qosqo.

Sallnow, Michael. 1987. *Pilgrims of the Andes: Regiona Cults in Cusco.* Washington, D.C.: Smithsonian Institution Press.

Savigliano, Marta. 1995. *Tango and the Political Economy of Passion.* Boulder: Westview.

Seligman, Linda. 1989. "To Be in Between: The Cholas as Market Women." *Comparative Studies of Society and History* 31, no. 4: 694–721.

Tamayo Herrera, José. 1980. *Historia del indigenismo cuzqueño: Siglos XVI–XX.* Lima: Instituto Nacional de Cultura.

——. 1981. *Historia social del Cuzco republicano.* 2nd. ed. Lima: Editorial Universo.

Ttupa Llavilla, Esteban. 1988. "Policarpo Caballero Farfán." In *Música Incaica: Sus Leyes y su Evolución Histórica,* 19–24. Lima: Corporacion de Servicios Integrales Turísticos Culturales.

Turino, Thomas. 1983. "The Charango and the Sirena: Music, Magic, and the Power of Love." *Latin American Music Review* 4, no. 1: 81–119.

——. 1984. "The Urban-Mestizo Charango Tradition in Southern Peru: A Statement of Shifting Identity." *Ethnomusicology* 28, no. 2: 253–70.

——. 1991. "The State and Andean Musical Production in Peru." In *Nation-States and Indians in Latin America,* ed. Greg Urban and Joel Sherser, 257–85. Austin: University of Texas Press.

Valcárcel, Luis E. 1924. *Inkánida: La Misión Peruana de Arte Inkaico en Bolivia, República Argentina i el Uruguai.* Vol. 1. Cuzco: Librería Tipografía "Cuzco."

——. 1981. *Memorias.* Lima: Instituto de Estudios Peruanos.

——. 1986. "Prologo a la Tercera Edición" de Uriel García. In *El Nuevo Indio,* 17–18. Cuzco: Municipalidad del Cuzco.

Valencia Espinoza, Abraham. 1994. "Pancho Gómez Negrón y el folklore cusqueño." *Revista dell Instituto American de Arte* 14: 153–61.

Varallanos, José. 1962. *El cholo y el Perú: Introduccioón al estudio sociológico de un hombre y un pueblo mestizos y su destino cultural.* Buenos Aires: Imprenta López.

Vidal De Milla, Delia. 1982. *Humberto Vidal Unda, Su Pensamiento, Su Obra, Su Pasión: El Cusco.* Cuzco: Inti Raimi.

Vidal Unda, Humberto. 1945. *Semana del Cuzco, Cita Continental en la Capital Arqueológica de América.* Special publication, Año 1 No.1 Cuzco.

——. 1958. *Visión del Cuzco, Monografía Sintética.* Cuzco: Editorial Garcilaso.

Vivanco, Alejandro. 1973. "El Migrante de Provincias Como Intérprete del Folklore Andino en Lima." B.A. thesis, Universidad Nacional Mayor de San Marcos, Lima.

Wade, Peter. 2000. *Music, Race, and Nation: Musica Tropical in Colombia.* Chicago: University of Chicago Press.

Walker, Charles. 1999. *Smoldering Ashes: Cuzco and the Creation of Republican Peru, 1780–1840.* Durham: Duke University Press.

Wara Céspedes, Gilka. 1984. "New Currents in *Música Folklórica* in La Paz, Bolivia." *Latin American Music Review* 5, no. 2: 217–42.

Williams, Raymond. 1977. *Marxism and Literature.* Oxford: Oxford University Press.

Index

Zoila S. Mendoza is an associate professor of Native American studies at the University of California, Davis.

Library of Congress Cataloging-in-Publication Data
Mendoza, Zoila S., 1960–
Creating our own : folklore, performance, and identity in Cuzco, Peru /
Zoila S. Mendoza.
p. cm.
Includes bibliographical references and index.
ISBN-13: 978-0-8223-4130-7 (cloth : alk. paper)
ISBN-13: 978-0-8223-4152-9 (pbk. : alk. paper)
1. Folklore—Peru—Cuzco. 2. Folklore—Performance—Peru—Cuzco.
3. Ethnicity—Peru—Cuzco. 4. National characteristics, Peruvian.
5. Nationalism—Peru—Cuzco. 6. Cuzco (Peru)—Social life and customs.
I. Title.
GR133.P4M46 2008
398.20985—dc22 2007033636